The Problem of College Readiness

EDITED BY

William G. Tierney and Julia C. Duncheon

SUNY
PRESS

Published by State University of New York Press, Albany

For information, contact State University of New York Press, Albany, NY
www.sunypress.edu

Production: Jenn Bennett
Marketing: Anne M. Valentine

Library of Congress Cataloging-in-Publication Data

The problem of college readiness / edited by William G. Tierney and Julia C. Duncheon.
     pages cm
   Includes bibliographical references and index.
   ISBN 978-1-4384-5723-9 (hc : alk. paper)—978-1-4384-5724-6 (pb : alk. paper)
   ISBN 978-1-4384-5725-3 (e-book) 1. Educational equalization—United States.
2. College preparation programs—United States. 3. Academic achievement—United
States. I. Tierney, William G., editor of compilation, author. II. Duncheon, Julia C.,
1984– editor of compilation, author.
   LC213.2.P755 2015
   379.2'6—dc23
                                      2014034930

10   9   8   7   6   5   4   3   2   1

CONTENTS

PART III
Conclusion

ILLUSTRATIONS

ACKNOWLEDGMENTS

We are grateful to the Rossier School of Education and the Pullias Center for Higher Education at the University of Southern California for the financial support to undertake this project. Monica Raad and Diane Flores in the Pullias Center, and Noel Alumit in the Research Office were extremely helpful in the final production and editing of the text. Our editor at SUNY, Beth Bouloukos, also was supportive throughout the project and a pleasure to work with from beginning to end. All royalties for the book will be donated for financial aid for low-income youth to attend a postsecondary institution.

Part I

INTRODUCTION

1

————◄◦►————

THE PROBLEM OF COLLEGE READINESS

JULIA C. DUNCHEON

Contemporary economic trends and social concerns have propelled postsecondary attainment into the center of the education policy agenda (Executive Office of the President, 2014). Although a high school diploma historically signified adequate training for the workforce (Baker, Clay, & Gratama, 2005), the modern knowledge-based economy increasingly requires tertiary degrees (Dohm & Shniper, 2007). College completion is associated with myriad benefits such as increased earnings and job satisfaction, higher levels of civic engagement, and lower crime rates (Baum & Ma, 2007; Camara, Wiley, & Wyatt, 2010; OECD, 2009). Yet postsecondary attainment remains stratified by race, ethnicity, and class (Rosenbaum & Becker, 2011). Educational stakeholders have thus focused on enhancing college access and success (Kirst & Venezia, 2004). As President Obama declared in 2009, "a good education is no longer just a pathway to opportunity—it is a prerequisite."

While larger proportions of high school graduates are entering college relative to prior generations, many students leave prior to degree completion (Ashtiani & Feliciano, 2012). Approximately 56% of four-year university students and 30% of two-year students obtain a degree (Symonds, Schwartz, & Ferguson, 2011). Table 1.1 presents data on students' high school to college pathways. High rates of remediation, or non-credit-bearing coursework for students underprepared in English and math, present

3

TABLE 1.1. High school to college pipeline: Nationwide outcomes for the year 2010

For every 100 9th graders	# Graduate from high school	# Enroll in college after high school	# Are still enrolled their sophomore year	# Graduate within 150% time
In the U.S.	74	46	31	21
In California	74	46	30	22

Source: National Center for Higher Education Management Systems (n.d.)

further cause for concern (Bettinger, Boatman, & Long, 2013). Nationally, remedial enrollment exceeds 20% in public four-year institutions and 50% in community colleges (Complete College America, 2012). Remediation is associated with increased likelihood of attrition and time-to-degree (Flores & Oseguera, 2013).

Underrepresented students—those who are first-generation, low-income, and/or of color—face particular challenges pertaining to higher educational access and completion. For instance, only about 30% of students from the bottom income quartile enroll in college relative to 80% from the top quartile (Bailey & Dynarski, 2011). In 2009, 35% of blacks and 29% of Latinas/os ages 18 to 24 were enrolled in higher education compared to 46% of whites (Kim, 2011). Despite the pervasive assumption that Asian students are the "model minority" (The Education Trust-West, 2012), the college enrollment rates of many Asian Pacific subgroup populations (e.g., Vietnamese, Hmong, Laotian, Cambodian, Pacific Islanders) trail behind those of whites (Teranashi, 2011). Underrepresented students also experience lower rates of completion on average relative to the general population (Aud et al., 2013). Low-income students are six times less likely than their higher-income peers to earn a bachelor's degree by age 25 (Bailey & Dynarkski, 2011). From 2010–2011, 39% of whites ages 25 to 29 held a bachelor's degree or higher compared to 20% of African Americans, 13% of Latinas/os (Aud et al., 2012), and 12%–14% of Laotians, Hmong, and Cambodians (Teranashi, 2013). Part of the problem is that underrepresented students are more likely than their traditional counterparts to attend less-selective institutions for which they are overqualified (e.g., community colleges; Roderick, Coca, & Nagaoka, 2011) or take remedial courses (Complete College America, 2012; see Table 1.2), factors that are associated with lower likelihood of graduation.

Enhancing higher educational attainment is not simply a matter of enrolling more students in college. High school students must graduate

TABLE 1.2. Average U.S. remediation rates among incoming college students, Fall 2006

	Entering two-year colleges	*Entering four-year colleges*
African American	67.7%	39.1%
Latina/o	58.3%	20.6%
White	46.8%	13.6%
Other race/ethnicity	48.9%	16.9%
Low-income	64.7%	31.9%
Total	51.7%	19.9%

Source: Complete College America (2012)

with the knowledge and skills necessary to pursue their postsecondary objectives (Achieve, 2011). Educational researchers and policymakers have thus focused on college readiness (Collins, 2009). A college-ready student is prepared to enter a postsecondary institution without need for remediation and navigate the system to obtain a degree (Conley, 2008; ConnectEd, 2012). Stakeholders aim to define the elements of readiness and enact policies to facilitate students' movement through the K-16 pipeline (Callan, Finney, Kirst, Usdan, & Venezia, 2006; Foley, Mishook, & Lee, 2013).

The college readiness agenda has revealed the misalignment between secondary and postsecondary contexts and encouraged greater rigor in high school curricula (ACT, 2005; Venezia & Voloch, 2012). Readiness discourse has also enhanced transparency around the skills and knowledge needed for postsecondary success (Venezia, Callan, Finney, Kirst, & Usdan, 2005), supporting more unified college preparation efforts across schools and classrooms (Achieve, 2004; Roderick, Nagaoka, & Coca, 2009). Encouraging all students to attend college also combats negative stereotypes about the achievement potential of traditionally underrepresented students (Dougherty, Mellor, & Smith, 2006). College readiness efforts thus reflect concern for educational equity (Symonds et al., 2011; Washington et al., 2012).

Yet despite consensus around the importance of college readiness, it remains an elusive concept—what exactly constitutes readiness, how it should be measured, and how it can be enhanced via policymaking are not clear-cut (Olson, 2006). As Lee (2012) has asserted, "there is a dearth of empirical research to inform national educational policies and standards for college readiness" (p. 52). Although college readiness gets enacted at the school and district level, states shape those responses. Accordingly, the

TABLE 1.3. Remediation rates among incoming students at
California State University, Fall 2013

	Needing remediation in math	Needing remediation in English
African American	53.8%	46.1%
Latina/o	38.8%	42.0%
White	15.4%	12.1%
Other race/ethnicity	23.6%	33.1%
Total	29.1%	32.1%

Source: CSU Proficiency Rates (n.d.)

collection of studies in this book addresses this concern through the lens of college readiness policy in one state—that of California. The national trends in high school to college pathways and remediation outlined above are reflected in California as well (see Tables 1.1 and 1.3). This volume provides insight into the current state of reform via studies of statewide policy design, implementation, and outcomes, as well as the experiences of underprepared students. Insofar as efforts to improve college readiness occur on a statewide level, documenting what takes place in one state enables readers to reflect on efforts in other states as well.

Investigating the policy landscape requires first examining the definitions, assumptions, and policies that characterize the college readiness agenda. First, what does it mean for a student to be college-ready? I discuss how the multifaceted nature of college readiness creates challenges for stakeholders. Second, how is college readiness measured? Which elements of readiness are addressed, and which are left out? I then turn to a discussion of college readiness policies designed to prepare high school students for postsecondary education. How have reforms addressed college readiness? What obstacles remain? Through considering these questions, I offer insight into the current state of the readiness agenda and its ongoing complexities. I close with previews of subsequent chapters.

Defining College Readiness

College readiness is a deceptively nuanced construct that differs from postsecondary eligibility (Connect Ed, 2012; Lombardi, Conley, Seburn, &

Downs, 2013). High schools have traditionally been responsible for making students eligible for higher education, which involves completing a particular course of study and required college admissions tests (Balfanz, 2009; Conley, 2012). Daniel Almeida offers further insight into the historical development of college readiness in chapter 2. However, because many eligible students do not obtain degrees (Attewell, Lavin, Domina, & Levey, 2006; Johnson, 2012), college readiness scholars have broadened the college access agenda to include persistence (Bragg & Durham, 2012; Flores & Oseguera, 2013).

College readiness is characterized according to a range of outcomes (Porter & Polikoff, 2012; Stemler, 2012). Conley (2007) and ACT (2007) have defined college readiness as the level of preparation needed to avoid remedial placement and succeed in credit-bearing college courses. Others have emphasized degree attainment: "students are college-ready when they have the knowledge, skills, and behaviors to complete a college course of study successfully" (Mijares, 2007, p. 1). Some have not specified specific outcomes: "an accumulation of knowledge and experiences that prepare students for college" (Maruyama, 2012, p. 253).

The readiness agenda has grown more complex with the recent integration of career goals. College and career readiness implies the need to prepare students for both higher education and the workplace (Hooley, Marriott, & Sampson, 2011; Lippman, Atienza, Rivers, & Keith, 2008). While some have suggested college readiness and career readiness are synonymous (Achieve, 2013; ACT, 2007), others have asserted they have subtle, or even significant, differences (Conley, 2012; ConnectEd, 2012). For instance, college coursework may require a broader knowledge base than vocational training (Rosenbaum, Stephan, & Rosenbaum, 2010). Although this book focuses on college readiness, conceptions of readiness vary depending on how college and career objectives are specified. Below I discuss how college readiness is characterized in the literature and the challenges associated with defining the construct.

The Elusive Nature of Defining College Readiness

College readiness researchers have shown that successful college students possess a diverse range of skills and knowledge (ACT, 2007; Bloom, 2010). Others also have outlined the specific components of college readiness (Conley, 2012; ConnectEd, 2012; McAlister & Mevs, 2012), which

TABLE 1.4. Components of college readiness

Cognitive academic factors	Non-cognitive academic factors	Campus integration factors
• Content knowledge	• Mindsets	• College knowledge
• Cognitive skills	• Behaviors	• Relationship to self and others

I summarize in three broad categories: cognitive academic factors, non-cognitive academic factors, and campus integration factors (see Table 1.4). Consistent with most readiness scholarship, I define non-cognitive as factors not measured by traditional achievement indicators (e.g., standardized exams; Bowles & Gintis, 1976). Campus integration factors may therefore be considered non-cognitive as well, but do not pertain directly to academics.

Cognitive academic factors. Cognitive academic factors include the content knowledge and cognitive skills required for success in entry-level college coursework (Barnett et al., 2012; Porter & Polikoff, 2012). First, students must acquire core content knowledge (Adelman, 1999, 2006; Conley, 2010). Students need to master the basics in main academic subjects and develop proficiency in math, reading, and writing (Byrd & Macdonald, 2005; Long, Iatarola, & Conger, 2008). Second, college readiness entails cognitive skills such as critical thinking, problem-solving, metacognition, communication skills, research skills, and systems thinking, which facilitate learning across disciplines (ConnectEd, 2012; NRC, 2012).

Non-cognitive academic factors. The academic preparation required for college readiness also includes non-cognitive abilities, or mind-sets and behaviors (Farrington et al., 2012). Mind-sets are the attitudes, beliefs, and emotions students have about themselves and schooling (Dweck, Walton, & Cohen, 2011). Examples include engagement, motivation, self-efficacy, and persistence (Robbins et al., 2004). Academic behaviors enable students to engage with content and maximize learning (Conley, 2012; Kuh, 2007). College-ready behaviors involve help-seeking, motivation, goal-setting, time management, self-efficacy, self-regulation, study skills, and task completion. Researchers have pointed out that these behaviors are transferable to the workplace, and thus also relevant to career readiness (McAlister & Mevs, 2012; NRC, 2012).

Campus integration factors. Although academic ability is essential to college readiness, students also need skills that help them adapt to a postsecondary setting, or campus integration factors. These factors, which may also be framed as non-cognitive, include college knowledge and relationship to self and others. I define each below.

College knowledge. College knowledge refers to understanding the procedural requirements and cultural expectations of higher education (Conley, 2005; Hooker & Brand, 2010). The processes of applying to college and securing financial aid can present large obstacles for high school seniors— particularly those who are low-income and/or first-generation (Corwin & Tierney, 2007; Perna & Steele, 2011). Bryan Rodríguez in chapter 7 explores the challenges associated with financial aid in greater depth. College-ready students understand how to complete college applications, select and enroll in their desired institution, and secure financial resources (ConnectEd, 2012; McAlister & Mevs, 2012). College knowledge also involves awareness of the culture, values, and expectations of postsecondary contexts, which differ from those of secondary schools (Conley, 2007). Research has shown that tacit cultural knowledge, such as knowing to visit office hours, utilize style guides to format papers, and submit assignments on time, is necessary for postsecondary success but may be unfamiliar to many first-generation students (Byrd & Macdonald, 2008; Collier & Morgan, 2008). College-ready students are familiar with the cultural and behavioral norms of higher education (Hooker & Brand, 2010).

Relationship to self and others. In addition to awareness of the postsecondary context, college readiness involves developing a strong relationship to oneself and others. First, students need a firm sense of self or a "productive self-concept" (ConnectEd, 2012, p. 15), which encompasses traits such as self-esteem and self-awareness. According to Conley (2012), students who are successful in postsecondary settings develop an academic- and/or career-oriented identity. College-ready students identify their goals, recognize their strengths and weaknesses, and understand how they fit into the larger campus community. Second, college-ready students possess social-emotional skills that enable positive relationship-building and community engagement (Aries & Seider, 2005; Sedlacek, 2004). Because college campuses serve diverse populations, students are expected to interact well with people from different backgrounds (Durlak, Weissberg, Dymnicki,

Taylor, & Schellinger, 2011; Murnane & Levy, 1996). College-ready students demonstrate interpersonal skills such as effective communication, teamwork, leadership skills, flexibility, and cultural sensitivity (ConnectEd, 2012; NRC, 2012). The ability to establish rapport with professors and build social capital is important to enable persistence, especially for first-generation students (Yamamura, Martinez, & Saenz, 2010).

In summary, college readiness is defined here as the preparation a student needs to enter college and persist to graduation without needing remediation. Readiness includes competencies in three areas: cognitive academic factors, non-cognitive academic factors, and campus integration factors. These components of readiness are summarized in Table 1.4.

Remaining Definitional Challenges

Although researchers have agreed that college readiness involves a combination of academic preparation and non-cognitive capacities, these skills are diverse, complex, and articulated in multiple ways (Olson, 2006; Washington et al., 2012). In addition, readiness develops and manifests differently for different students (Conley, 2012). The absence of a universal, operational definition leads stakeholders to interpret college readiness based on their individual experiences and goals (McAlister & Mevs, 2012). For instance, Washington et al. (2012) studied the implementation of a high school course developed in Virginia to enhance students' college readiness. Findings revealed large variation in course design due to teachers' varying perceptions of college readiness. For example, some prioritized academic outcomes, others focused on student motivation, and others emphasized knowledge transfer across contexts.

The ambiguity around readiness is particularly problematic for first-generation students and their families. Research has found that parents from different backgrounds have diverse, often conflicting perspectives on college readiness (Cortez, Martinez, & Saenz, 2013; ENCORE, 2009). One study by ENCORE (2009) found that high-income, native English-speaking parents spoke of college readiness in terms of skills (e.g., critical thinking, strong study habits), while low-income, Spanish-speaking parents understood readiness in terms of measurable outcomes (e.g., exam scores, high school graduation). Students and parents require clearer understandings of what college readiness entails to access adequate preparatory experiences (Yamamura et al., 2010). Consequently, one remaining challenge for researchers and policymakers is enhancing transparency and clarity around the components of college readiness (Maruyama, 2012).

Some scholars have argued that dominant college readiness models fail to adequately address the high school context or the cultural identities of students, families, and communities (Carter, Locks, & Winkle-Wagner, 2013; Castro, 2013). By focusing on the skills students should have, readiness frameworks de-emphasize the structural conditions that create inequitable access to college preparation (Welton & Martinez, 2013). Studies focusing on college knowledge tend to adopt a deficit model, portraying students of color as lacking social or cultural capital or college aspirations (Castro, 2013). Researchers consequently recommend policies designed to remedy deficiencies rather than build on the existing cultural assets of underrepresented youth (Liou, Antrop-Gonzalez, Cooper, 2009). Most quantitative studies of college readiness employ dichotomous variables to account for race (e.g., Latino/Hispanic, or not), which oversimplify the multifaceted nature of cultural identity (Welton & Martinez, 2013). Few studies acknowledge the heterogeneity of college preparatory practices among students from similar racial/ethnic backgrounds. Mainstream conceptions of readiness may therefore perpetuate a set of normative assumptions around college-going (Castro, 2013). Greater consideration of the contexts, needs, and experiences of non-dominant students may improve college readiness models.

Measuring College Readiness

Although college readiness involves non-cognitive elements, it is typically measured based on indicators of academic performance (McAlister & Mevs, 2012). Measures of academic achievement are useful for two primary reasons. First, research has cited rigorous academic preparation as a key predictor of postsecondary outcomes (Adelman, 1999, 2006; Long, Iatarola, & Conger, 2008; Perna, 2005). How students perform in high school is strongly associated with their likelihood of doing well in college courses. Second, assessments of student performance are relatively easy to obtain and standardize (Porter & Polikoff, 2012). In what follows, I first discuss the common indicators used to measure readiness and then areas for future improvement.

Indicators for Measuring College Readiness

Course-taking, GPA, and class rank. One approach is to examine high school students' course-taking patterns, such as the level of course rigor and fulfillment of four-year college admissions requirements (Porter & Polikoff, 2012; Roderick et al., 2009). Research has identified the rigor of curriculum as the strongest indicator of college performance (DesJardins & Lindsay, 2008), and the effect of rigorous course-taking is even larger for African American and Latina/o students than for their white peers (Adelman, 1999). Taking advanced courses while in high school has consistently been associated with higher likelihood of postsecondary success (Karp, Calcagno, Hughes, Jeong, & Bailey, 2007; Struhl & Vargas, 2012). Thus, students who have completed a college preparatory curriculum may be considered college-ready (Lee, 2010). High school grade point average (GPA) and class rank are additional indicators used to assess a student's level of readiness for college (Astin & Oseguera, 2012). Research has established a relationship between these measures of high school performance and college GPA (Cimetta, D'Agostino, & Levin, 2010; DesJardins & Lindsay, 2008; Strayhorn, 2010).

Standardized testing. In addition to course-taking patterns, GPA, and class rank, test performance is often employed to assess readiness (Camara et al., 2010; Wiley, Wyatt, & Camara, 2010). Researchers have developed benchmark scores on college admissions tests (e.g., ACT and SAT) to predict a student's likelihood of postsecondary achievement (Wyatt, Kobrin, Wiley, Camara, & Proestler, 2011). Cut scores have also been established on state and/or institutional assessments such as remedial placement exams (e.g., ACCUPLACER and COMPASS) to signify readiness (Grubb et al., 2011; Venezia & Voloch, 2012)—an approach Lisa Garcia will examine in chapter 5. Standardized test performance is often used to determine college course assignment (Howell, Kurlaender, & Grodsky, 2010). Students who do not exceed a designated cut score on college admissions tests, Advanced Placement exams, or institutional remedial placement assessments may be considered not ready and placed into remediation (Calcagno & Long, 2008).

Postsecondary outcomes. The aforementioned academic indicators may be more or less predictive depending on how a researcher defines college success. As Porter and Polikoff (2012) have pointed out, various postsecondary outcomes can serve as proxies for whether a student was ready for college. Assignment to remediation is one postsecondary outcome used to gauge students' readiness. Other scholars use college freshman GPA, which is measured on a four-point scale by most institutions and only requires following high school graduates for one year. When researchers have the capacity to collect longitudinal data, longer-term postsecondary outcomes may be used to evaluate students' readiness. For instance, studies may consider degree completion, time-to-degree, or the cumulative GPA of graduating seniors (Porter & Polikoff, 2012). In summary, college readiness is typically measured based on indicators of academic achievement at both the secondary and postsecondary levels.

Remaining Measurement Challenges

Although common indicators offer insight into students' achievement levels, there is no consensus around how college readiness should be measured (Conley, 2007; Maruyama, 2012). Below I discuss recommendations for (a) improving academic indicators and (b) developing indicators for noncognitive competencies.

Improving academic readiness indicators. Many researchers have highlighted shortcomings of existing academic indicators and offered suggestions for improvement (Maruyama, 2012; Nichols & Berliner, 2008). I address each in the following subsections.

Course-taking, GPA, and class rank. Although rigorous course-taking is strongly associated with success in college, this indicator is difficult to assess due to variation across schools and classrooms (ACT, 2007; Maruyama, 2012; Porter & Polikoff, 2012). Researchers may quantify the number and types of college preparatory courses that appear on students' transcripts, but course titles do not convey the level of rigor or breadth of content students experienced (Finkelstein & Fong, 2008; Wyatt, Wiley, Camara, & Proestler, 2011). One challenge is the absence of a standardized measure for academic rigor. Wyatt et al. (2011) utilized SAT scores and test-takers' high school grades to establish an academic rigor index (ARI), but the ARI was created based on test-takers' course titles, and thus could not account for instructional variation across classrooms. The variation in academic rigor across educational contexts speaks to the weaknesses inherent in measuring readiness based on GPA and class rank (Porter & Polikoff,

2012). A high school GPA of 4.0 may signal that a student is hardwork-ing, but does not necessarily indicate that a student mastered college-ready academic content and honed college-ready academic skills.

Standardized testing. Scholars have suggested that standardized test performance is insufficient to accurately reflect a student's level of academ-ic preparation, citing both philosophical arguments and concerns around validity and reliability (Maruyama, 2012; Stemler, 2012). Standardized testing has sparked general criticism for conflating exam performance with student learning (Crouse & Trusheim, 1988; Kim & Sunderman, 2005; Nichols, Glass, & Berliner, 2005). Students may perform well on particular tests without mastering course content or acquiring a broad range of skills and knowledge. Benchmarks on standardized exams also portray college readiness as a dichotomous variable—ready, or not—rather than a complex set of competencies that develop over time (Barnes & Slate, 2013). At the same time, standardized testing has been associated with reinforcing unequal systems of power (Fraizer, 2003). College admissions exam scores have been associated with socioeconomic status, as high-income parents can provide their children with supplemental test preparation (e.g., tutor-ing; Huot & Williamson, 1997; Lehman, 1999).

Additional areas for improvement relate to the validity and reliabil-ity of standardized assessments for measuring college readiness. Research finds that college admissions tests are only minimally useful in predicting postsecondary achievement (Allensworth & Easton, 2007; Niu & Tienda, 2010). Since institutions vary by type, selectivity, and criteria for admis-sions and course placement, benchmarks may signal readiness for some universities but not for others (ACT, 2010; Lee, 2012). Another challenge is that college admissions tests are disconnected from federal and state standards (Achieve, 2007). Because the SAT and ACT tests are norm ref-erenced, scores reflect how students compare to other test-takers rather than what content they have mastered (Atkinson & Geiser, 2009). Ef-forts to improve the alignment of assessments to curriculum have been complicated by the variation in readiness standards across states and test-ing organizations, although the Common Core may encourage greater uniformity (Porter, McMaken, Hwang, & Yang, 2011; Le, 2002; Rolfhus, Decker, Brite, & Gregory, 2010). Remedial placement exams, which are often institution-specific and cannot be standardized across contexts, also raise concerns around validity (Porter & Polikoff, 2012).

Postsecondary outcomes. Postsecondary outcomes commonly used to de-termine college readiness also have limitations (Porter & Polikoff, 2012).

For example, remedial placement may not accurately measure readiness because many students assigned to college-level courses do not persist (Ashtiani & Feliciano, 2012), and remedial courses vary across institutions (Levin & Calcagno, 2008). I further explore the challenges associated with remedial assessment and placement in chapter 6. Variation in coursework across colleges and universities limits the utility of measuring readiness based on freshman GPA. Using freshman grades also requires selecting a benchmark GPA that differentiates ready students from their not-ready peers; the challenge is determining what level of achievement (e.g., passing vs. earning a B average) denotes readiness. Long-term outcomes, such as graduation and time-to-degree, are useful given the emphasis on college completion. However, using these indicators necessitates tracking students for multiple years, and this type of data is often difficult to obtain (Porter & Polikoff, 2012).

Given these challenges, scholars have advocated for using multiple measures and improving existing indicators to more accurately assess students' academic readiness (Hodara, Jaggars, & Karp, 2012). Coupling high school test scores with course grades, for instance, is important to give greater weight to teachers' judgments of students' ability (Maruyama, 2012). Researchers are also developing college and career readiness assessments based on the Common Core standards (Achieve, 2012). The College Career Ready School Diagnostic (CCRSD) developed by Conley and colleagues (2010) assesses the extent to which schools offer college preparatory opportunities (Conley, McGaughy, Kirtner, Van Der Valk, & Martinez-Wenzl, 2010), and has shown evidence of reliability and internal validity (Lombardi et al., 2013). Such comprehensive assessments are promising but have yet to be adopted on a wide scale. Further research is needed to maximize the effectiveness of these measures.

Measuring non-cognitive readiness competencies. As discussed above, college readiness is not simply the acquisition of academic content knowledge or skills (Conley, 2012). Measures of academic performance may therefore "fail to fully capture the developmental process required for all young people to complete high school and enter, succeed in, and graduate from postsecondary education and training" (Hooker & Brand, 2012, p. 77).

Research on attrition has revealed that many students who drop out of college were actually in good academic standing (Johnson, 2012). For instance, Tinto (1993) found that academic failure accounts for only 15%-25% of dropouts. Most students drop out for reasons such as poor social integration, dissatisfaction with the institutional environment, or financial concerns (Tinto, 1993). A study by the American Institutes for Research (AIR) reported that only 10% of students who dropped out prior to degree completion had less than a C grade point average (GPA; Johnson, 2012). Attewell, Heil, and Reisel (2010) found that across two-year and four-year institutions, no single, dominant factor is associated with degree attainment, and factors related to graduation vary widely. Relying on measures of academic performance may not fully illustrate students' likelihood of postsecondary completion.

Scholars have suggested that non-cognitive competencies may be particularly important for the long-term educational success of first-generation youth (Deke & Haimson, 2006; Kyllonen, 2008; Lerman, 2008; Sedlacek, 2008). One qualitative study investigated first-generation college students' perspectives on college readiness (Byrd & Macdonald, 2005). Participants stressed the importance of time management, goal-setting, help-seeking, and self-advocacy more frequently than academic skills like math and reading. College knowledge is another aspect of readiness that academic indicators do not capture (Hooker & Brand, 2010). Postsecondary requirements such as taking admissions tests, meeting particular deadlines, and selecting a well-matched college are often difficult for students to navigate (Corwin & Tierney, 2007). How much aid students receive and students' perceptions of college costs also affect college outcomes (Perna & Steele, 2011). Even high-achieving students may be unable to matriculate successfully if unaware of admissions and financial aid procedures (Lin, 2006). Almeida's study in part II of this volume offers insight into the challenges first generation students face in acquiring college knowledge.

The shortcomings of current measurement systems stem not from the focus on academic preparation but rather from the conflation of academic readiness with college readiness (Maruyama, 2012). Indicators of academic preparation are often purported to measure college readiness in mainstream policy discourse. Yet while academically ready students may be positioned to perform well in college courses, they are not inherently college-ready (Karp & Hughes, 2008; McAlister & Mevs, 2012). Additional indicators that account for non-cognitive, nonacademic competencies may facilitate more comprehensive approaches to college preparation and provide clearer information for students and their families (Conley, 2010). As ConnectEd (2012) asserts, "assessments are needed that can measure the full array of knowledge and skills in the proposed [college readiness frameworks]" (p. 17). The subsequent section examines how college readiness has been translated to policy.

Developing College Readiness Policy

Attention to college readiness has sparked reforms to smooth students' transitions from high school to postsecondary education (Cline, Bissel, Hafner, & Katz, 2007; Domina & Ruzek, 2013). Federal legislation such as Race to the Top and the American Recovery and Reinvestment Act of 2009 has prioritized college and career readiness (Bloom, 2010; Yamamura et al., 2010). To be sure, college readiness policy broadly defined may arguably assume many forms, such as expanding charter schools (Hoxby, Murarka, & Kang, 2009), developing early college high schools (Hoffman & Vargas, 2010), hiring more qualified teachers (Howell, 2011), and creating longitudinal data tracking systems (Adelman, 2010). These reform initiatives are beyond the scope of this chapter. I focus on two policies that explicitly address college readiness in public high schools, which prepare the majority of underserved students for higher education: college for all curriculum and college readiness assessment. I discuss the accomplishments and challenges of each below.

College Readiness Policies Targeting Public High Schools

College for all curriculum. One college readiness policy approach is encompassed in the mantra "college for all," implying that all high school students should graduate prepared to pursue postsecondary degrees (Carnevale, 2008; Osterman, 2008). This goal suggests the need to expose all students to a college preparatory curriculum (Hoffman, Vargas, Venezia, & Miller, 2007; Venezia, Kirst, & Antonio, 2004). College for all is embodied in state- and district-level policies focused on college preparatory course-taking and accelerated learning programs (Allensworth, Nomi, Montgomery, & Lee, 2009; An, 2013). A college preparatory curriculum involves minimum coursework in core academic subjects (e.g., four years of English and at least three years of math) that make students eligible for postsecondary entrance (Venezia & Jaeger, 2013). Historically, high school students planning to pursue higher education have been encouraged to complete these courses. Traditionally underrepresented students have been less likely than their higher-income white counterparts to be ushered into the college preparatory track and more likely to be steered into vocational courses (McDonough, 1997; Oakes, 2005).

Policymakers have aimed to combat this trend and increase college-going by implementing stricter curricular requirements (Achieve, 2011; Venezia & Jaeger, 2013). Twenty-one states and the District of Columbia will have mandated college preparatory course-taking by the year 2015 (Achieve, 2012; Balfanz, 2009, 2012; Mazzeo, 2010). Many school districts such as Los Angeles Unified and San Jose Unified in California have also instituted default curriculum standards (Finkelstein & Fong, 2008). These reforms aim to ensure that all high school graduates meet the course-taking requirements for entrance into four-year institutions. Such policies are motivated by research showing that schools in which all students take college preparatory coursework have higher achievement outcomes and more equitable learning opportunities for low-income students of color (Lee, Burkam, Smerdon, Chow-Hoy, & Geverdt, 1997; Lee, Croninger, & Smith, 1997).

Accelerated learning programs such as dual enrollment (DE) and Advanced Placement (AP) expose high school students to college-level academics and the opportunity to earn college credits (An, 2013; Struhl & Vargas, 2012; Ward & Vargas, 2012). DE courses utilize a college syllabus, confer college credits to students who pass the class, and may be offered on a postsecondary campus (Speroni, 2011). AP courses have a standardized curriculum intended to be college-level, and students can earn college credits if they pass the optional exam at the end of the year. Studies comparing the outcomes of AP or DE course-takers to non-course-takers find that participation in college-level classes increases the probability that students will enroll and succeed in a postsecondary institution (Iatarola, Conger, & Long, 2011; Karp et al., 2007). Though initially developed to target high-achieving students, accelerated learning programs have been viewed as a strategy to increase college readiness (An, 2013; Hoffman et al., 2008). Policymakers have encouraged schools to offer these courses to a broader population of students (Ward & Vargas, 2012). To summarize, college for all reforms include requiring college preparatory curriculum for all students and expanding access to accelerated learning programs.

College readiness assessment. Another prevalent college readiness initiative has focused on assessing high school students' proficiency prior to college matriculation (Dougherty, 2008; Venezia & Voloch, 2012; Zinth, 2012). These efforts reflect concern that many students do not know they are underprepared until they enter college and place into remediation (Knudson, Zitzer-Comfort, Quirk, & Alexander, 2008). The idea is that if students learn they are not ready earlier, they can improve their skills before high school graduation, reducing remedial need at the college level. Assessment initiatives often involve interventions for struggling students.

Many states have employed existing testing mechanisms—K-12 state assessments or college placement tests—to support postsecondary preparation (Achieve, 2012; Martinez & Klopott, 2005). California's Early Assessment Program (EAP) is one such policy that has received national attention (McLean, 2012; Venezia & Voloch, 2012) and will be discussed by Garcia later in this volume. The EAP added college readiness indicators to the 11th grade California Standards Test (CST). Participating seniors who have not met proficiency in English may enroll in the Expository Reading and Writing Course (ERWC) designed by K-12 teachers and California State University (CSU) faculty (Knudson et al., 2008). A similar course is being developed for math. The EAP also provides professional development for high school teachers. While the program has not significantly lowered remediation rates, researchers have identified some evidence of its effectiveness (Achieve, 2009; McLean, 2012). One study found that EAP decreased students' likelihood of placing into remediation by four percentage points in math and six percentage points in English (Howell et al., 2010). Hafner, Joseph, and McCormick (2010) reported that ERWC participation increased students' learning outcomes and improved teachers' knowledge of postsecondary literacy standards.

Other states have implemented similar reforms. Florida requires high school students that score within a specified range on its state exam to take a college readiness assessment during their junior year (Barnett & Fay, 2013; Burdman, 2011). Students who do not meet college-ready proficiency must enroll in College Success and College Readiness classes, which impart postsecondary developmental education curriculum. New Mexico legislation adopted in 2003 mandated the alignment of high school curricula with the placement tests employed at public colleges and universities (Dounay, 2006). Since 2001, 11th-graders in Colorado and Illinois have been required to take the ACT, an approach that has been associated with increased college-going rates in both states (ACT, 2005). The City University of New York's (CUNY) At Home in College Program (AHC) offers math and English preparatory classes for public high school students who

TABLE 1.5. The college readiness policy agenda for public high schools

College for all curriculums	College readiness assessment
• Mandated college preparatory course-taking	• Early signals based on college readiness indicators
• Accelerated learning programs	• CCR assessments aligned with Common Core State Standards

have not met college readiness benchmarks on the SAT or the state assessments (Venezia & Voloch, 2012). Students then take the CUNY Placement Exam in January of their senior year and have a second opportunity to pass the test in the spring. AHC has been associated with decreased remedial need at CUNY.

While some states have employed existing testing mechanisms to support college preparation, the Common Core State Standards (CCSS) initiative has spurred the development of college and career readiness assessments (Lee, 2010; Rothman, 2011). These standards, adopted by 45 states since 2009, outline the skills and knowledge needed for success in college-level English and math coursework (ConnectEd, 2012; Dougherty et al., 2006). The federal government awarded two multistate consortia more than $362 million to design these assessment systems for the 2014–15 school year (U.S. Department of Education, 2010).

The two consortia, the Partnership for the Assessment of Readiness for College and Careers (PARCC) and Smarter Balance, have taken different approaches, but their systems share some similarities (Doorey, 2012). Both feature end-of-the-year summative assessments, optional interim assessments, professional development, model curricula, and formative tasks for instructional use. The consortia also include cutoff scores on the 11th-grade assessments that indicate college readiness in English and math (Barnett & Fay, 2013). These assessments are particularly important given that fewer than 2% of math items and 20% of English items on existing state tests measure the high-order skills required for college and career readiness (Yuan & Le, 2012). Researchers have found that PARCC and Smarter Balance assessments reflect the goals of deeper learning, or the transferable college- and work-ready skills that enable success (Herman & Linn, 2013; Pellegrino & Hilton, 2012).

In summary, integrating high school assessments and college readiness indicators represents a second policy trend to improve students' likelihood

of postsecondary success. Table 1.5 summarizes the college readiness policy interventions discussed above.

Remaining Policy Challenges

College for all curriculum. Although mandating high curricular standards
may broaden access to college preparation, scholars have raised some concerns around placing all students on a college-bound track (Barnes & Slate,
2013; Glass & Nygreen, 2011; Roderick, Coca, Moeller, & Kelley-Kemple,
2013). Research indicates that of the 47 million job openings projected
by 2018, more than two-thirds will require some postsecondary education (Carnevale, Smith, & Strohl, 2010). Nearly half of the jobs requiring attainment beyond high school—14 million—will demand workers
with an associate's degree or occupational certificate (Barton, 2008). Yet by
mandating course-taking patterns required for entering four-year institutions, current reforms de-emphasize educational and vocational alternatives and potentially disadvantage students geared for community colleges
(Barnes & Slate, 2013)—obstacles Rodríguez discusses in further detail in
chapter 3. Rosenbaum (2001) has argued that "college for all" is confusing and deceptive for many youth, who are encouraged to plan for college
regardless of their past achievement and personal goals. Some researchers
have recommended enabling students to pursue multiple postsecondary
pathways (Rosenbaum, 2001; Symonds et al., 2011). Opponents of tracking warn that different paths result in the marginalization of traditionally
underrepresented youth (Nieto, 1999; Oakes, 2005; Spring, 2000), which
is a legitimate concern. Nevertheless, policies focusing on bachelor's degree
attainment rather than higher education generally seem misaligned with
projected economic demand and may fail to acknowledge the goals of all
students.

　　College for all initiatives also raise the stakes for students and may
create particular challenges for underserved youth (Balfanz, 2012; Rosenbaum, 2001). Academic achievement rates and course-taking patterns
are already stratified by race and class (Ashtiani & Feliciano, 2012). One
study of California high schools found that the proportion of white seniors
who had completed the college preparatory curriculum exceeded that of
Latina/o and African American seniors by at least 15 percentage points in
both English and math (Finkelstein & Fong, 2008). Likelihood of meeting
these requirements also varied substantially across schools, with students

in low-performing schools significantly less likely to complete college preparatory courses. Different students therefore have unequal opportunities to meet the same high standards, and the personal consequences of failing to meet those standards (e.g., inability to graduate high school) may fall disproportionately on the most marginalized youth (Rosenbaum & Becker, 2011).

As a result, college for all policies may inadvertently push underserved students out of the K-12 system (Berliner, 2006; Rosenbaum et al., 2010). Research on dropouts finds that students who leave high school early are often struggling academically (Balfanz, 2012; Neild & Balfanz, 2006; Rumberger, 2011). Dropout rates run as high as 50% in urban districts that serve primarily low-income students of color (Balfanz & Legters, 2004; Greene & Forster, 2003). In a study of Chicago schools, which mandated college preparatory coursework beginning in 1997, Mazzeo (2010) found that struggling students earned lower grades and were more likely to fail ninth-grade classes after the reform. High school graduation and postsecondary enrollment rates also decreased. While Allensworth et al. (2009) found that mandatory college preparatory curriculum did not exacerbate the dropout rate in Chicago schools, Algebra I failure rates among low-ability students increased. Struggling students may also be funneled out of the traditional school system. For instance, after San Jose Unified School District mandated a college preparatory curriculum, black and Latina/o students were disproportionately transferred to alternative high schools (Lin, 2006). Providing additional academic supports is imperative to ensure that underserved high school students can succeed (Asch, 2010; Symonds et al., 2011).

Another concern is that completing a college preparatory curriculum does not guarantee readiness, evidenced by high rates of remediation in four-year institutions (Dougherty, 2008; Flores & Oseguera, 2013; Howell, 2011). For example, a study of Chicago Public Schools (CPS) found that many rising 12th-graders had already fulfilled their college preparatory course requirements and opted to take relatively easy classes (e.g., electives; Roderick et al., 2013). Racial and economic disparities widened in the fourth year of high school because first-generation students did not know the importance of taking advanced courses for college transition. Students may also complete college preparatory course requirements but remain ineligible for more selective four-year institutions if they do not take the SAT or complete other admissions requirements (Lin, 2006).

Research has also found that high school courses with advanced labels may be only nominally rigorous, especially in low-performing schools (Achieve, 2012; ACT, 2007; Ewing, 2006). AP courses vary in difficulty level across schools and classrooms, and passing rates on AP exams are stratified by race and class (Dougherty, Mellor, & Jian, 2005). Students taking AP courses in lower-quality schools are significantly less likely than their more privileged counterparts to pass the exams, and many do not even take the test (Dougherty et al., 2005). Students may therefore earn high grades in advanced classes without having encountered or mastered rigorous coursework. For these reasons, mandating college preparatory curriculum and/or encouraging participation in accelerated learning programs must be accompanied by additional strategies to ensure that (a) coursework is actually challenging, (b) struggling students receive extra support, and (c) all students meet non-course-related admissions requirements.

College readiness assessment. While aligning high school state assessments with college readiness indicators has sparked improvement on many fronts, testing alone does not enhance students' college preparedness (Darling-Hammond & Adamson, 2013; McLean, 2012; Venezia, Bracco, & Nodine, 2010). The assumption that undergirds college readiness assessments is that students who know they are behind will take the necessary steps to improve their skills. Yet some research suggests that information does not always encourage or enable students to act (Tierney & Garcia, 2011; McLean, 2012). In one report on California's Early Assessment Program, McLean (2012) highlighted the need to enhance students' responsiveness to their test results because the program does not require students to enroll in preparatory courses. Tierney and Garcia (2011) also conducted a study of EAP and found that participating students were generally unaware that they had taken a college readiness exam and received feedback. Consequently, EAP did not motivate changes in students' behavior during their senior year. Many of the participants' schools did not offer the academic support class, and their teachers and counselors often did not know students' EAP results. Tierney and Garcia (2011) highlighted the importance of conveying testing information to students in a way that is meaningful and accessible, effectively delivering academic supports, and strengthening secondary-postsecondary partnerships.

Teacher professional development is also critical to ensure that college readiness indicators facilitate students' improvement (Callan et al., 2006;

Darling-Hammond & Adamson, 2013; Knudson et al., 2008; Venezia & Jaeger, 2013). Because teachers are responsible for delivering the supplemental curriculum, they play a central role in enabling the success of early assessment programs (Knudson et al., 2008). A 2012 report on EAP suggested the need to involve more high school teachers in professional development (McLean, 2012). Darling-Hammond (2007) has shown that teachers need curricular resources and training to align their instructional practices with higher-level skills and content. Indeed, if teachers are unsure of how to align their instruction with postsecondary standards—or even what postsecondary standards are—high school students that learn they are not ready cannot access the support they need.

Another challenge is the timing of these tests. Many of these college readiness assessments are administered during students' junior year, but scholars have pointed out that 11th grade may be too late for students to learn they are underprepared for college-level work (Venezia & Voloch, 2012). Struggling students, particularly those who may be community college–bound, are often performing far below grade level and cannot achieve proficiency by the end of their senior year. Given that students who drop out often fall behind early in their high school careers (Neild & Balfanz, 2006), college readiness indicators and academic interventions may be more beneficial if offered in earlier grades (Dougherty & Rutherford, 2010).

Although the PARCC and Smarter Balance assessment systems may measure college-ready skills more effectively than existing tests, researchers have expressed concerns regarding the availability of resources (Darling-Hammond & Adamson, 2013; Doorey, 2012; Sawchuk, 2010). Darling-Hammond and Adamson (2013) highlighted affordability and feasibility as potential challenges to the implementation of new assessment systems. High-quality assessments that test more complex learning tasks and require human scoring are more costly than low-quality assessments that rely primarily on multiple-choice questions. States will need to engage in cost-saving practices and resource reallocation to reap the benefits of new assessments. Regarding feasibility, Darling-Hammond and Adamson (2013) advocated for including teachers in scoring processes and better integrating formative and summative assessments. Without thoughtful integration of curriculum, assessment, and professional development, college- and career-ready assessment systems are unlikely to motivate improved teaching and learning.

Another concern is that assessment efforts and their accompanying interventions tend to focus exclusively on academic preparation (Roderick et al., 2009; Venezia & Voloch, 2012). While obtaining information on students' math and English performance is crucial, meeting proficiency benchmarks is only one ingredient of postsecondary readiness (Zhao, 2009). Non-cognitive competencies such as acquiring college knowledge are essential to college readiness (Hooker & Brand, 2012), but students who participate in college readiness assessment programs do not necessarily receive additional forms of college-going support (e.g., college counseling). Increasing college readiness requires that school personnel help students understand both the academic and nonacademic facets of college (Barnes, Slate, & Rojas-LeBouef, 2010).

College for all initiatives and assessment efforts have potential to improve high school students' college preparation—and in many instances already have. Yet challenges remain for first-generation youth in particular who continue to face barriers on their path to college. Broadening the scope of existing reforms such that students can successfully pursue a range of postsecondary options may be worthwhile. The success of current initiatives depends on enhancing the capacity of schools, staff, and teachers to support students' postsecondary goals.

Moving College Readiness Forward

I have suggested here that college readiness is a nuanced construct. Although use of the term has become commonplace in research, policy, and practice, what college readiness means and how it can be enhanced are questions that lack clear answers. I have offered a broad definition of college readiness that we use for the purpose of this book: College readiness is the preparation required to enroll in college and persist to graduation without need for remediation. Readiness consists of a variety of competencies that fall into three main categories: cognitive academic factors, non-cognitive academic factors, and campus integration factors. Some authors in this volume focus on particular aspects of students' readiness, but all assume that college readiness cannot be fully captured by one indicator or category of skills.

Indeed, the multifaceted nature of college readiness defies simple and straightforward policy solutions. Educational stakeholders are still working to identify effective strategies for moving students through the K-16 pipeline. The good news, however, is that current efforts to define, measure, and legislate college readiness have made considerable progress. The college readiness agenda has raised awareness around the importance of postsecondary attainment, sparked K-12 curricular reform, and motivated more students to pursue ambitious educational goals. Despite ongoing complexities and challenges, college readiness offers a mechanism for improving educational quality and enhancing equal opportunity.

The chapters in this volume offer various perspectives on the issue of college readiness. In the ensuing chapters we offer a bit of history as a way to continue the conversation about what is meant by preparation for college. We then use by way of example what is taking place in California in order to underscore state actions. By no means are we suggesting that what California does, or is doing, is a model for the rest of the nation. We also are not suggesting that everything we consider here is the sum of what a state such as California is doing. To the contrary, what we have attempted here is to offer analyses on multiple levels to highlight the interrelatedness and complexity of issues that surround college readiness. We are reacting against analyses that reduce college readiness to a "magic bullet," as if one act on one level—helping high school students read at grade level, for example—will solve the dilemma of ensuring more of America's children are prepared for college. As part II demonstrates, actions are occurring on multiple levels, and the way to think about them is also multifaceted.

The remainder of part I discusses the historical and contemporary challenges associated with college access and completion. Daniel Almeida explores the historical roots of the college readiness agenda in chapter 2. Documenting educational trends since the establishment of the U.S. higher education system, Almeida illustrates how postsecondary access has expanded in response to changing workforce demand, shifting demographic trends, and heightened concern for equitable educational opportunity. This chapter provides the historical and conceptual context necessary for understanding college readiness today.

In chapter 3, Bryan Rodríguez builds on Almeida's historical analysis by examining 19th- and 20th-century reforms that shaped the educational trajectories of underserved students in particular. Rodríguez frames his discussion around a group of students he refers to as the "least ready," or those who enter community colleges significantly underprepared and require multiple levels of remediation. These students differ from those who transfer to a four-year institution or graduate within a four-year time horizon with an A.A./A.S. degree or certificate. The term "least ready" is not intended to advance a deficit perspective—indeed, that some students enter community college several levels behind reflects a failure on the part of the school system to provide adequate preparation rather than a failure on the part of the individual student (Castro, 2013). Students who are "least ready" address a central dilemma facing state policymakers: What should be done to help students who enter two-year colleges significantly underprepared and become trapped in cycles of remedial coursework? Chapter 3 documents how compulsory schooling laws and the California Master Plan for Higher Education of 1960 have shaped educational opportunity for these most vulnerable students. Collectively, chapters 2 and 3 provide historical perspective on the rise of the college readiness agenda and the challenges that remain for students at risk of non-completion.

Part II features empirical and theoretical work focusing on high school preparation and higher education reform in California in order to highlight how one state is dealing with such an initiative. California is a useful model for analysis of state-level college readiness policy given its size, diversity, and expansive higher education system. In chapter 4, Daniel Almeida investigates the preparatory experiences of college-bound seniors attending public high schools in Los Angeles. Focusing on students' acquisition of college knowledge—the information required to apply to, select, and enroll in a postsecondary institution and secure financial aid—Almeida documents the particular challenges that low-income, first-generation students face as they prepare to transition to college from low-performing schools.

In chapter 5, Lisa Garcia examines the California State University's (CSU) Early Assessment Program (EAP), referenced earlier, which was designed to provide high school students early signals regarding their college readiness. Garcia focuses on the history, development, implementation, and outcomes of the EAP, highlighting its accomplishments and shortcomings. Ultimately, she argues that information alone—absent substantial academic interventions that support improvement—is insufficient to increase the college readiness of high school students.

Chapter 6 examines a more recent CSU policy, the Early Start Program, which targets high remediation rates by requiring underprepared students to begin coursework over the summer prior to their first fall semester. I present findings from an inquiry into the implementation of this policy. Focusing on the sense-making of English and composition faculty members, I explore how ground-level actors first resisted and ultimately complied with the CSU mandate. I suggest that literacy remediation in particular occupies contested terrain in higher education and reflects the chasm between policy and practice. I highlight variation across campuses with respect to remedial assessment and instruction.

In chapter 7, Bryan Rodríguez explores higher education reform with a focus on California's community colleges. He investigates how recent policy shifts in financial aid and two-year college course registration are shaping the experiences of the least ready students. Using rich qualitative data based on a sample of two-year college students placed into the lowest levels of remediation, Rodríguez identifies the unique challenges that severely underprepared students face in persisting to degree attainment or transfer to a four-year institution. In particular, he suggests that diminishing access to financial aid and new restrictions on college course registration have created additional barriers for students who already struggle academically.

William Tierney concludes the volume with a discussion of the way forward in chapter 8. He offers commentary on the preceding chapters and considers future directions for college readiness scholars, policymakers, and practitioners, drawing on the lessons learned from California. Certainly, the analyses presented in this book cannot fully address the numerous and diverse issues associated with college readiness. However, through consideration of historical trends and the current policy landscape in California across the secondary and postsecondary systems, we offer insight into the progress that has been made and the challenges that remain for increasing postsecondary access, readiness, and completion.

References

Achieve, Inc. (2004). The expectations gap: A 50-state review of high school graduation requirements. Washington, DC: Achieve, Inc.

Achieve, Inc. (2007). *Aligned expectations? A closer look at college admissions and placement tests.* Washington, DC: Author.

Achieve. (2009, October). *An analysis of the Early Assessment Program Assessments for Algebra II, Summative High School Mathematics, and English.* Retrieved on February 13, 2013 from http://www.stanford.edu/group/pace/PUBLICATIONS/CDP/AchieveFINALEAPReport Oct2009.pdf

Achieve, Inc. (2011). *Closing the expectation gap 2011: Sixth annual 50-state progress report on the alignment of high school policies with the demands of college and careers*. Retrieved from http://www.achieve.org/files/AchieveClosingtheExpectationsGap2011.pdf

Achieve, Inc. (2012). Closing the expectations gap: 50-state progress report on the alignment of K-12 policies and practice with the demands of college and careers. American Diploma Project Network. Achieve.

Achieve, Inc. (2013). Make the Case: College Ready AND Career Ready. Retrieved from http://www.futurereadyproject.org/sites/frp/files/Flex-CollegeReady%26CareerReady.pdf

Adelman, C. (1999). *Answers in the tool box: Academic intensity, attendance patterns, and bachelor's degree attainment*. Washington, DC: U.S. Department of Education.

Adelman, C. (2006). *The toolbox revisited: Paths to degree completion from high school through college*. Washington, DC: U.S. Department of Education.

Adelman, C. (2010). *College—and career—ready: Using outcomes data to hold high schools accountable for student success*. Washington, DC: Education Sector Reports.

Allensworth, E. M., & Easton, J. Q. (2007). *What matters for staying on-track and graduating in Chicago public high schools*. Chicago: Consortium on Chicago School Research.

Allensworth, E., Nomi, T., Montgomery, N., & Lee, V. E. (2009). College preparatory curriculum for all: Consequences of ninth grade course taking on academic outcomes in Chicago. Educational Evaluation and Policy Analysis, 31(4), 367–391.

American College Testing (ACT). (2005). *Course count: Preparing students for postsecondary success*. Iowa City, IA.

American College Testing (ACT). (2007). *Rigor at risk: Reaffirming quality in the high school core curricula*. Iowa City, IA: Author.

American College Testing (ACT). (2010). *College readiness standards for EXPLORE, PLAN, and ACT*. Iowa City, IA: Author.

An, B. P. (2013). The influence of dual enrollment on academic performance and college readiness: Differences by socioeconomic status. *Research in Higher Education, 54*, 407–432.

Aries, E., & Seider, M. (2005). The interactive relationship between class identity and the college experience: The case of lower income students. *Qualitative Sociology, 28*, 419–443.

Asch, C. M. (2010). The inadvertent bigotry of inappropriate expectations. *Education Week, 29*(35), 35.

Ashtiani, M., & Feliciano, C. (2012). *Low-income young adults continue to face barriers to college entry and degree completion*. Los Angeles:

Pathways to Postsecondary Success: Maximizing Opportunities for Youth in Poverty Research Brief. Number 1

Astin, A. W., & Oseguera, L. (2012). Pre-college and institutional influences on degree attainment. In A. Seidman (Ed.), *College student retention* (2nd ed., pp. 119–145). Lanham: Rowman & Littlefield Publishers.

Attewell, P., Heil, S., & Reisel, L. (2010). Competing explanations of undergraduate completion. *American Educational Research Journal, 47,* 1–22.

Attewell, P., Lavin, D., Domina, T., & Levey, T. (2006). New evidence on college remediation. *Journal of Higher Education, 77,* 886–924.

Atkinson, R. C., & Geiser, S. (2009). Reflections on a century of college admission tests. *Educational Researcher, 38,* 665–676.

Aud, S., Hussar, W., Kena, G., Bianco, K., Frohlich, L., Kemp, J., & Tahan, K. (2012). *The condition of education 2011.* (NCES 2011-033). Washington, DC: U.S. Department of Education.

Aud, S., Hussar, W., Johnson, F., Kena, G., Roth, E., Manning, E., Wang, X., & Zhang, J. (2013). *The condition of education 2012.* Washington, DC: U.S. Department of Education, Institute of Education Sciences, National Center for Education Statistics. Retrieved from https://nces.ed.gov/pubsearch/pubsinfo.asp?pubid=2012045

Bailey, M. J., & Dynarski, S. (2011). Inequality in postsecondary education. In G. J. Duncan & R. J. Murnane (Eds.), *Whither opportunity? Rising inequality, schools, and children's life chances* (pp. 117-132). New York: Russell Sage Foundation.

Baker, D. B., Clay, J. N., & Gratama, C. A. (2005). *The essence of college readiness: Implications for students, parents, schools, and researchers.* Bothell, WA: The BERC Group.

Balfanz, R. (2009). Can the American high school become an avenue of advancement for all? *The Future of Children, 19*(1), 17–36.

Balfanz, R. (2012). Doing it all: Raising graduation rates and standards. In *Getting to 2014: The choices and challenges ahead* (pp. 5–8). Retrieved from www.educationsector.com

Balfanz, R. & Legters, N. (2004). Locating the dropout crisis. Baltimore: Center for Social Organization of Schools, Johns Hopkins University. Retrieved September 1, 2004, from www.csos.jhu.edu/tdhs/rsch/Locating_Dropouts.pdf.

Barnes, W., & Slate, J. R. (2013). College-readiness is not one-size-fits-all. *Current Issues in Education, 16*(1), 1–13.

Barnes, W., Slate, J. R., & Rojas-LeBouef, A. M. (2010). College-readiness and academic preparedness: The same concepts? Current Issues in Education, 13(4). Retrieved from http://cie.asu.edu/

Barnett, E., & Fay, M. (2013). The Common Core State Standards: Implications for community colleges and student preparedness for college (An NCPR Working Paper). New York: National Center for Postsecondary Research. http://ccrc.tc.columbia.edu/publications/common-°©-core-°©-state-°©-standards-°©-implications.html.

Barnett, E. A., Corrin, W., Nakanishi, A., Bork, R. H., Mitchell, C., Sepanik, S. (2012). *Preparing High School Students for College An Exploratory Study of College Readiness Partnership Programs in Texas*. Washington, DC: National Center for Postsecondary Research, U.S. Department of Education.

Barton, P. E. (2008). How many college graduates does the U.S. labor force really need? *Change 40*(1), 16–21.

Baum, S., & Ma, J. (2007). *Education pays: The benefits of higher education for individuals and society*. New York: The College Board.

Berliner, D. C. (2006). Our impoverished view of educational research. *Teachers College Record, 108*(6), 949–995.

Bettinger, E. P., Boatman, A., & Long, B. T. (2013). Student supports: Developmental education and other academic programs. *The Future of Children, 23*(1), 93–115.

Bloom, T. (2010). *College and career readiness: A systemic P-20 response*. Arlington, VA: Naviance.

Bowles, S., & Gintis, H. (1976). *Schooling in capitalist America: Educational reform and the contradictions of economic life*. New York: Basic Books.

Bragg, D. D., & Durham, B. (2012). Perspectives on access and equity in the era of (community) college completion. *Community College Review, 40*(2), 106–125.

Burdman, P. (2011). Testing ground: How Florida schools and colleges are using a new assessment to increase college readiness. Boston: Jobs for the Future. Retrieved from http://www.jff.org/sites/default/files/ATD_AE_TestingGround_100311.pdf.

Byrd, K. L., & Macdonald, G. (2005). Defining college readiness from the inside out: First-generation college student perspectives. *Community College Review, 33*(1), 22–37. doi: 10.1177/009155210503300102

Calcagno, J. C., & Long, B. T. (2008) *The impact of postsecondary remediation using a regression discontinuity approach: Addressing endogenous sorting and noncompliance (NCPR Working Paper)*. New York: National Center for Postsecondary Research.

California State University (CSU) Proficiency Rates (n.d.). "First time freshmen remediation systemwide." Retrieved from http://www.asd.calstate.edu/remediation/12/Rem_Sys_fall2012.htm

Callan, P. M., Finney, J. E., Kirst, M. W., Usdan, M. D., & Venezia, A. (2006). *Claiming common ground: State policymaking for improving college readiness and success.* San Jose, CA: The National Center for Public Policy and Higher Education.

Camara, W., Wiley, A., & Wyatt, J. (2010). College readiness and preparation: Developing a multidimensional metric based on college outcomes. Paper presented at the National Conference on Large Scale Assessment (CCSSO).

Carnevale, A. (2008) College for All? *Change.* Retrieved from http://www9.georgetown.edu/grad/gppi/hpi/cew/pdfs/college%20for%20all.pdf

Carnevale, A. P., Smith, N., & Strohl, J. (2010). *Help wanted: Projections of jobs and education requirements through 2018.* Washington, DC: Georgetown University Center on Education and the Workforce.

Carter, D. F., Locks, A. M., & Winkle-Wagner, R. (2013). From when and where I enter: Theoretical and empirical considerations of minority students' transition to college. In M. B. Paulsen (Ed.), *Higher Education: Handbook of Theory and Research,* vol. 28, (pp. 93–149). Dordrecht, The Netherlands: Springer.

Castro, E. L. (2013). Racialized readiness for college and career: Toward an equity grounded social science of intervention programming. *Community College Review, 41*(4), 292–310.

Cimetta, A. D., D'Agostino, J. J., & Levin, J. R. (2010). Can high school achievement tests serve to select high school students? *Educational Measurement: Issues and Practice, 29,* 3–12.

Cline, Z., Bissell, J., Hafner, A., & Katz, M. (2007). Closing the college readiness gap. *Leadership, 37,* 30–33.

Collier, P. J., & Morgan, D. L. (2008). "Is that paper really due today?": differences in first-generation and traditional college students' understandings of faculty expectations. *Higher Education, 55,* 425–446.

Collins, M. L. (2009). *Setting up success in developmental education: How state policy can help community colleges improve student success outcomes.* Boston: Jobs for the Future.

Complete College America. (2012). *Remediation: Higher Education's Bridge to Nowhere.* Washington, DC: Author.

Conley, D. T. (2005). *College knowledge: What it really takes for students to succeed and what we can do to get them ready.* San Francisco: Jossey-Bass.

Conley, D. T. (2007). *Redefining college readiness.* Eugene, OR: Educational Policy.

Conley, D. T. (2008). Rethinking college readiness. *New Directions for Higher Education, 2008*(144), 3-13. doi:10.1002/he.321

Conley, D. T. (2010). *College and career ready: Helping all students succeed beyond high school.* San Francisco: Jossey-Bass.

Conley, D. T. (2012). *A complete definition of college and career readiness.* Eugene, OR: Educational Policy Improvement Center.

Conley, D. T., McGaughy, C., Kirtner, J., Van Der Valk, A., & Martinez-Wenzl, M. T. (2010). *College readiness practices at 38 high schools and the development of the CollegeCareerReady School Diagnostic tool.* Paper presented at the 2010 annual conference of the American Educational Research Association, Denver, CO.

Connect Ed California. (2012). *College and career readiness: What do we mean?* Berkeley, CA: ConnectEd.

Cortez, L. J., Martinez, M. A., & Saenz, V. B. (2013). Por los ojos de madres: Latina mothers' understandings of college readiness. *International Journal of Qualitative Studies in Education,* 1–24.

Corwin, Z. B., & Tierney, W. G. (2007). *Getting there—and beyond: Building a culture of college-going in high schools.* Los Angeles: Center for Higher Education Policy Analysis.

Crouse, J., & Trusheim, D. (1988). *The case against the SAT.* Chicago: University of Chicago Press.

Darling-Hammond, L. (2007). Race, inequality and educational accountability: The irony of "No Child Left Behind." *Race, Ethnicity and Education,* 10(3), 245–260.

Darling-Hammond, L., & Adamson, F. (2013). Developing assessments of deeper learning: The costs and benefits of using tests that help students learn. Stanford, CA: Stanford Center for Opportunity Policy in Education.

Deke, J. & Haimson, J. (2006). Expanding Beyond Academics: Who Benefits and How? Trends in Education Research, Issue Brief #2. Princeton, NJ: Mathematica Policy Research. Retrieved from http://www.mathematica-mpr.com/publications/PDFs/expandbeyond.pdf.

Desjardins, S. L., & Lindsay, N. K. (2008). Adding a statistical wrench to the "Toolbox." *Research in Higher Education, 49,* 172–179.

Dohm, A., & Shniper, L. (2007, November). *Occupational employment projections to 2016. Bureau of Labor Statistics.* Retrieved February 23, 2013, from http://www.bls.gov/opub/mlr/2007/11/art5full.pdf

Domina, T., & Ruzek, E. (2013). Paving the way: K-16 partnerships for higher education diversity and high school reform. *Educational Policy, 26,* 243–267.

Doorey, N. A. (December 2012/January 2013). Coming soon: A new generation of assessments. *Educational Leadership, 70*(4).

Dougherty, C. (2008). They can pass, but are they college ready? Washington, DC: Data Quality Campaign. Retrieved April 24, 2009, from http://www.dataqualitycampaign.org/resources/310

Dougherty, C., Mellor, L., & Jian, S. (2005). The relationship between Advanced Placement and college graduation. Austin, TX: National Center for Educational Accountability.

Dougherty, C., Mellor, L., & Smith, N. (2006, May). *Identifying appropriate college-readiness standards for all students* (Issue Brief No. 2). Austin, TX: National Center for Educational Accountability.

Dougherty, C., & Rutherford, J. (2010). Six guiding principles for school improvement efforts. Austin, TX: National Center for Educational Achievement.

Dounay, J. (2006 April). Embedding college readiness indicators in high school curriculum and assessments. (Policy Brief). Denver, CO: Education Commission of the States. Retrieved from http://www.google.com/url?sa=t&rct=j&q=&esrc=s&source=web&cd=4&ved=0CEEQFjAD&url=http%3A%2F%2Ffiles.eric.ed.gov%2Ffulltext%2FED493713.pdf&ei=4kpoUsOYD8GriQLjy4GoBg&usg=AFQjCNGKM2dh84d6Ym9zurQ_4YPkP5baGg&sig2=VS_wtUABxWGrlEIkr-IdJA&bvm=bv.55123115,d.cGE&cad=rja

Durlak, J. A., Weissberg, R. P., Dymnicki, A. B., Taylor, R. D., & Schellinger, K. B. (2011). The Impact of Enhancing Students' Social and Emotional Learning: A Meta-Analysis of School-Based Universal Interventions. *Child Development, 82*(1), 405–432.

Dweck, C. S., Walton, G. M., & Cohen, G. L. (2011). *Academic tenacity: Mindsets and skills that promote long-term learning.* Seattle, WA: Gates Foundation. Retrieved from http://collegeready.gatesfoundation.org/Learning/LearningContent/AcademicTenacityMindsetandSkillsthatPromote

ENCORE Research Report. (2009). *Understanding the perceptions of college readiness in the Rio Grande Valley of Texas.* Prepared by the Texas Valley

Communities Foundation. Retrieved from http://www.getencore.org/docs/ENCORE_Research_Report_2009.pdf

Ewing, M. (2006 November). The AP program and student outcomes: A summary of research. [RN-29]. New York: College Board.

Executive Office of the President. (January 2014). Increasing college opportunity for low-income students: Promising models and a call to action. Washington, DC: Author. Retrieved from http://www.whitehouse.gov/sites/default/files/docs/white_house_report_on_increasing_college_opportunity_for_low-income_students_1-16-2014_final.pdf

Farrington, C. A., Roderick, M., Allensworth, E., Nagaoka, J., Keyes, T. S., Johnson, D. W., & Beechum, N. O. (2012). *Teaching adolescents to become learners. The role of noncognitive factors in shaping school performance: A critical literature review.* Chicago: University of Chicago Consortium on Chicago School Research. Retrieved from https://ccsr.uchicago.edu/publications/teaching-adolescents-become-learners-role-noncognitive-factors-shaping-school

Finkelstein, N. D., & Fong, A. B. (2008). *Course-taking patterns and preparation for postsecondary education in California's public university systems across minority youth.* (Issues & Answers Report, REL 2008–No. 035). Washington, DC: U.S. Department of Education, Institute of Education Sciences, National Center for Education Evaluation and Regional Assistance, Regional Educational Laboratory West. Retrieved from http://ies.ed.gov/ncee/edlabs

Flores, S. M., & Oseguera, L. (2013). Public policy and higher education attainment in a twenty-first-century racial demography: Examining research from early childhood to the labor market. In M.B. Paulsen (ed.), *Higher Education: Handbook of Theory and Research* (pp. 513–560), New York: Springer.

Foley, E., Mishook, J., & Lee, J. (2013). Developing college readiness within and across school districts: The federal role. *The Next Four Years: Recommendations for Federal Education Policy, 36*(Winter/Spring 2013), 7–17.

Fraizer, D. (2003). The politics of high-stakes writing assessment in Massachusetts why inventing a better assessment model is not enough. Journal of Writing Assessment, 1(2), 105–121.

Glass, R. D., & Nygreen, K. (2011). Class, race, and the discourse of "college for all": A response to "Schooling for Democracy." *Democracy and Education, 19*(1), 1–8.

Greene, J. P., & Forster, G. (2003). Public high school graduation and college readiness rates in the United States (Education Working Paper No. 3). New York: Manhattan Institute for Policy Research, Center for Civic Innovation.

Grubb, W. N., Boner, E., Frankel, K., Parker, L., Patterson, D., Gabriner, R., Hope, L., Shorring, E., Smith, B., Taylor, R., Walton, I., & Wilson, S. (2011). Assessment and alignment: The dynamic aspects of developmental education. [Working Paper #7]. Stanford, CA: Policy Analysis for California Education (PACE).

Hafner, A., Joseph, R., & McCormick. J. (2010). College readiness for all: Assessing the impact of English professional development on teaching practice and student learning. *Journal of Urban Learning, Teaching and Research, 6*(3), 23–45.

Herman, J., & Linn, R. (2013). *On the road to assessing deeper learning: The status of smarter balanced and PARCC assessment consortia* (Vol. 823). Los Angeles: National Center for Research on Evaluation, Standards, and Student Testing (CRESST).

Hodara, M., Jaggars, S. S., & Karp, M. M. (2012). Improving developmental education assessment and placement: Lessons from community colleges across the country (CCRC Working Paper No. 51). New York: Columbia University, Teachers College, Community College Research Center.

Hoffman, N., Vargas, J. A., Venezia, A., & Miller, S. M. (Eds.). (2007). *Minding the gap: Why integrating high school with college makes sense and how to do it.* Cambridge, MA: Harvard Education Press.

Hoffman, N., & Vargas, J. (2010). *A policymaker's guide to early college designs: Expanding a strategy for achieving college readiness for all.* Boston: Jobs for the Future.

Hooker, S., & Brand, B. (2010). College knowledge: A critical component of college and career readiness. *New Directions for Youth Development, 2010*(127), 75–85.

Hooley, T., Marriott, J., & Sampson, J. P. (2011). Fostering college and career readiness: How career development activities in schools impact on graduation rates and students' life success. Derby, UK: International Centre for Guidance Studies.

Howell, J. S. (2011). What influences students' need for remediation in college? Evidence from California. *Journal of Higher Education, 82,* 293–318.

Howell, J., Kurlaender, M., & Grodsky, E. (2010). Postsecondary preparation and remediation: Examining the effect of the Early Assessment Program at California State University. *Journal of Policy Analysis and Management, 29*(4), 726–748.

Hoxby, C. M., Murarka, S., & Kang, J. (2009). How New York City's charter schools affect achievement: Second report in series. Cambridge, MA: New York City Charter Schools Evaluation Project. Retrieved from http://www.nber.org/~schools/charterschoolseval/how_NYC_charter_schools_affect_achievement_sept2009.pdf.

Huot, B., & Williamson, M. (1997). Rethinking portfolios for evaluating writing: Issues of assessment and power. In K. Yancey & B. Huot (Eds.), Assessing writing across the curriculum: Diverse approaches and practices. Greenwich, CT: Ablex.

Iatarola, P., Conger, D., & Long, M. C. (2011). Determinants of high schools' advanced course offerings. *Educational Evaluation and Policy Analysis, 33*(3), 340–359.

Johnson, N. (2012). *The institutional costs of student attrition.* Washington, DC: American Institutes for Research.

Karp, M. M., & Hughes, K. L. (2008). Supporting college transitions through collaborative programming: A conceptual model for guiding policy. *Teachers College Record, 110,* 838–866.

Karp, M., Calcagno, J. C., Hughes, K., Jeong, D. W., & Bailey, T. (2007). *The postsecondary achievement of participants in dual enrollment: An analysis of student outcomes in two states.* Louisville, KY: National Research Center for Career and Technical Education.

Kim, J. S., & Sunderman, G. L. (2005). Measuring academic proficiency under the No Child Left Behind Act: Implications for educational equity. *Educational Researcher, 34*(8), 3–13.

Kim, Y. M. (2011). *Minorities in higher education: Twenty-fourth status report, 2011 supplement.* Washington, DC: American Council on Education. Retrieved from http://www.acenet.edu/news-room/Pages/Minorities-in-Higher-Education-2011-supplement.aspx

Kirst, M., & Venezia, A. (Eds.). (2004). *From high school to college: Improving opportunities for success in postsecondary education.* San Francisco: Jossey-Bass.

Knudson, R. E., Zitzer-Comfort, C., Quirk, M., & Alexander, P. (2008). The California Early Assessment Program. *The Clearing House: A Journal of Educational Strategies, Issues, and Ideas, 81*(5), 227–231.

Kuh, G. D. (2007, Winter). What student engagement data tell us about college readiness. *Peer Review, 9*(1), 4–8.

Kyllonen, P. (2008). Enhancing noncognitive skills to boost academic achievement. Educational Testing in America: State Assessments, Achievement Gaps, National Policy and Innovations Session III: Innovations in Testing. Princeton NJ: Education Testing Service.

Le, V. (2002). *Alignment among secondary and post-secondary assessments in five case study states.* Santa Monica, CA: RAND.

Lee, J. (2010). Tripartite growth trajectories of reading and math achievement: Tracking national academic progress at primary, middle, and high school levels. *American Educational Research Journal, 47,* 800–832.

Lee, J. (2012). College for all: Gaps between desirable and actual P-12 math achievement trajectories for college readiness. *Educational Researcher, 41*(2), 43–55.

Lee, V., Burkham, D. Smerdon, B., Chow-Hoy, T., & Geverdt, D. (1997). *High school curriculum structure: Effects on coursetaking and achievement in mathematics for high school graduates.* Ann Arbor, MI: University of Michigan.

Lee, V., Croninger, R. G., & Smith, J. B. (1997). Course-taking, equity, and mathematics learning: Testing the constrained curriculum hypothesis in U.S. secondary schools. *Education Evaluation and Policy Analysis, 19*(2), 99–121.

Lehman, N. (1999). *The big test: The secret history of the American meritocracy.* New York: Farrar, Straus & Giroux.

Lerman, R. (2008). Are skills the problem? Reforming the education and training system in the United States. In T. Bartik & S. Houseman (Eds.)., *A Future of Good Jobs.* (pp. 17–80). Upjohn Institute. Retrieved from http://www1.american.edu/cas/econ/faculty/lerman/Ch%20%202%2%20Lerman.pdf

Levin, H.S., & Calcagno, J.C. (2008). "Remediation in the Community College: An Evaluator's Perspective." *Community College Review, 35*(3), 181-207.

Lippman, L., Atienza, A., Rivers, A., & Keith, J. (2008). *A developmental perspective on college and workplace readiness.* Washington, DC: Child Trends.

Liou, D. D., Antrop-Gonzalez, R., & Cooper, R. (2009). Unveiling the promise of community cultural wealth to sustaining Latina/o students' college-going information networks. *Educational Studies, 45,* 534–555.

Lin, B. (2006). Access to A-G curriculum at San Jose Unified School District. Center for Latino Policy Research, Research Brief Vol. 2(1).

Lombardi, A. R., Conley, D. T., Seburn, M. A., & Downs, A. M. (2013).

College and career readiness assessment: Validation of the key cognitive strategies framework. *Assessment for Effective Intervention, 38*(3), 163–171.

Long, M. C., Iatarola, P., & Conger, D. (2008). Explaining gaps in readiness for college-level math: The role of high school courses. *Education Finance and Policy, 4*(1), 1–33.

Martinez, N., & Klopott, S. (2005). *The link between high school reform and college access and success for low-income minority youth.* American Youth Policy Forum. Retrieved from http://www.aypf.org/publications/HSReformCollegeAccessandSuccess.pdf

Maruyama, G. (2012). Assessing college readiness: Should we be satisfied with ACT or other threshold scores? *Educational Researcher, 41*(7), 252–261.

Mazzeo, C. (2010). *College prep for all? What we've learned from Chicago's efforts.* Chicago: Consortium on Chicago School Research.

McAlister, S., & Mevs, P. (2012). *College readiness: A guide to the field.* Providence, RI: Annenberg Institute for School Reform at Brown University.

McLean, H. (2012). *California's Early Assessment Program: Its successes and the obstacles to successful program implementation.* Stanford, CA: Policy Analysis for California Education.

McDonough, P. (1997). *Choosing college: How social class and school structure opportunity.* Albany, NY: State University of New York Press.

Mijares, A. (2007). Defining college readiness. Retrieved October 8, 2007, from http://www.edsource.org/assets/files/convening/CollegeBoard_brief.pdf

Murnane, R. J., & Levy, F. (1996). *Teaching the new basic skills: Principles for educating children to thrive in a changing economy.* New York: Free Press.

National Center for Higher Education Management Systems (NCHEMS) (n.d.). "Student pipeline: Transition and completion rates from 9th grade to college for the year 2010." Retrieved from http://www.higheredinfo.org/dbrowser/index.php?submeasure=119&year=2010&level=nation&mode=data&state=0

National Research Council (NRC). (2012). *Education for Life and Work: Developing Transferable Knowledge and Skills in the 21st Century.* Washington, DC: The National Academies Press.

Neild, R. C., & Balfanz, R. (2006). *Unfulfilled promise: The dimensions and characteristics of Philadelphia's dropout crisis.* Philadelphia: Philadelphia Youth Transitions Collaborative.

Nichols, S. N., & Berliner, D. C. (2008). Why has high-stakes testing so easily slipped into contemporary life? *Phi Delta Kappan, 89*(9), 672–676.

Nichols, S. N., Glass, G. V., & Berliner, D. C. (2005). High-stakes testing and student achievement: Does accountability pressure increase student learning? *Educational Policy Analysis Archives, 14*(1). Retrieved from http://epaa.asu.edu/epaa/vi4n1/

Nieto, S. (1999). *The light in their eyes: Creating multicultural learning communities.* New York: Teachers College Press.

Niu, S. X., & Tienda, M. (2010). Minority student academic performance under the uniform admission law: Evidence from the University of Texas at Austin. *Educational Evaluation and Policy Analysis, 32*(1), 44–69.

Noble, J. P., & Camara, W. J. (2003). Issues in college admissions testing. In J. E. Wall & G. R. Walz (Eds.), *Measuring up: Assessment issues for teachers, counselors, and administrators* (pp. 283–296). Greensboro, NC: ERIC Counseling and Student Services Clearinghouse.

Oakes, J. (2005). *Keeping track: How schools structure inequality* (2nd ed.). New Haven, CT: Yale University Press.

Obama, B. (2009). *Remarks of President Barack Obama as prepared for delivery address to joint session of congress.* (24 February 2009). Washington, D.C.: Office of the Press Secretary. Retrieved from http://www.whitehouse.gov/the_press_office/Remarks-of-President-Barack-Obama-Address-to-Joint-Session-of-Congress

OECD. (2009). *Education at a glance: OECD indicators.* Paris: OECD.

Olson, L. (2006, April). Views differ on defining college prep: How to gauge readiness sparks vexing questions. *Education Week, 25*(33), 1, 26, 28–29.

Osterman, P. (2008, August 12). *College for All? The Labor Market for College-Educated Workers.* Washington, DC: Center for American Progress.

Parker, T. L., Bustillos, L. T., & Behringer, L. B. (2010). Remedial and developmental education policy at a crossroads. Boston: Getting Past Go & Policy Research on Preparation Access and Remedial Education (PRePARE). Retrieved from http://www.gettingpastgo.org/docs/Literature-Review-GPG.pdf

Pellegrino, J. W., & Hilton, M. L. (Eds.). (2012). *Education for life and work: Developing transferable knowledge and skills in the 21st century.* Washington, DC: National Academies Press.

Perna, L. W. (2005). The key to college access: Rigorous academic preparation. In W. G. Tierney, Z. B. Corwin, & J. E. Colyar (Eds.), Preparing for college: Nine elements of effective outreach (pp. 113–134). Albany, NY: State University of New York Press.

Perna, L. W., & Steele, P. (2011). The role of context in understanding the contributions of financial aid to college opportunity. *Teachers College Record, 113,* 893–933.

Porter, A., McMaken, J., Hwang, J., & Yang, R. (2011). Assessing the Common Core Standards: Opportunities for improving measures of instruction. *Educational Researcher, 40,* 186–188.

Porter, A. C., & Polikoff, M. S. (2012). Measuring academic readiness for college. *Educational Policy, 26*(3), 394–417.

Robbins, S. B., Lauver, K., Davis, D., Davis, H. L., Langley, R., & Carlstrom, A. (2004). Do psychosocial and study skill factors predict college outcomes? A meta-analysis. *Psychological Bulletin, 130*(2), 261-288. doi: 10.1037/0033-2909.130.2.261

Roderick, M., Nagaoka, J., & Coca, V. (2009). College readiness for all: The challenge for urban high schools. *The Future of Children, 19*(1), 185–210.

Roderick, Coca, & Nagaoka, (2011). Potholes on the road to college: High school effects in shaping urban students' participation in college application, four-year college enrollment, and college match. *Sociology of Education, 84*(3), 178–211.

Roderick, M., Coca, V. Moeller, E., & Kelley-Kemple, T. (2013). *From high school to the future: The challenge of senior year in Chicago public schools.* Chicago: The University of Chicago Consortium on Chicago School Research.

Rolfhus, E., Decker, L. E., Brite, J. L., & Gregory, L. (2010). *A systematic comparison of the American Diploma Project English language arts college readiness standards with those of the ACT, College Board, and Standards for Success.* Washington, DC: Institute of Education Sciences.

Rosenbaum, J. E. (2001). *Beyond college for all: Career paths for the forgotten half.* New York: Russell Sage Foundation.

Rosenbaum, J. E., & Becker, K. I. (2011). The early college challenge: Navigating disadvantaged students' transition to college. *American Educator,* (Fall 2011).

Rosenbaum, J. E., Stephan, J. L., & Rosenbaum, J. E. (2010). Beyond one-size-fits-all college dreams: Alternative pathways to desirable careers.

American Educator, 34(3), 1–12. Retrieved from http://www.aft.org/pdfs/americaneducator/fall2010/Rosenbaum.pdf

Rothman, R. (2011). *Something in common: The common core standards and the next chapter in American education.* Boston: Harvard Educational Press.

Rumberger, R. W. (2011). *Dropping out: Why students drop out of high school and what can be done about it.* Cambridge, MA: President and the Fellows of Harvard College.

Sawchuk, S. (2010, February 3). States rush to join testing consortia. *Education Week.* Available from http://www.edweek.org

Sedlacek, W. E. (2004). Beyond the big test: Noncognitive assessment in higher education. San Francisco: Jossey-Bass.

Sedlacek, W. E. (2008). Using noncognitive variables in K-12 and higher education. *University of Michigan Summit on College Outreach and Academic Success: Summary report from meetings at the School of Education*, August 11–12, 2008 (pp. 35–42). Ann Arbor, MI: University of Michigan.

Speroni, C. (2011). *Determinants of students' success: The role of advanced placement and dual enrollment programs.* An NCPR Working paper. New York: National Center for Postsecondary Research.

Spring, J. (2000). *American education.* Boston: McGraw Hill.

Stemler, S. E. (2012). What should university admissions tests predict? *Educational Psychologist, 47*(1), 5–17.

Strayhorn, T. L. (2010). When race and gender collide: The impact of social and cultural capital on the academic achievement of African American and Latino males. *The Review of Higher Education, 33*(3), 307–332.

Struhl, B., & Vargas, J. (2012). *Taking college courses in high school: A strategy for college readiness: The college outcomes of dual enrollment in Texas.* Boston: Jobs for the Future.

Symonds, W. C., Schwartz, R. B., & Ferguson, R. (2011). *Pathways to prosperity: Meeting the challenge of preparing young Americans for the 21ˢᵗ century.* Boston: Pathways to Prosperity Project and Harvard Graduate School of Education. Retrieved from http://www.gse.harvard.edu/news_events/features/2011/Pathways_to_Prosperity_Feb2011.pdf

Teranashi, R. (2011). *The relevance of Asian Americans and Pacific islanders in the college completion agenda.* New York: National Commission on Asian American Pacific Islander Research in Education and Asian and Pacific Islander American Scholarship Fund.

Teranashi, R. (2013). *iCount: A data quality movement for Asian Americans and Pacific Islanders in higher education.* Princeton, NJ: Educational Testing Service.

The Education Trust-West (August 2012). *Overlooked and underserved: Debunking the Asian "model minority" myth in California schools.* Oakland, CA: Author.

Tierney, W. G., & Garcia, L. D. (2011). Remediation in higher education: The role of information. *American Behavioral Scientist, 55*(2), 102–120.

Tinto, V. (1993). *Leaving college: Rethinking the causes and cures of student attrition.* Chicago: University of Chicago Press.

U.S. Department of Education. (2010, September). *U.S. Secretary of Education Duncan announces winners of competition to improve student assessments* [press release]. Retrieved from www.ed.gov/news/pressreleases/us-secretary-education-duncan-announces-winners-competition-improve-student-asse

Venezia, A., & Jaeger, L. (2013). Transitions from high school to college. *The Future of Children, 23*(1), 117–136.

Venezia, A., & Voloch, D. (2012). Using college placement exams as early signals of college readiness: An examination of California's Early Assessment Program and New York's At Home in College Program. *New Directions for Higher Education, 158,* 71–79.

Venezia, A., Kirst, M., & Antonio, A. (2004). *Betraying the college dream: How disconnected K-12 and post-secondary systems undermine student aspirations.* San Francisco: Jossey-Bass.

Venezia, A., Callan, P. M., Finney, J. E., Kirst, M. W., & Usdan, M. D. (2005). *The governance divide: A report on a four-state study on improving college readiness and success.* San Jose, CA: The National Center for Public Policy and Higher Education.

Venezia, A., Bracco, K. R., & Nodine, T. (2010). One-shot deal. Students' perceptions of assessment and course placement in California's community colleges. San Francisco: WestEd.

Ward, D. S., & Vargas, J. (2012). Using dual enrollment policy to improve college and career readiness: A web tool for decision makers. Policy Brief. Boston, MA: Jobs for the Future.

Washington, H. D., Barnett, E. A., Fay, M. P., Mitchell, C., Pretlow, J., & Bork, R. H. (2012). Preparing students for college learning and work: Investigating the capstone course component of Virginia's college and career readiness initiative. NCPR Working Paper, December 2012. National Center for Postsecondary Research.

Welton, A. D., & Martinez, M. A. (June 2013). Coloring the college pathway: A more culturally responsive approach to college readiness and access for students of color in secondary schools. *Urban Review.* Advance online publication.

Wiley, A., Wyatt, J., & Camara, W. J. (2010). *The development of a multi-dimensional college readiness index* (Research Report No. 2010-3). New York: The College Board.

Wyatt, J. N., Wiley, A., Camara, W. J., & Proestler, N. (2011). *The development of an index of academic rigor for college readiness.* New York: The College Board.

Wyatt, J. N., Kobrin, J., Wiley, A., Camara, W. J., & Proestler, N. (2011). *SAT Benchmarks: Development of a college readiness benchmark and its relationship to secondary and postsecondary school performance* (Research Report No. 2011-5). New York: The College Board.

Yamamura, E. K., Martinez, M. A., & Saenz, V. B. (2010). Moving beyond high school expectations: Examining stakeholders' responsibility for increasing Latino/a students' college readiness. *The High School Journal, 93*(3), 126–148.

Yuan, K. & Le, V. (2012). *Estimating the Percentage of Students Who Were Tested on Cognitively Demanding Items Through the State Achievement Tests.* Santa Monica, CA: RAND Corporation.

Zhao, Y. (2009). Comments on the common core standards initiative. *AASA Journal of Scholarship & Practice, 6*(3), 46–54.

Zinth, J. D. (2012). State polices to increase rigor and relevance in high schools. In B. Smerdon & K. M. Borman (Eds.). *Pressing forward: Increasing and expanding rigor and relevance in America's high schools* (pp. 29–48). Charlotte, NC: Information Age Publishing.

2

THE ROOTS OF COLLEGE READINESS

An Old Problem with New Complexities

DANIEL J. ALMEIDA

Entering the term "college readiness" into any academic search engine today yields thousands of hits, but the phrase was first referenced (only once) in the educational literature in the March 1948 issue of The School Review. In an article titled "Curriculum Articulation for Secondary and Higher Education," the author wrote:

> College people condemned the high schools for paying less attention to college preparation. High-school educators pointed out that most secondary-school students were not college bound and that, according to scientific evidence, it was the aptitudes, work habits, and quality of preparation of students rather than the program of studies pursued which made for college readiness (Wheat, 1948, p. 1).

Articulation refers to "the close coupling of courses and educational experiences in a sequential manner for the purpose of obtaining continuity of student development" (Wheat, 1948, p. 147). One wonders how long articulation, college readiness, and, by extension, remediation have been concerns in the discourse of higher education. Some may surmise that the debate concerning college readiness began around the time of The School Review article's publication. Others may point to the first official remedial writing program implemented at the University of California, Berkeley at the end of the 19th century (Maxwell, 1979). Whereas the term "college readiness" had yet to enter the lexicon, the issue of how to prepare students for postsecondary studies has existed since the earliest colleges in the United States.

In chapter 1, Julia Duncheon discussed the challenges and complexities of the contemporary college readiness agenda. My purpose here is to demonstrate that the concept of college readiness in higher education is not entirely new, but has evolved over time. The nation's first tertiary institutions, like their European predecessors, existed primarily to educate elite members of society and prepare clergy. The American model, however, grew increasingly democratic as the institution adopted a mission to serve the public good and responded to the needs of an advancing society (Geiger, 1999). As higher education changed to accommodate more diverse student groups in an increasing number of disciplines, the concept of college readiness evolved as well (Brubacher & Rudy, 2002).

This chapter explores the roots of college readiness, identifying its historical and conceptual foundations in the American education system. I first discuss the construct of college readiness—that is, the skills and knowledge students need to be successful in higher education—and how this definition has changed over time. I then examine the evolution of secondary education in the United States and highlight its role in preparing students for college. I specifically attend to vocational education, tracking, racial desegregation, and the subsequent resegregation of public schools, as these issues have had a significant impact on the differing levels of college preparation, access, and readiness.

Part 1: What Is Meant by College Readiness?

As Duncheon described in chapter 1, college readiness is the preparation required to enter college-level courses and persist to degree attainment. Because the term "preparation" is vague, education scholars and practitioners have conceptualized what readiness entails in different ways. One approach is to avoid explicitly defining the concept (Olson, 2006). A second perspective focuses on cognitive abilities and academic preparation as measured by standardized assessments and high school record (Porter

& Polikoff, 2012). The third manner of characterizing college readiness—which we adopt in this volume—is more comprehensive; readiness involves non-cognitive factors pertaining to academics (e.g., study skills) and campus integration (e.g., social-emotional capacities) in addition to cognitive skills (Conley, 2008; Roderick, Nagaoka, & Coca, 2009; Sedlacek, 2008). Drawing on this more expansive interpretation, I trace the origins of the cognitive and non-cognitive factors that have become associated with college readiness. I begin with the two main subjects—English and math—that comprise the cognitive aspect, and then turn to the importance of non-cognitive variables.

The Significance of Reading and Writing in English

Unlike today, reading and writing in English were not emphasized in the earliest institutions of higher learning (Dempsey, 1985). The core of the postsecondary curriculum during the colonial era consisted of Latin and Greek; coursework involved memorization and recitation of classical language and literature (Brubacher & Rudy, 2002). Students spent most of their study time methodically translating texts, focusing on grammar and sentence structure (Dempsey, 1985). College readiness at these early colleges thus pertained to proficiency in Latin and Greek, the languages of instruction. As university curriculum shifted to include modern humanities and science subjects, English literacy skills became increasingly crucial to college success. Reading became particularly critical in the 20th century with the introduction of general survey courses, which required students to consume large amounts of text (Maxwell, 1979).

The rise of the library also enhanced the importance of reading in higher learning (Dempsey, 1985). In colonial times, the availability of books was limited; at Harvard, for example, only faculty, college overseers, and seniors were even allowed inside the library. Once tertiary institutions embraced the German tradition of research and graduate education toward the end of the 19th century, the library's role became increasingly vital (Cohen & Kisker, 2010; Geiger, 1999; Veysey, 1965). College students needed to read a wide array of texts for their studies (Dempsey, 1985), and libraries began to make their resources readily available to students and faculty alike. The broader accessibility of books enabled faculty to assign lengthy reading and writing assignments. As English literacy skills became fundamental to the postsecondary curriculum, students' reading and writing deficits became more apparent to college faculty (Dempsey, 1985; Maxwell, 1979).

The work of American psychologists who trained in Europe toward the end of the 19th century drew further attention to the issue of college literacy (Dempsey, 1985). Research aimed to measure college students' reading and writing abilities as well as identify interventions to facilitate improvement. The importance of reading in particular came to the fore beginning in 1877 with the Library Journal's publishing of an article titled "How to Read in College," followed by the introduction of a survey technique for skimming text quickly. Decades later, when World War II servicemen needed condensed eight-week course schedules, the method known as SQ3R (Survey, Question, Read, Recite, Review) became a popular strategy for teaching reading comprehension (Maxwell, 1979).

As composition became the primary mode of expression and evaluation, the faculty at Harvard began to realize the weaknesses in first-year students' formal writing (Brubacher & Rudy, 2002). The university instituted the first freshman English course in 1874, and other institutions predictably followed Harvard's lead (Maxwell, 1979). In 1898, the University of California, Berkeley was the first to implement a non-credit-bearing writing program to remediate students' skills before enrolling them in college-level classes. Many universities established entire preparatory departments to support under-performing students before enrolling them in college-level curriculum (Cohen & Kisker, 2010).

By 1915, 350 institutions had created preparatory departments, many of which enrolled more students than college-level courses (Brubacher & Rudy, 2002; Maxwell, 1979). These preparatory departments focused much of their attention on the remediation of students' literacy skills. By the 1930s, remedial reading clinics appeared in public secondary schools and subsequently on many college campuses, including the most elite institutions (Casazza & Silverman, 1996). In addition, private preparatory schools were created for underprepared high school graduates to increase their readiness for college-level coursework (Dempsey, 1985; Maxwell, 1979). Reading and writing continue to be central components of college readiness as proficient literacy skills are essential across disciplines.

Like literacy, mathematical aptitude represents a central cognitive element of college readiness with strong historical roots. I now describe how advancements in science and technology led to greater emphasis on math in higher education, which helps to explain the contemporary emphasis on math preparation to support college achievement.

The Increasing Importance of Mathematics

Mathematics was one of the few subjects offered in the classical curriculum that dominated colleges is the colonial era (Brubacher & Rudy, 2002). However, math achievement was not a requirement for admission; generally, students only had to demonstrate proficiency in Latin and Greek. In 1745, Yale became the first institution to include the subject on its entrance examination (Casazza & Silverman, 1996).

Decisions to include subjects in higher education curriculum were often driven by perceived practicality (Cohen & Kisker, 2010). Mathematics became more integral to college coursework toward the end of the colonial period, as the Industrial Revolution heightened demand for workers with mathematical skills. Meanwhile, farmers expressed discontent with the available curricular options, which were largely irrelevant to their needs. The U.S. Congress responded to these trends by passing the Morrill Land Grant Act in 1862 (Williams, 1991).

The rationale of the Morrill Act was to create a more democratic system of higher education (Williams, 1991), and it established institutions throughout the country to make higher education available to millions more Americans (Stephens, 2001). The land grant institutions offered subjects designed to meet the needs of farmers and industrialists through an emphasis on computational skills and mathematical concepts (Williams, 1991). In contrast to older, established institutions that served more homogenous student bodies, these new universities expanded access to students from a wider array of demographic and academic backgrounds (Stephens, 2001). Accommodating students who had traditionally been excluded from higher education, however, made the issue of college readiness more challenging. The land grant colleges struggled as enrollments grew sluggishly, large numbers of students enrolled in remedial courses, and institutions experienced high levels of attrition (Williams, 1991).

Attention to mathematics surged across all levels of education in response to Cold War competition between the United States and the Soviet Union (Maxwell, 1979). Advances in areas such as computer technology and data processing further cemented the prominence of mathematics, requiring that students take more math courses and gain a more sophisticated knowledge of the subject. These trends prompted the College Entrance Examination Board (known today as the College Board) to issue an influential report in 1959 recommending significant changes to how and when specific areas of math were taught (Center for the Study of Mathematics

Curriculum, 2004). The recommendations raised the standard for college preparatory math, suggesting that high school students prepare to enroll in calculus during their first year of college rather than algebra, trigonometry, and/or geometry.

As a result, many universities stopped providing these lower-level math courses, and students who were not prepared for calculus were often sent to junior colleges to improve their skills before enrolling in college-level math (Maxwell, 1979). This curricular change came in the 1960s during dramatic shifts in postsecondary student demographics. The GI Bill granted access to higher education to millions of war veterans, and many institutions began recruiting students from diverse racial, economic, and academic backgrounds, many of whom lacked sufficient college preparatory math in their high schools (Maxwell, 1979; Turner & Bound, 2003). This combination of higher mathematics standards and broader recruitment strategies meant that more students—especially those from low-income families and underrepresented minority groups—were entering higher education underprepared.

As the U.S. education system evolved to meet the needs of a changing society, student preparation for postsecondary English and math became a central concern. Academic preparation continues to be crucial to success in higher education and is the strongest predictor of college attainment (Adelman, 2006). Only 10% of college dropouts, however, have a GPA below a C average (Johnson, 2012). This surprising fact suggests that persistence for the vast majority of college students depends on non-cognitive factors, or competencies that support academic performance and/or campus integration but may not be measured by cognitive tests (Bowles & Gintis, 1976). I turn to these components of college readiness below.

The Recognition of Non-Cognitive Factors in College Readiness

Even the creators of the SAT—a test designed to measure the cognitive abilities of college applicants in English and mathematics—acknowledged the limits of the exam in predicting college readiness (Sedlacek, 2008). The test makers referred to the SAT as a "supplementary record" and stated that "[t]o place too great emphasis on test scores is as dangerous as the failure to properly evaluate any score or rank in conjunction with other measures and estimates which it supplements" (Brigham, 1926, pp. 44–45).

In the literature, college success was first linked to non-cognitive variables in the 1940s (e.g., Eysenck, 1947). However, as early as the late 1800s, education leaders began to realize that factors such as study habits and attitudes (or what Duncheon referred to as academic mind-sets in chapter 1; Farrington et al., 2012) mattered to collegiate achievement. As President John Bradley of Illinois College wrote, "it is less important what one studies than how he studies" (Bradley, 1876, p. 199, as cited in Dempsey, 1985).

At the turn of the 19th century, research in psychology began to explore the role of study habits and attitudes in college students' achievement (Dempsey, 1985). Though many studies of this era were criticized for methodological concerns, researchers began to acknowledge that factors other than intelligence were affecting the grades of college students (Fleming, 1932; Harris, 1931, 1940). Examples included self-sufficiency and emotional steadiness. Emergent knowledge regarding the impact of non-cognitive variables on college performance led to the development of instruments to assess them. In the 1950s, new assessments such as the Brown-Holtzman Survey of Study Habits and Attitudes (SSHA) were designed to measure student attitudes about studying (Maxwell, 1979). This tool was used for counseling students who may have been college-ready in math and English but lacked important non-cognitive skills.

Increased attention to non-cognitive factors in higher education reflected three goals: (a) improving the prediction of student performance, (b) enhancing retention, and (c) increasing the admission rates of underrepresented students of color (Thomas, Kuncel, & Crede, 2007). Models accounting for both cognitive and non-cognitive skills have been more predictive of students' future success than models assessing cognitive abilities alone, like the SAT or ACT (Oswald, Schmitt, Kim, Ramsay, & Gillespie, 2004; Sternberg, Bonney, Gabora, & Merrifield, 2012). According to Astin (1975), nonacademic factors that affect retention include: family background, financial costs, religious affiliation, study habits, and institutional characteristics. Tinto's (1993) model of college student persistence also acknowledged individual characteristics (e.g., academic self-esteem), along with prior qualifications and academic and social support, which together influence whether students succeed in college.

As more underrepresented groups pursued higher education during the mid- to late-20th century, scholarly interest in non-cognitive factors increased to improve the accuracy of college readiness assessment. Research has shown that measures of cognitive ability, such as standardized

assessments and high school grades, are less predictive of college achievement and completion for students of color than for their white counterparts (Burton & Ramist, 2001; Hoffman & Lowitzki, 2005; Steele,
1997; Zwick & Sklar, 2005). Other studies have found that these racial
disparities may be reduced by including non-cognitive factors (Oswald et
al., 2004; Sternberg et al., 2012). In their work studying the differences
between college students of color and their white counterparts, Sedlacek
and Brooks (1976) listed seven key non-cognitive variables for evaluating
the college readiness of underrepresented students. These non-cognitive
factors included: (a) positive self-concept, (b) realistic self-appraisal, (c)
capacity to understand and deal with racism, (d) preference for long-term,
rather than short-term, goals, (e) access to a strong support person, (f)
leadership potential, and (g) civic and community engagement.

A growing body of literature has explored non-cognitive attributes in
relation to college readiness (e.g., Arbona & Novy, 1990; Credé, & Kuncel, 2008; Duckworth, Peterson, Matthews, & Kelly, 2007; Hood, 1992;
Le, Casillas, Robbins, Langley, 2005; Sternberg et al., 2012; Strayhorn,
2013; Tracey & Sedlacek, 1984; Willingham, 1985). Court cases in the
late 1990s supported the use of non-cognitive factors in college admissions decisions (e.g., Farmer v. Ramsay et al., 1998; Castenada et al. v.
The University of California Regents, 1999; Sedlacek, 2008). Today, university mission statements, marketing materials, and public documents
underscore the importance of nonacademic factors in higher education
(Schmitt, 2012). According to Schmitt's (2012) examination of colleges
and universities, 12 dimensions are valuable to college success: (a) mastery
of general principles, (b) intellectual interest and curiosity, (c) artistic appreciation, (d) multicultural appreciation, (e) leadership, (f) interpersonal
skills, (g) social responsibility, (h) physical and psychological health, (i)
career orientation, (j) adaptability, (k) perseverance, and (l) ethics. Notably,
though dimensions (a) and (b) are related to academic ability, the majority
emphasizes non-cognitive traits. Yet while scholars, faculty, and employers
generally acknowledge the value of non-cognitive factors, college readiness
is still predominantly assessed based on cognitive indicators (Kyllonen,
2005; Stemler, 2012).

What role does secondary education play in fostering students' college
readiness? In part 2 of this chapter, I explore the evolution and key features
of secondary education in the U.S. I focus on vocational tracking and racial
segregation—issues that are at the root of disparities in college readiness.

Part 2: The Role of Secondary Education in College Readiness

During the colonial period before secondary education was prominent in the U.S., students who entered college often came directly from Latin grammar schools or had private tutors, often clergymen (Brubacher & Rudy, 2002). The narrow purview of university curriculum and homogeneity of the student body at that time, referenced earlier in this chapter, meant that preparation for college primarily entailed teaching Latin and Greek to elite white males. Concern for students' different levels of college readiness did not surface until the mid-18th century, when colleges added modern subjects to the traditional curriculum and more groups began to enter higher education.

As the number of postsecondary institutions grew during the 1800s, debates ensued over which subjects to include in the curriculum and how to teach them (Cohen & Kisker, 2010). While some wanted new universities to imitate East Coast liberal arts colleges for reasons of legitimacy, others argued that the traditional classics courses were too theoretical and irrelevant to many new students (Brubacher & Rudy, 2002). Course offerings and their difficulty levels thus became increasingly diverse and admissions requirements became more variable as a result. The differentiation of admissions standards meant that individual institutions defined college readiness differently. Given this variation, secondary schools "could not make general preparation to meet such a diversity of demands without having almost as many senior classes as colleges for which their graduates were preparing" (Brubacher & Rudy, 2002, p. 242).

The Early High Schools

While public and state support for elementary schools was pervasive throughout the 19th century, the same was not true for secondary schools (Rumberger, 2011). Many states, including California, directed the majority of their education funding to the elementary level, which limited the capacity of high schools (Brubacher & Rudy, 2002). As late as 1870, approximately 500 secondary schools existed in the entire United States, serving a mere 50,000 students (Boyer, 1983). While some early high schools aimed to prepare the elite for higher education, most secondary schools did not train students for college (Rumberger, 2011; Wheat, 1948).

As a result, finding sufficient numbers of college-ready students proved challenging for postsecondary institutions (Cohen & Kisker, 2010).

High school enrollment increased dramatically during the late 19th and early 20th centuries and reached 2.2 million by 1920 (U.S. Department of Education, 2011). The rise in enrollment coincided with the practice of social promotion—passing students to subsequent grade levels regardless of ability to keep similar ages together in classrooms—which became prominent in the 1920s and 1930s (Tyack, 1974). Social promotion enabled more unprepared students to enter high school and affected the structure of the curriculum. High school coursework became more differentiated to meet societal needs by preparing "working-class youth and immigrants for working-class jobs and citizenship" (Rumberger, 2011, p. 22). While some, mostly elite, secondary students were preparing for college, a high school diploma was still a terminal degree for the vast majority of young people (Brubacher & Rudy, 2002).

The Rise of Vocational Education and Tracking

Secondary education now had two goals—preparing some students for college and training the majority to enter the workforce. In the late 19th century, the latter goal became the primary focus of most high schools, which prioritized vocational education at the expense of college preparatory coursework (U.S. Department of Education, 2003). This trend was largely motivated by the need to accommodate more students due to the advent of compulsory schooling and the influx of immigration (Tyack, 1974). Meanwhile, the business community and the labor movement championed career training for the masses to meet industrial workforce demand (Rumberger, 2011). The U.S. government expressed its support by passing the Smith-Hughes Act in 1917, allocating federal funding to promote vocational education.

Curricular tracking thus became the norm in high schools by the early 20th century (Tyack, 1974). It was not uncommon for high school students to spend only half their time in academic subjects like English and the rest in applied tracks (e.g., machine shop or bookkeeping) (Rumberger, 2011). Only a small proportion of students were educated in the college preparatory track. Female students were typically tracked into courses such as home economics, bookkeeping, or shorthand, which prepared them for roles consistent with societal expectations. When tracked by ability, female students were generally placed at all levels in lower grades, but tracked out of science and math in high school, leaving them less prepared for college relative to their male peers (Broussard & Joseph, 1998). The use of intelligence tests, originally developed to assess recruits for World War I, strengthened the custom of tracking in comprehensive high schools—a practice that exists in various forms to this day (Oakes, 2005).

As a result of differentiated curricula, rising high school enrollments did not produce the numbers of college-ready students that institutions of higher education were seeking. Yet because universities needed to compete for students' tuition dollars to stay open, even the most selective Ivy League institutions were forced to admit underprepared students in large numbers (Cohen & Kisker, 2010; Maxwell, 1979). While tracking contributed to differing levels of academic preparation, the problem of poor college preparation among students of color was exacerbated by school segregation, which I address below.

From Desegregation to Resegregation

Historically, black students have been much more likely than white students to have a poor secondary school background with little college preparation (Brown & Davis, 2001). The U.S. Supreme Court's 1896 decision in Plessy v. Ferguson upheld racial segregation in public schools (Allen, Jewell, Griffin, & Wolf, 2007). Although the phrase "separate but equal" was used to justify segregated schooling, the education that most black students received in public schools was far inferior to that of their white counterparts. Before the court reversed its ruling some 68 years later with Brown v. Board of Education, over 40% of students, primarily in the South, were educated in a legally segregated school, and many more were segregated due to racial residential patterns (Allen et al., 2007; Clotfelter, 2004).

In the decades that followed the Brown decision, U.S. public education was characterized by more interracial contact than ever before (Allen et al., 2007). Research has shown that racially and economically integrated schools positively affect the academic achievement and long-term outcomes of students of color, including preparation for college (Rothstein, 2013). The Civil Rights Act of 1964 gave the federal government a powerful tool—funding—with which to encourage school desegregation

(Orfield, 1969). As a result, the proportion of African American students attending schools with more than 90% minority enrollment dropped dramatically in the early 1970s (Orfield, 1983).

The racial integration of public schools, however, did not occur without conflict (Clotfelter, 2004). While the intense opposition in southern states was unsurprising given the region's history of slavery, forms of protest surfaced throughout the United States. Clotfelter (2004) outlined four factors that hindered school desegregation: (a) white antipathy—both overt and latent—to interracial contact, (b) multiple methods by which whites could circumvent the intentions of the policy (e.g., moving to the suburbs, sending children to private schools), (c) willingness of state and local officials to comply with white resistance, and (d) wavering commitment from the federal government to enforce desegregation laws. These factors not only impeded integration in the 1960s but also caused what many term as the "resegregation" of public education beginning in the 1970s (Orfield, Frankenberg, & Lee, 2003). Resegregation, in turn, led to more inequitable college preparation for students from different racial backgrounds.

School districts have become more and more segregated despite the nation's growing diversity; between 1986 and 2000, African American and Latina/o students became increasingly segregated from white students (Orfield et al., 2003). Latina/o students are now the most segregated group by race, income, and language. Residential patterns and school choice are largely to blame for the increase in segregation. In addition, more conservative judges who favor race-neutral policies have been appointed to the U.S. Supreme Court and the lower courts, which have overturned or weakened civil rights–era desegregation rulings (Orfield et al., 2003; Reardon, Yun, & Kurlaender, 2006). Race-neutral policies, which generally utilize income and socioeconomic status to make school assignments, have done little, if anything, to improve racial integration (Reardon et al., 2006).

Students may also experience segregation within schools that are racially diverse via tracking (Rumberger, 2011). One study reported that only 26% of high school graduates had completed a college preparatory program, while 56% had taken a general curriculum, and 18% had been placed in vocational education (Planty, Bozick, & Ingels, 2006). Oakes (2005) found that virtually all schools continue to sort their students in some way, highlighting racial disparities in course-taking; white students tend to be placed in high-ability classrooms with college preparatory curriculum, whereas African American and Latina/o students are disproportionately represented in the lower tracks.

Segregation and tracking therefore contribute to educational inequality and by extension unequal college preparation (Broussard & Joseph, 1998; Orfield et al., 2003). The racial and socioeconomic composition of a school has been associated with many factors related to educational opportunity, including financial resources, test scores, quality teachers, and graduation rates (Orfield et al., 2003; Rumberger, 2011). One study examined the effects of tracking on labor market returns and found that 70% of individuals who were placed in the academic track during high school enjoyed higher paying careers (e.g., administrative, sales, professional, technical or managerial positions) compared to only 45% and 48% of the general and vocational tracks, respectively (Broussard & Joseph, 1998). In addition, only 10% of academic track students ended up in service industry jobs, which generally offer lower pay and benefits, compared to approximately 20% of students in the other two tracks. Segregation among and within public secondary schools thus has far-reaching implications for students' long-term outcomes, including their readiness for college (Rothstein, 2013).

Conclusion: Bridging the Gap

Despite increased attention to college readiness in recent decades, underprepared students have always enrolled in higher education (Maxwell, 1979). As the nation expanded and the economy evolved, so did the nature of higher education, including the types of institutions created, the courses offered, and the students who enrolled. Postsecondary education became increasingly democratic, expanding access to new groups of students with varying levels of academic preparation and unique needs. The concept of college readiness thus grew more complex to assume the wide range of cognitive and non-cognitive factors recognized today. Secondary education—largely responsible for preparing students for college—evolved as well, but in a direction inconsistent with many of the changes in higher education. Segregated schooling and the emphasis on ability-tracking have had detrimental effects on college readiness, particularly for underrepresented students of color and those from low-income communities.

Elementary, secondary, and higher education in the United States originated independent of each other (Wheat, 1948). Not surprisingly, the three entities have had different purposes and are only loosely related. Recognizing the gaps between the sectors, leaders have made various attempts over time to smooth articulation (Brubacher & Rudy, 2002). For example, one strategy popular during the 19th century was the certificate system, where universities sent representatives to high schools to oversee curriculum and teaching, and to determine whether the high school was "certified" (Henderson, 1912). Students graduating from a high school deemed certified by a university were granted admission. Another significant effort to lessen the breach between secondary and higher education was the standardization of college admissions requirements using Carnegie units for high school curricula (Shedd, 2003).

Still, the size and diversity of the United States and the relative autonomy of colleges and universities have created wide variability in higher education (Brubacher & Rudy, 2002). This variation contributes to ongoing confusion surrounding college readiness, and the gap between secondary and postsecondary education remains. If U.S. higher education is to continue with its democratic ethos, innovative strategies are needed to better align secondary and postsecondary education. Otherwise institutions of higher education are likely to continue to struggle to address the needs of underprepared students, and inequity will persist in higher education outcomes.

References

Adelman, C. (2006). The toolbox revisted: Paths to degree completion from high school through college. Washington, DC: U.S. Department of Education.

Allen, W. R., Jewell, J. O., Griffin, K. A., & Wolf, D. S. S. (2007). Historically black colleges and universities: Honoring the past, engaging the present, touching the future. *Journal of Negro Education, 76*(3).

Arbona, C., & Novy, D. M. (1990). Noncognitive dimensions as predictors of college success among black, Mexican-American, and white students. *Journal of College Student Development, 31*(5), 415–422.

Astin, A. W. (1975). *Preventing students from dropping out.* San Francisco: Jossey-Bass.

Bowles, S., & Gintis, H. (1976). *Schooling in capitalist America: Educational reform and the contradictions of economic life.* New York: Basic Books.

Boyer, E. L. (1983). *High school: A report on secondary education in America.* New York: Harper & Row.

Brigham, C. C. (1926). The scholastic aptitude test of the college entrance examination board. In T. S. Fiske (Ed.), *The work of the college entrance examination board, 1901–1925*. New York: Ginn & Co.

Broussard, C. A., & Joseph, A. L. (1998). Tracking: A form of educational neglect? *Children & Schools, 20*(2), 110–120.

Brown, M. C., & Davis, J. E. (2001). The historically black college as social contract, social capital, and social equalizer. *Peabody Journal of Education, 76*(1), 31–49.

Brubacher, J. S., & Rudy, W. (2002). *Higher education in transition: A history of American colleges and universities* (4th ed.). New Brunswick, NJ: Transaction.

Burton, N. W., & Ramist, L. (2001). *Predicting success in college: SAT studies of classes graduating since 1980*. New York: College Entrance Examination Board.

Casazza, M. E., & Silverman, S. L. (1996). *Learning assistance and developmental education: A guide for effective practice*. San Francisco: Jossey-Bass.

Center for the Study of Mathematics Curriculum. (2004) Program for College Preparatory Mathematics: Report of the Commission on Mathematics College Entrance Examination Board, 1959 Retrieved from http://www.mathcurriculumcenter.org/PDFS/CCM/summaries/college_prep_summary.pdf

Clotfelter, C. T. (2004). *After brown: The rise and retreat of school desegregation*. Princeton, NJ: Princeton University Press.

Cohen, A. M., & Kisker, C. B. (2010). *The shaping of American higher education: Emergence and growth of the contemporary system*. San Francisco: Jossey-Bass.

Conley, D. T. (2008). Rethinking college readiness. *New Directions for Higher Education, 2008*(144), 3–13.

Credé, M., & Kuncel, N. R. (2008). Study habits, skills, and attitudes: The third pillar supporting collegiate academic performance. *Perspectives on Psychological Science, 3*(6), 425–453.

Dempsey, B. J. L. (1985). *An update on the organization and administration of learning assistance programs in US senior institutions of higher education*. Houston, TX: University of Houston-University Park.

Duckworth, A. L., Peterson, C., Matthews, M. D., & Kelly, D. R. (2007). Grit: Perseverance and passion for long-term goals. *Journal of Personality and Social Psychology, 92*(6), 1087.

Eysenck, H. J. (1947), Student selection by means of psychological tests: A critical survey. *British Journal of Educational Psychology, 17*: 20–39.

Farrington, C. A., Roderick, M., Allensworth, E., Nagaoka, J., Keyes, T. S., Johnson, D. W., & Beechum, N. O. (2012). *Teaching adolescents to become learners. The role of noncognitive factors in shaping school performance: A critical literature review*. Chicago: University of Chicago Consortium on Chicago School Research. Retrieved from https://ccsr. uchicago.edu/publications/teaching-adolescents-become-learners-role-noncognitive-factors-shaping-school

Fleming, E. G. (1932). College achievement, intelligence, personality, and emotion. *Journal of Applied Psychology, 16*(6), 668–674.

Frankenberg, E., Lee, C., & Orfield, G. (2003). *A multiracial society with segregated schools: Are we losing the dream?* (p. 4). Civil Rights Project. Cambridge, MA: Harvard University.

Geiger, R. (1999). The ten generations of American higher education. In Altbach, P. G., Berdahl, R. O., Gumport, P. J. (Eds.) *American Higher Education in the Twenty-first Century: Social, Political, and Economic Challenges*. (pp. 38–69). Baltimore: Johns Hopkins University Press.

Hanford, G. H., & College Board, New York, NY. (1991). *Life with the SAT: Assessing our young people and our times* College Board Publications, Box 886, New York, NY.

Harris, D. (1931). *The relation to college grades of some factors other than intelligence*. ProQuest, UMI Dissertations Publishing.

Harris, D. (1940). Factors affecting college grades: a review of the literature, 1930–1937. *Psychological Bulletin, 37*(3), 125.

Henderson, J. L. (1912). *Admission to college by certificate* (No. 50). New York: Teachers College, Columbia University.

Hoffman, J. L., & Lowitzki, K. E. (2005). Predicting college success with high school grades and test scores: Limitations for minority students. *The Review of Higher Education, 28*(4), 455–474.

Hood, D. W. (1992). Academic and noncognitive factors affecting the retention of black men at a predominantly white university. *The Journal of Negro Education, 61*(1), 12–23.

Johnson, N. (2012). The institutional costs of student attrition. Research Paper. Delta Cost Project at American Institutes for Research. Retrieved from http://www.deltacostproject.org/resources/pdf/Delta-Cost-Attrition-Research-Paper.pdf

Kyllonen, P. (2005). The case for noncognitive assessments. *R & D Connections*, 1–7.

Le, H., Casillas, A., Robbins, S. B., & Langley, R. (2005). Motivational and skills, social, and self-management predictors of college outcomes: Constructing the Student Readiness Inventory. *Educational and Psychological Measurement, 65*(3), 482–508.

Maxwell, M. (1979). *Improving student learning skills: A comprehensive guide to successful practices and programs for increasing the performance of underprepared students.* San Francisco: Jossey-Bass.

Oakes, J. (2005). *Keeping track: How schools structure inequality.* New Haven, CT: Yale University Press.

Orfield, G. (1969). *The reconstruction of southern education: The schools and the 1964 civil rights act.* New York: Wiley-Interscience.

Orfield, G. (1983). *Public school desegregation in the United States, 1968–1980.* Washington, DC: Joint Center for Political Studies.

Orfield, G., Frankenberg, E. D., & Lee, C. (2003). The resurgence of school segregation. *Educational Leadership, 60*(4), 16–20.

Olson, L. (2006, April). Views differ on defining college prep: How to gauge readiness sparks vexing questions. *Education Week, 25*(33), 1, 26, 28–29.

Oswald, F. L., Schmitt, N., Kim, B. H., Ramsay, L. J., & Gillespie, M. A. (2004). Developing a biodata measure and situational judgment inventory as predictors of college student performance. *Journal of Applied Psychology, 89*(2), 187–207.

Planty, M., Bozick, R., Ingels, S. J. (2006). Academic pathways, preparation, and performance: A descriptive overview of transcripts from the high school graduating class of 2003–04 (NCES 2007-316) Washington, DC: National Center for Education Statistics, U.S. Department of Education.

Porter, A. C., & Polikoff, M. S. (2012). Measuring academic readiness for college. *Educational Policy, 26*(3), 394–417.

Reardon, S. F., Yun, J. T., & Kurlaender, M. (2006). Implications of income-based school assignment policies for racial school segregation. *Educational Evaluation and Policy Analysis, 28*(1), 49–75.

Roderick, M., Nagaoka, J., & Coca, V. (2009). College readiness for all: The challenge for urban high schools. *The Future of Children, 19*(1), 185–210.

Rothstein, R. (2013). Why our schools are segregated. *Educational Leadership, 70*(8), 50.

Rumberger, R. W. (2011). *Dropping out: Why students drop out of high school and what can be done about it.* Cambridge, MA: Harvard University Press.

Schmitt, N. (2012). Development of rationale and measures of noncognitive college student potential. *Educational Psychologist, 47*(1), 18–29.

Sedlacek, W. (2008). *The noncognitive variable system.* Presented as part of a symposium: Access to college: Race conscious policies and the consequences of colorblindness. American Educational Research Association Convention, New York.

Sedlacek, W. E., & Brooks, G. C., Jr. (1976). *Racism in American education: A model for change.* Chicago: Nelson-Hall.

Shedd, J. M. (2003). The history of the student credit hour. *New Directions for Higher Education, 2003*(122), 5–12.

Steele, C. M. (1997). A threat in the air: How stereotypes shape intellectual identity and performance. *American Psychologist, 52*(6), 613.

Stemler, S. E. (2012). What Should University Admissions Tests Predict? *Educational Psychologist, 47*(1), 5–17.

Sternberg, R. J. (1985). Beyond IQ: A triarchic theory of human intelligence. New York: Cambridge University Press.

Sternberg, R. J., Bonney, C. R., Gabora, L., & Merrifield, M. (2012). WICS: A model for college and university admissions. *Educational Psychologist, 47*(1), 30–41.

Stephens, D. (2001). Increasing access: Educating underprepared students in US colleges and universities past, present, and future. Retrieved from http://faculty.etsu.edu/stephen/misc/increasingaccess.htm

Strayhorn, T. L. (2013). What role does grit play in the academic success of black male collegians at predominantly white institutions? *Journal of African American Studies, 18*(1), 1–10.

Thomas, L. L., Kuncel, N. R., & Credé, M. (2007). Noncognitive variables in college admissions: The case of the non-cognitive questionnaire. *Educational and Psychological Measurement, 67*(4), 635–657.

Tinto, V. (1993). Leaving College: Rethinking the causes and cures of student attrition. (2nd ed.). Chicago: University of Chicago Press.

Tracey, T. J., & Sedlacek, W. E. (1987). Prediction of college graduation using noncognitive variables by race. *Measurement and Evaluation in Counseling and Development, 19*, 177–184.

Turner, S., & Bound, J. (2003). Closing the gap or widening the divide: The effects of the GI bill and world war II on the educational outcomes of black Americans. *The Journal of Economic History, 63*(01), 145–177.

Tyack, D. B. (1974). *The one best system: A history of American urban education*. Cambridge, MA: Harvard University Press.

U.S. Department of Education. (2011). Historical summary of public elementary and secondary school statistics: Selected years, 1869–70 through 2008–09 [Table 35]. Washington DC: U.S. National Center for Education Statistics. Retrieved from http://nces.ed.gov/programs/digest/d11/tables/dt11_035.asp

U.S. Department of Education. (2003). From there to here: The road to reform of American high schools. Washington, DC: Author. Retrieved from http://www2.ed.gov/about/offices/list/ovae/pi/hsinit/papers/history.pdf

Veysey, L. R. (1965). *The emergence of the American university*. Chicago: University of Chicago Press.

Wheat, L. B. (1948). Curriculum articulation for secondary and higher education. *The School Review, 56*(3), 146–155.

Willingham, W. W. (1985). *Success in college: The role of personal qualities and academic ability*. New York: College Entrance Examination Board.

Williams, R. L. (1991). *The origins of federal support for higher education: George W. Atherton and the land-grant college movement*. University Park, PA: Pennsylvania State Press.

Zwick, R., & Sklar, J. C. (2005). Predicting college grades and degree completion using high school grades and SAT scores: The role of student ethnicity and first language. *American Educational Research Journal, 42*(3), 439–464.

3

◄◦►

THE CHALLENGE OF THE LEAST READY

A Historical Perspective

BRYAN ADÁN RODRÍGUEZ

As Almeida noted in chapter 2, the question of how to improve academic outcomes for America's youth has driven considerable policy debate, educational reform, and academic research over the past two centuries. Throughout this period, educational policymakers and researchers have confronted the challenge of improving educational opportunity and achievement. State and federal educational policies such as compulsory schooling regulations of the 19th century and the California Master Plan for Higher Education of 1960 were designed to provide students from all backgrounds with greater access to academic institutions. However, significant educational hurdles remain for many students—in particular those who are the least ready for postsecondary education.

College readiness, as noted in chapter 1, refers to the skills and knowledge a student needs to succeed in higher education. The least ready is defined here as students who attend two-year institutions and are at risk of not transferring or graduating due to placement into the lowest levels of remediation. My concern is not with those students who attend four-year institutions or graduate from a community college with an A.A./A.S. degree or certificate. Rather, I am concerned with those students who, among all college students at open-access two-year institutions, face the greatest

65

barriers to graduation due to significant under-preparedness in math and/ or English. Thus, although college readiness entails a range of cognitive and non-cognitive skills, for the purposes of this chapter and consistent with the approach of state and institutional policymakers, I focus on academic readiness as measured by cognitive indicators (e.g., standardized test scores and remedial course placement).

By using the term "least ready," I am not suggesting that students in this subgroup are somehow lacking or in deficit. To the contrary, placement into the lowest levels of remediation suggests inequitable or inadequate access to opportunities that develop college-ready competencies as opposed to a problem with the individual. I use the term "least ready" to acknowledge the reality state policymakers presently confront: some students who enter community college have had such poor academic preparation that their chances of completing remedial sequences and persisting to graduation are particularly low. These students are less academically ready for college than their counterparts who perform on the college level or only require one remedial course. Those who are least ready are also vulnerable to dropping out of two-year colleges due to financial obstacles, such as rising budgetary constraints and decreases in student aid and college affordability. To inform policy efforts that may support this group of students, this analysis and my subsequent chapter in part II focus on the least ready.

While Almeida discussed the historical evolution of college readiness generally, I offer historical perspective on the role of educational policy in shaping opportunity for students who are significantly underprepared for college. I first identify the least ready students and discuss how the term has evolved over time. I then examine schooling policies of the 19th and 20th centuries that extended educational access to students who have traditionally been underserved and underprepared. Second, I discuss the least ready today by considering their academic outcomes and the challenges they face in pursuing postsecondary education. I conclude by highlighting the social and economic repercussions of failing to provide adequate educational opportunities to this demographic of students.

Who Are the Least Ready?

Much has been written on the key elements of college success and what it means to be academically ready for college (ACT Policy Report, 2004; Conley, 2007; Horn & Nuñez, 2000). As mentioned above, college readiness has been defined as the level of preparation a student needs to complete college-level coursework and persist to degree attainment (Baber, Castro, & Bragg, 2010; Conley, 2007; 2010). Academic readiness includes a variety of domains such as cognitive performance, content knowledge, behaviors, and mind-sets. An academically ready student is able to "understand what is expected in a college course, can cope with the content knowledge that is presented, and can take away from the course the key intellectual lessons and dispositions the course was designed to convey and develop" (Conley, 2007, p. 5–6). High school GPA, high school class rank, and college admissions test scores (e.g., the SAT) have been used to assess readiness, though these indicators cannot account for the non-cognitive factors that support persistence (Greene & Forster, 2003; Wiley, Wyatt, & Camara, 2010).

The population discussed here, the least ready, is broadly defined as community college students who enroll in remedial coursework and lack the preparation needed to transfer to a four-year college or attain a two-year college degree (Conley, 2007). Yet there are gradations of academic readiness even within this category. The least ready students are defined specifically as those who place into lower-level remedial courses (California Community Colleges Chancellor's Office, 2012). Of the population who places into remedial courses, students who place multiple levels below transfer level are the least likely to complete remedial courses and the least likely to graduate or transfer (Community College Survey of Student Engagement, 2008). While students entering community colleges with the least preparation may come from all backgrounds, they are disproportionately low-income students of color (EdSource, 2010). This analysis thus provides insight into how educational policies influence underserved student populations. Because these students tend to take classes multiple times or drop out, the legislature continues to wonder if state monies should be spent in a way that does not appear to reach its goal of graduation or transfer.

American education has evolved significantly since the birth of compulsory education laws in the 19th century. Before attending secondary schools was common practice, receiving an education often meant attending K-8 schools in which basic skills were taught—students learned to read, write, and do simple math. The idea that students were either ready or not ready for K-8 schooling is conceivable. Two centuries ago, the least ready students would have likely failed to complete a primary education. Yet today's education system features multiple tiers of schooling, types of institutions, education providers, and areas of study. Meanwhile, the economy increasingly requires higher levels of degree completion. Given that K-16 schooling has transformed over the past two centuries, I argue that the nature of academic readiness, and those who are categorized as the least ready, have changed as well. I focus ultimately on those who are the least prepared and most vulnerable in two-year postsecondary institutions.

Contextualizing Schooling and the Least Ready

The education literature has well documented the challenges associated with preparing America's youth for success in school (Coleman, 1966; Tyler, 1974). Scholars have long debated the notion that education is society's "great equalizer" (Mann, 1868, p. 669). Some researchers have suggested that public schools in the 19th and 20th centuries were intentionally designed to sustain social and economic inequalities (Bowles & Gintis, 1976; Katz, 1975). That is, schooling institutions reproduce existing socioeconomic disparities within a capitalist society. Scholars such as Bowles and Gintis (1976) asserted that schooling was used as a tool for social reproduction, such that children from middle- and upper-class families attained social mobility through education while disadvantaged children of working-class families did not. Others contended (Jencks, 1979) that family background rather than school quality was the key determinant of students' academic performance and their transition into the labor market (Vinovskis, 1992). These authors suggested that promoting access to education among disadvantaged students required altering children's home environment. The implication was that policymakers needed to focus on broader social and economic factors outside of school.

Although this chapter considers how state and federal policies have facilitated greater equity and opportunity for all youth, I acknowledge that whether schools serve the function of expanding equity or perpetuating existing inequity is subject to debate. Nevertheless, over the past two centuries, educational policies have generally provided increasing access to individuals who were once excluded from the educational system.

Historical Overview: Legislation That Expanded Educational Access

The following historical overview focuses on two pieces of legislation: compulsory education regulations of the 19th century and the California

Master Plan for Higher Education of 1960. Together, these two policies reflect a movement to promote broader access to education.

Compulsory Education Regulations of the 19th Century

Prior to 1851, the United States lacked a uniform system of public schooling. There were an array of primary schools catering to boys, girls, and people of different economic backgrounds (Katz, 1976). Secondary and post-secondary schooling options were rare and generally limited to wealthy white men.

The growth of urban centers and industrial establishments during the first half of the 19th century dramatically transformed the social landscape of American culture and public policy. The influx of immigration from European nations such as Ireland, Poland, and Germany in the 1830s and 1840s led to significant demographic shifts in American cities throughout the Northeast. The cultural and linguistic heterogeneity of urban centers in the U.S. prompted "systematic solutions on chaotic urban conditions" (Katz, 1976, p. 1). For example, historian Karl Kaestle describes New York during the 19th century:

> The city's population multiplied tenfold from 1800 to 1850, and the tremendous increase in the scale of problems, combined with the alienation and segregation of the well-to-do from the poor, increased people's reliance on institutional solutions to social problems. Re-formers tried to rationalize charity, standardize schools, and incarcerate vagrants. These were symptoms of a general effort to impose systematic solutions on chaotic urban conditions (Katz, 1976, p. 1).

Housing shortages, harsh living conditions, and high crime rates characterized immigrant enclaves in urban centers in the Northeast. The large immigrant population required increased local financial resources for the urban poor. According to Katz (1976), in 1837, New York City spent an estimated $279,999 in services to support low-income residents, approximately 60% of whom were immigrants. By 1860, the proportion of immigrants rose to 86%. Increasing diversity encouraged a "new receptivity" (Katz, 1976, p. 15) for a standardized education system among educators, policymakers, and industrialists.

School reform advocates such as Horace Mann and Henry Barnard led the common school movement and garnered support for a system that would seek to unify Christian morality and democratic ideals (Hunt & Maxson, 1981). Pressure from business interests also fueled the common school movement. Manufacturers favored a uniform school system to instill in children respect and obedience to authority, values which were considered fundamental to successful employment (Bowles & Gintis, 1976). The revisionist perspective described by Bowles and Gintis suggests that the standardization of American schools was crucial not only for the prosperity of the industrial sector of the economy, but also for future economic growth across all sectors of the labor market.

However, the forces behind the development of compulsory education were not merely economic (Tyack, 1976). Problematizing the tendency for scholars to employ one particular theory or perspective to explain educational trends, Tyack (1976) wrote, "it seems useful to entertain alternative modes of explanation as a way of avoiding the reductionism that selects evidence to fit a particular thesis" (p. 356). Therefore, a complex interplay of political, organizational, and economic factors motivated the growth of compulsory education laws. Massachusetts was the first state to enact compulsory education legislation in 1852, and other states followed suit in the following decades. By 1918, all 50 states implemented compulsory education laws requiring that children, typically ages 8 to 14, attend school (Graham, 1974). By the 1930s and 1940s, many states required that students attend high school. By the 1950s, secondary school attendance "had become so customary that school-leavers were routinely seen as 'dropouts'" (Tyack, 1976, p. 359).

Today, regardless of race/ethnicity, social class, or religion, each school-aged child in the United States has access to a K-12 education. Disadvantaged students, who would otherwise not have an opportunity to receive an education prior to compulsory education regulations, now had a right to receive an education. Decades later in the 20th century, policymakers began focusing on generating educational opportunities beyond K-12 schooling for more students.

Donahoe Higher Education Act/ CA Master Plan for Higher Education of 1960

While the compulsory schooling laws of the 19th century ensured that children received primary and secondary education, the California Master

Plan for Higher Education of 1960 targeted the postsecondary context. Historically, the development of "new public institutions was not the result of well-thought-out plans but was often based on politics" (Johnson, 2010, p. 4). The Master Plan, by contrast, provided a systematic framework for the state's public tertiary institutions to expand higher education access for California's rapidly growing population.

The Master Plan established a three-tier system of higher education entities: the University of California (UC), California State University (CSU), and California Community College (CCC). The fundamental principles of the Master Plan were to (a) create a system of affordable higher education available to all regardless of a student's ability to pay, in which academic progress would only be limited by individual proficiency, and (b) differentiate the functions of the three entities so that each could focus on different areas of academics/training—a strategy to conserve public resources on duplicate efforts (University of California Office of the President, 2013). The plan also initiated the California Grant (Cal Grant), a financial aid program that provided assistance to California undergraduates and vocational training students.

When the Master Plan was established, an estimated 11% of working-age adults in California had a college degree. The Master Plan's goal of enhancing "access, affordability, and quality" (Johnson, 2010, p. 4) granted the top 12.5% of high school graduates entrance to a University of California campus and the top 33.3% of high school graduates entrance to a California State University campus. The University of California would serve as the state's primary research university, offering bachelor's, master's, doctoral, and professional degrees. The California State University would provide a majority of undergraduate education and some master's programs. The California Community College system would offer lower-division academic coursework for transfer to a four-year university or completion of vocational, career technical education, basic skills education, and enrichment courses.

Some scholars have argued that differentiated systems of higher education perpetuate inequality by only allowing certain students access to the most elite institutions (Bastedo & Gumport, 2003). While concern for equity certainly warrants attention, the Master Plan's establishment of an open access community college system represented an important advancement toward creating postsecondary opportunity for students who were not academically ready for selective four-year schools. As Johnson (2010) explained, the Master Plan established "the principle of universal access to postsecondary education in California at the community college level," such that all students who were "capable of benefitting from instruction" were granted entrance (p. 11). The Master Plan continues to govern California's system of public higher education. Today's 112 community college campuses remain open access; individuals can walk on to a campus and pursue a postsecondary degree at little or no cost, after accounting for financial aid.

The California Community Colleges comprise the largest system of higher education in the U.S., offering the only entry point to four-year universities for a majority of students in the state (Martinez-Wenzl & Marquez, 2012). The system serves approximately 2.4 million students, or two-thirds of California's college student population and nearly one-quarter of all community college students in the nation (California Community Colleges Chancellor's Office, 2012). In 1960, the Master Plan committee anticipated significant increases in student enrollment. One of the fundamental components of the plan was long-term, state-funded financial support. For the two decades following the plan's inception, "California and its residents supported the system's growth through capital expenditures for new buildings, including new campuses, and provided funds for operating expenses, most notably for instruction, that kept student fees among the lowest in the nation" (Johnson, 2010, p. 5).

However, as Johnson (2010) went on to say, "today, that commitment has changed" (p. 5). Amid recent financial turmoil and wavering political support for public education, federal and state funding cuts are threatening the open-door policy in the community college system (Mullin, 2012). Due to budgetary constraints, the California Community College system has limited course offerings, increased tuition, decreased the number of available seats, and reduced faculty/administration personnel (Bohn, Reyes, & Johnson, 2013). Despite policymakers' and educators' ongoing efforts to improve student outcomes, many resources that have been traditionally allocated to community college students are now being diverted elsewhere.

Future Growth and the Role of the Least Ready

U.S. educational policies have trended toward providing the least ready with greater access to academic institutions—first to K-12 schools and more recently to higher education. Legislation such as compulsory schooling regulations of the 19th and 20th centuries and the California Master

Plan for Higher Education of 1960 have expanded educational opportunity for traditionally underserved student populations. In recent decades, K-12 schools have made progress toward developing college-going cultures and encouraging more students to pursue higher education (Roderick, Nagaoka, & Coca, 2009). Nearly 90% of today's high school students from all racial/ethnic groups aspire to go to college (Callan et al., 2006). Yet while more students are entering college, their greatest obstacle is not gaining admission but rather becoming academically ready for postsecondary schooling (Adelman, 2006).

Statistics on college access and completion suggest that many students are lost along the high school to college pipeline and point to the problem of widespread under-preparedness (Kantrowitz, 2012). Once the global leader in higher educational attainment among individuals ages 24 to 35, the U.S. has been surpassed by several industrialized nations and now ranks fifth. Postsecondary completion rates have become stagnant despite longstanding patterns of generational increases. Attainment gaps also persist among students who are academically underprepared—many of whom come from socioeconomically disadvantaged backgrounds—and their college ready counterparts (National Center for Public Policy and Higher Education, 2008).

California specifically confronts low rates of college completion. As Duncheon referenced in chapter 1 (Table 1.1), only 44 out of every 100 students who enter ninth grade in California will enter college (NCHEMS, n.d.). Of those 44 students, 26 will enroll in community college and only 8 will graduate with an associate's degree within three years. According to the National Center for Education Statistics (2010), tens of thousands of California community college students drop out annually. The result is that "young adults in California are [now] less likely than older adults to have graduated from college" (Johnson, 2010, p. 3). Such data reflect what scholars have termed the aspirations-attainment gap; while more students aspire to attend college than ever before, many will not graduate with a postsecondary degree (Roderick et al., 2009).

The low rate of two-year college completion can be attributed in large part to students' under-preparedness for postsecondary coursework (Bailey, Jeong, & Cho, 2010). Many scholars have problematized a one-size-fits-all college-going agenda that promotes universal bachelor's degree attainment, which may have particularly harmful consequences for students who are least academically prepared (Ravitch, 2010; Rosenbaum, Stephan, & Rosenbaum, 2010; Symonds, Schwartz, & Ferguson, 2011; Zhao, 2009).

Some students may be better suited for one level of postsecondary education and not necessarily for another (Barnes & Slate, 2013).

While higher education struggles with low graduation rates, workforce demand for college-educated employees has grown substantially and is projected to increase (Johnson & Sengupta, 2009). The fastest growing sectors of the American economy require individuals to have at least some postsecondary education (Carnevale & Desrochers, 2003). Roughly 45 years ago, 72% of U.S. jobs were held by workers with a high school diploma or less. By 2018, only 38% of jobs in the United States will be available to workers without some postsecondary education (Holzer & Lerman, 2009). Yet less than 47% of Americans are projected to have at least an associate's degree by 2025. According to the Lumina Foundation (2012), the American economy will be more than 23 million degree-holders short of meeting workforce needs. Other projections estimate a "shortfall of 14 million workers who have the knowledge and skills needed to compete for middle-income jobs in a global economy" by the year 2020 (Callan et al., 2006, p. 3). Consistent with national trends, California's economic growth will demand approximately 1 million more college graduates in 2025 than are expected to be supplied (Johnson & Sengupta, 2009).

Federal and state policymakers thus have incentive to improve college readiness rates, particularly among students with the greatest risk of non-completion (Callan et al., 2006). Future economic growth hinges largely on the capacity of the tertiary education sector to produce graduates that can perform the jobs of the future. The least ready students attending two-year colleges represent a significant segment of the workforce. Facilitating degree attainment among the least ready is also important to enable social mobility for these students. Unless the level of academic preparation students receive improves, the extent to which the American workforce will be able to compete globally is expected to decline significantly (Callan et al., 2006).

The Least Ready Today

Students who enter college academically underprepared typically enroll in remediation, or non-credit-bearing math and English courses that serve as prerequisites to baccalaureate-level coursework. Students who are academically underprepared are less likely to complete their degree or transfer relative to their college-ready counterparts (Bailey et al., 2010). Of those who place into remediation, students who place multiple levels below transfer level are the least likely to complete their remedial courses and graduate or transfer (Community College Survey of Student Engagement, 2008).

The least ready are typically nontraditional students—older, attending school part-time, and balancing full-time work and childcare. Thus while many of the least ready students come directly from high school, a significant number are adults who have been in the workforce and are returning to school (California Community Colleges Chancellor's Office, 2012). Approximately 18% of students in math courses four levels below transfer (arithmetic) are above the age of 25; by contrast, only 2% of students in math courses one level below transfer (intermediate algebra) were above the age of 25 (EdSource, 2010).

The rate of remedial course-taking in community colleges in the state of California exceeds 80%, and students demonstrate varied levels of under-preparedness. Although there are a number of ways to measure academic preparation (e.g., high school grades, course-taking), most community colleges in California and across the nation rely on subject-specific standardized tests such as ACCUPLACER or COMPASS for course placement. Approximately 92% of two-year colleges use scores on assessment tests for placement into remedial courses (Hughes & Scott-Clayton, 2011). The least ready students score significantly lower than the remedial cut-point. They place into courses three levels or more below transfer level in math, English writing, English as a second language (ESL) writing, and/or English as a second language (ESL) reading.

In the fall of 2010, 14.6% of the 350,129 first-time students entering the California Community College system were considered prepared for college-level math (see Table 3.1). The remaining students, roughly 85.4%, were placed into remedial math courses. The least ready students are represented in levels 3-6—the furthest from a transfer-level math course. Although none of the students were placed six levels below transfer, 1.9% of students placed five levels below transfer, 18.7% placed four levels below, and 20.1% placed three levels below (California Community Colleges Chancellor's Office, 2012). Therefore, an estimated 142,500 students, or 40.7% of the student population, placed at least three levels below transfer level.

Research suggests that students who place into the lowest levels of math remediation are less likely than their better prepared peers to complete the course sequences necessary for graduation or transfer (Bailey et al., 2010). Only 46% of the community college students in California who

TABLE 3.1. Percentage of students who tested into each level
of math and English, Fall 2010

Course placement	Math total students: 350,129	English total students: 319,892
Transfer level	14.6%	28.4%
1 level below transfer	20.6%	35.1%
2 levels below transfer	24.2%	20.3%
3 levels below transfer*	20.1%	13.8%
4 levels below transfer*	18.7%	1.7%
5 levels below transfer*	1.9%	0.6%
6 levels below transfer*	0.0%	0.0%
7 levels below transfer*	n/a	0.0%

Source: California Community Colleges Chancellor's Office (2012)
*Represented as the least ready

enter one level below transfer level in math (intermediate algebra) receive a certificate or degree or transfer to a four-year institution (California Community Colleges Student Task Force, 2012). The completion rate among students who enter community college four levels below transfer level (arithmetic) drops to 25.5%. One study using a sample of about 50,000 students in the Los Angeles Community College District (LACCD) reported similar trends (Fong, Melguizo, Prather, & Bos, 2013); students who placed one level below transfer (intermediate algebra) had a 54% pass rate for the course, while only 7% of students who were placed four levels below transfer level (arithmetic) completed intermediate algebra (see Table 3.2). Complete College America (2012) reported that just 16% of students required to take three developmental math courses completed their full math sequence within three years. According to EdSource (2010), 51% of students who placed into intermediate algebra (one level below transfer) transferred or completed their degree. By contrast, only 18% of students who placed into arithmetic (four levels below transfer) were able to transfer or complete their degree.

Similar patterns in course-taking and completion emerge for English remediation. Of the 319,892 first-time students who entered California community colleges in 2010, approximately 28.4% were considered prepared for college-level English writing (see Table 3.1). The least ready students who placed three-to-seven levels below transfer comprise 16.1%

TABLE 3.2. Percentage of students who passed each level
of remedial math based on initial placement

Initial remedial course placement	Percentage who passed arithmetic	Percentage who passed pre-algebra	Percentage who passed elementary algebra	Percentage who passed intermediate algebra
Intermediate algebra (1 course below transfer level)	---	---	---	54%
Elementary algebra (2 courses below transfer level)	---	---	51%	28%
Pre-algebra (3 courses below transfer level)	---	46%	25%	12%
Arithmetic (4 courses below transfer level)	39%	23%	14%	7%

Adapted from Fong, Melguizo, Prather, and Bos (2013); this author is grateful to these scholars for permission to reproduce their figures

TABLE 3.3. Number of least ready students by subject in
California community colleges, Fall 2010

Subject	Number of least ready students
Math	142,503
English writing	51,503
English reading	41,026
ESL writing	12,890
ESL reading	12,613

Source: California Community Colleges Chancellor's Office (2012)

of first-time course-takers. According to Bettinger and Long (2007), 75% of students who are required to take three remedial English remediation courses fail to successfully complete their course sequences.

The numbers of least ready students in California by subject area are shown in Table 3.3. Although there is potential overlap among students by subject, these figures offer approximations of how many students require multiple levels of remediation upon college entrance. Math courses appear to serve the most significantly underprepared students (142,503), while the number of least ready students in writing is roughly 51,503.

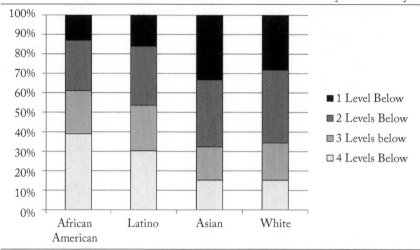

FIGURE 3.1. Distribution of students across remedial math levels by race/ethnicity

Source: EdSource, 2010.

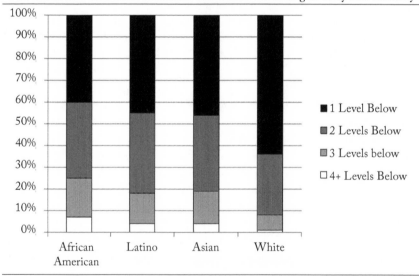

FIGURE 3.2. Distribution of students across remedial writing levels by race/ethnicity

Source: EdSource, 2010.

Consistent with trends in remedial course-taking generally, African American and Latina/o students enroll in lower-level remedial courses at a higher rate compared to their peers (Adelman, 2006; Brown & Niemi, 2007; EdSource, 2010). African American and Latina/o students are twice as likely to be placed in the lowest math (i.e., arithmetic) and writing level course compared to their white peers (see Figures 3.1 and 3.2). Similarly, African American and Latina/o students are half as likely to be enrolled in intermediate algebra compared to their white and Asian peers. As a result, students from these racial/ethnic groups disproportionately encounter the obstacles associated with entering college significantly behind academically.

What Challenges Do the Least Ready Face?

Developing basic skills such as reading, writing, and math allows students to pursue higher-skilled employment in the job market or apply knowledge/skills in future academic coursework (California Community Colleges Chancellor's Office, 2012). However, the least ready students face obstacles that are not only academic but also financial, social, and cultural that diminish their likelihood of completing their remedial coursework and persisting to degree attainment (EdSource, 2010). Financial hardships in particular impede progress for many underprepared students.

One of the challenges associated with remediation is that students must pay for their remedial courses, but often do not accrue credits that count toward a degree. Students who place into lower-level remedial courses must consequently pay for and pass several courses for no credit before completing a series of subject courses (Strong American Schools, 2008); the timeline for finishing these remedial courses can last several semesters or potentially several years. According to Strong American Schools (2008), the total cost to students taking remedial courses is roughly $708 to $886 million in remedial education tuition and fees. The fact that remedial courses cost money but do not count toward graduation is particularly problematic for underprepared students who are disproportionately socioeconomically disadvantaged. The least ready students are nearly twice as likely to come from low-income backgrounds compared to the general community college student population (EdSource, 2010).

The least ready students also may be less likely than their better-prepared peers to benefit from financial aid. As mentioned in the prior section, many of the least ready students are adults returning to school, and these students are often enrolled only part-time due to work obligations (EdSource, 2010). Students assigned to arithmetic (i.e., lower-level math), for example, are nearly four times more likely than students assigned to intermediate algebra (i.e., higher-level math) to be enrolled in six units or less. This figure is particularly important because students who are enrolled in six units or less often do not qualify for state or federal financial aid. Particularly given recent trends in rising tuition costs and decreasing financial aid availability (Oliff, Palacios, Johnson, & Leachman, 2013), affording college presents a significant barrier to completion for many students. Many of the least ready students must work additional hours, pay for childcare, and take out student loans in order to take college classes. These nonacademic obstacles exacerbate the academic challenges the least ready students already face.

Conclusion

Today, policymakers, researchers, and practitioners are working to enhance educational opportunity and achievement, particularly for students from traditionally underrepresented backgrounds. Throughout the past two centuries, state and federal education policies such as compulsory education regulations of the 19th century and the California Master Plan for Higher Education of 1960 have facilitated greater access to academic institutions for these student populations. Still, significant educational hurdles remain for many—especially the least ready students. At a time of tight fiscal budgets, policymakers continue to look at areas where goals are not being reached. As I noted, the subject of this chapter are those students who are most at-risk when they enter community college. Of consequence, state legislators have continued to express concern about what needs to be done. Results range from eliminating these students from attending a community college since their chances of graduating are slim to providing intensive support services to ensure that they do graduate. Obviously, any policy has budget implications. Regardless, postsecondary under-preparedness is likely to continue preventing matriculation and degree completion for these students without interventions to enhance institutional supports.

References

ACT Policy Report. (2004). *The role of academic and non-academic factors in improving college retention.* Iowa City, IA.

Adelman, C. (2006). *The toolbox revisited: Paths to degree completion from high school through college.* Washington, DC: U.S. Department of Education.

Baber, L. D., Castro, E. L., & Bragg, D. D. (2010, August). *Measuring success: David Conley's college readiness framework and the Illinois College and Career Readiness Act.* Champaign, IL: Office of Community College Research and Leadership, University of Illinois at Urbana-Champaign.

Bailey, T. (2009). Challenge and opportunity: Rethinking the role and function of developmental education in community college. *New Directions for Community Colleges, 145,* 11–30.

Bailey, T., Jeong, D. W., & Cho, S. (2010). Referral, enrollment, and completion in developmental education sequences in community colleges. *Economics of Education Review, 29,* 255–270.

Barnes, W., & Slate, J. R., (2013). College-readiness is not one-size-fits-all. *Current Issues in Education, 16*(1), 1–13.

Bastedo, M. N., & Gumport, P. J. (2003). Access to what? Mission differentiation and academic stratification in U.S. public higher education. *Higher Education, 46,* 341–359.

Bettinger, E. P., & Long, B. T. (2007). Remedial and developmental courses. In S. Dickert-Conlin & R. Rubenstein (Eds.), *Economic inequality and higher education* (pp. 69–100). New York: Russell Sage Foundation.

Bohn, S., Reyes, B., & Johnson, H. (2013). *The impact of budget cuts on California's community colleges.* San Francisco: Public Policy Institute of California. Retrieved from http://www.ppic.org/main/publication.asp?i=1048

Bowles, S. & Gintis, H. (1976). *Schooling in capitalist America: Education reform and the contradictions of economic life.* New York: Basic Books.

Brown, R., & Niemi, D. (2007). *Investigating the alignment of high school and community college tests in California.* San Jose, CA: The National Center for Public Policy and Higher Education.

Callan, P. M., Finney, J. E., Kirst, M. W., Usdan, M. D., & Venezia, A. (2006). *Claiming common ground: State policymaking for improving college readiness and success.* San Jose, CA: The National Center for Public Policy and Higher Education.

California Community Colleges Chancellor's Office. (2012). *Basic skills accountability: Supplement to the ARCC Report*. Sacramento, CA: California Community Colleges Chancellor's Office.

California Community Colleges Student Task Force. (2012). *Advancing student success in the California community colleges*. Retrieved from http://www.californiacommunitycolleges.cccco.edu/Portals/0/StudentSuccessTaskForce/REPORT_SSTF_FINAL_122911.pdf

Carnevale, A., & Desrochers, D. (2003). *Standards for what? The economic roots of K–16 reform*. Princeton, NJ: Education Testing Service. Retrieved from http://www.transitionmathproject.org/assets/docs/resources/standards_for_what.pdf.

Coleman, J. S. (1966). *Equality of educational opportunity study (EEOS)*. Ann Arbor, MI: Inter-university Consortium for Political and Social Research.

Community College Survey of Student Engagement (CCSSE). (2008). *High expectations and high support*. Austin, TX: The University of Texas at Austin, Community College Leadership Program.

Complete College America (2012). *Remediation: Higher education's bridge to nowhere*. Washington, DC: Complete College America.

Conley, D. T. (2007). *Redefining college readiness*. Eugene, OR: Educational Policy Improvement Center.

Conley, D. T. (2010). *College and career ready: helping all students succeed beyond high school*. San Francisco: Jossey-Bass.

EdSource. (2010). *Course-taking patterns, policies, and practices in developmental education in the California Community Colleges*. Mountain View, CA: EdSource.

Fong, K., Melguizo, T., Bos, H., & Prather, G. (2013). *A different view on how we understand progression through the developmental math trajectory*. (CCCC Policy Brief #3). Rossier School of Education, University of Southern California: California Community College Collaborative. Retrieved from http://www.sccommunitycollege.com/

Graham, P. A. (1974). *Community and class in American education: 1865-1918 (studies in the history of American education)*. New York: John Wiley & Sons.

Greene, J. P., & Forster, G. (2003). *Public high school graduation and college readiness rates in the United States*. New York: Manhattan Institute for Policy Research.

Holzer, H. J., & Lerman, R. I. (2009). *The future of middle skill jobs*. Washington, DC: Brookings Institution.

Horn, L., & Nuñez, A. M. (2000). *Mapping the road to college: First-generation students' math track, planning strategies, and context of support* (NCES 2000–153). Washington, DC: National Center for Education Statistics.

Hughes, K. L., & Clayton, J. S. (2011). Assessing developmental assessment in community colleges (assessment of evidence series). *Community College Review, 39*(4), 327–351.

Hunt, T. C., & Maxson, M. M. (1981). *Religion and morality in American schooling.* Lanham, MD: Rowman & Littlefield.

Jencks, C. (1979). *Who gets ahead? The determinants of economic success in America.* New York: Basic Books.

Johnson, H. (2010). *Higher education in California: New goals for the Master Plan.* San Francisco: Public Policy Institute of California.

Johnson, H., & Sengupta, R. (2009). *Closing the gap: Meeting California's need for college graduates.* San Francisco: Public Policy Institute of California. Retrieved from www.ppic.org/content/pubs/report/R_409HJR.pdf

Katz, M. S. (1975). *Class, bureaucracy & schools: The illusion of educational change in America.* New York: Praeger.

Katz, M. S. (1976). *A history of compulsory education laws. Fastback Series* (No. 75, Bicentennial Series). Retrieved from http://www.eric.ed.gov/ERICWebPortal/contentdelivery/servlet/ERICServlet?accno=ED119389.

Kantrowitz, M. (2012). *The college completion agenda may sacrifice college access for low income, minority and other at-risk.* Student Financial Aid Policy Analysis. Retrieved from http://www.finaid.org/educators/20120910completionagenda.pdf

Lumina Foundation. (2012). *A stronger nation through higher education.* Indianapolis, IN: Author.

Mann, H. (1868). *Life and works of Horace Mann* (Vol. 3). London: Forgotten Books.

Martinez-Wenzl, M., & Marquez, R. (2012). *Unrealized promises: Unequal access, affordability, and excellence at community colleges in Southern California.* Los Angeles: The Civil Rights Project/Proyecto Derechos Civiles.

Mullin, C. M. (2012, February). *Why access matters: The community college student body* (Policy Brief 2012-01PBL). Washington, DC: American Association of Community Colleges.

National Center for Education Statistics. (2010). *The condition of education*

2010 in brief (NCES 2010-029). Washington, DC: National Center for Education Statistics, Institute of Education Sciences, U.S. Department of Education.

National Center for Public Policy and Higher Education. (2008). *Measuring up 2008: Technical guide for measuring up 2008.* San Jose, CA: Author.

National Center for Public Policy and Higher Education. (2013). *Income of U.S. workforce projected to decline.* San Jose, CA: Author.

NCHEMS (National Center for Higher Education Management Systems). (2013). *Student pipeline -transition and completion rates from 9th grade to college.* Retrieved from http://www.higheredinfo.org/dbrowser/index.php?measure=72

Oliff, P., Palacios, V., Johnson, I., & Leachman, M. (2013). *Recent deep state higher education cuts may harm students and the economy for years to come.* Washington, DC: Center on Budget and Policy Policies.

Ravitch, D. (2010). *The death and life of the great American school system: How testing and choice are undermining education.* New York: Basic Books.

Roderick, M., Nagaoka, J., & Coca, V. (2009). College readiness for all: The challenge for urban high schools. *The Future of Children, 19*(1), 185–210.

Rosenbaum, J. E., Stephan, J. L., & Rosenbaum, J. E. (2010). Beyond one-size-fits-all college dreams: Alternative pathways to desirable careers. *American Educator, 34*(3), 1–12.

Strong American Schools (2008). *Bridge to nowhere.* Washington, DC: Author.

Symonds, W. C., Schwartz, R. B., & Ferguson, R. (2011). *Pathways to prosperity: Meeting the challenge of preparing young Americans for the 21st century.* Boston: Pathways to Prosperity Project and Harvard Graduate School of Education.

Tyack, D. B. (1976). Ways of seeing: An essay on the history of compulsory schooling. *Harvard Educational Review, 46*(3), 355–389.

Tyler, R. W. (1974). The federal role in education. *Public Interest, 34,* 164–187.

University of California Office of the President. (2013). *California Master Plan for higher education: Major features.* Oakland, CA.

Vinovskis, M. A. (1992). Schooling and poor children in 19th century America. *American Behavioral Scientist, 35*(3), 313–331.

Wiley, A., Wyatt, J., & Camara, W. J. (2010). *The development of a multidimensional college readiness index* (Research Report No. 2010-3). New

York: The College Board. Retrieved from http://professionals.collegeboard.com/profdownload/pdf/10b_2084_DevMultiDimenRR_WEB_100618.pdf

Zhao, Y. (2009). *Catching up or leading the way: American education in the age of globalization.* Alexandria, VA: ASCD.

Part II

—◄○►—

USING THEORY, POLICY, AND PRACTICE TO ANALYZE A STATE RESPONSE

4

———◄○►———

College Readiness
and Low-Income Youth

The Role of Social Capital in Acquiring College Knowledge

DANIEL J. ALMEIDA

Our assumption here is that the United States needs more college-ed-ucated citizens to compete in the global knowledge-based economy (Howell, Kurlaender, & Grodsky, 2010; Tierney & Garcia, 2010). A high school education is no longer sufficient training for a majority of occupations in the 21st century (Baker, Clay, & Gratama, 2005; Dohm & Shniper, 2007). Approximately 60% of all U.S. jobs require some higher education, an increase from 30% just 40 years ago (Hyslop & Tucker, 2012). California's economic situation is even more precarious than the nation's; the Public Policy Institute of California projected that "the gap between the demands of California's economy and supply of college-educated workers poses a serious threat to the state's economic future" (Johnson, 2009, p. 3).

Motivated by these trends, President Barack Obama (2009) set a goal for all U.S. citizens to complete at least one year of postsecondary education and challenged Americans to once again lead the world in college attainment by 2020. Despite the growing emphasis on postsecondary education, college completion rates have been fairly stable over the last several decades (Adelman, 2006; Howell et al., 2010; Turner, 2005). The

89

graduation rates of first-generation students—those who are first in their family to attend college—are even lower than those of students whose parents have a college education; only 27.4% of first-generation college students graduate within four years, compared to 42.1% of students with college-educated parents (DeAngelo &, Franke, 2011). While graduation rates among all income groups have increased in recent decades, the rate of increase between the 1960s and 1980s was 18% for high-income students relative to only 4% for students from low-income families (Bailey & Dynarski, 2011). The president's goal of college for all is unrealistic unless high schools prepare students to succeed once they matriculate.

As we suggested in part I, college readiness is the preparation required to enroll in a postsecondary institution without need for remediation and to persist to graduation. Most readiness indicators focus on cognitive ability and academic preparedness using standardized assessments or high school record (Porter & Polikoff, 2012). Although academic preparation is crucial to postsecondary success (Adelman, 2006), research has shown that up to 90% of college dropouts were in good academic standing (i.e., earning a C average or better; Johnson, 2012). Whether the vast majority of college students persist to degree attainment may therefore depend on nonacademic factors, or what Duncheon referred to as campus integration factors (see chapter 1). One crucial area within this category is college knowledge—that is, an understanding of the procedural and cultural aspects of higher education (Conley, 2008). College knowledge includes understanding: (a) the application process, (b) the options available for higher education, (b) how to access financial aid, (c) academic requirements, and (d) the difference in culture between secondary and postsecondary education (Bell, Rowan-Kenyon, & Perna, 2006; Conley, 2008; Hooker & Brand, 2010; Roderick, Nagaoka, & Coca, 2009).

The first part of this volume considered the conceptual and historical underpinnings of the college readiness agenda and the challenges facing underserved students. Part II contains studies of the current college readiness context in California; this chapter and Lisa Garcia's subsequent chapter focus on postsecondary preparation in high schools. Chapters 6 and 7, by Julia Duncheon and Bryan Rodríguez, respectively, explore college readiness policies at the postsecondary level. While Garcia investigates an academic intervention for high school students, I focus on a non-cognitive area of college readiness. Specifically, I examine how high school seniors from low-income communities in Los Angeles who will be the first in their families to attend college develop college knowledge. Drawing on a social capital framework, I answer the following research question: How do low-income, first-generation students acquire college knowledge? I focus on low-income students whose parents did not attend college because this population faces unique challenges in accessing postsecondary education (Perna, 2000; Plank & Jordan, 2011; Roderick et al., 2009). Compared to students from middle- and upper-income backgrounds, low-income students are less likely to have not only the economic capital necessary to pay for college, but also access to college-relevant social capital that aids students in preparing for and enrolling in college (Farmer-Hinton, 2008; McDonough & Calderone, 2006; Tierney & Venegas, 2006). Understanding how low-income, first-generation youth acquire college knowledge may help policymakers and practitioners better prepare these students for postsecondary transition.

In what follows, I begin by reviewing literature concerning the college knowledge component of college readiness, specifically as it relates to first-generation, low-income youth. I then outline the theory of social capital, its relation to other forms of capital, and its application to acquiring college knowledge. Next, I explicate the research design and limitations of the study. The subsequent section presents the study's findings, followed by a discussion operationalizing key constructs of social capital to analyze the results. I conclude with implications and directions for future research.

College Knowledge: A Critical Component of College Readiness

Access to college knowledge is not distributed evenly throughout society, and misinformation about college is prevalent among many high school students and their parents (Conley, 2008). Students who are first in their families to attend college and those from urban or low-income communities are less likely than their more privileged peers to receive information about college (Bell et al., 2009) and obtain the social capital needed to understand the world of postsecondary education (Hooker & Brand, 2010). A college-going culture, or a school environment "in which all students have the expectation that they will go to college and [that] helps them to develop the know-how to go," (McAlister & Mevs, 2012, p. 12) is crucial for students to acquire college knowledge. However, first-generation, low-income students are often concentrated in low-performing schools that are less likely than their higher-performing counterparts to feature a strong college-going culture (Roderick et al., 2009).

The vast majority of students graduating from high school (92%) expect to pursue a postsecondary degree (Adelman, 2006). Yet many first-generation, low-income youth who are academically qualified and have high aspirations have minimal access to information about the college application process and thus have more difficulty gaining admittance to a postsecondary institution (Roderick et al., 2009). One study, for example, found that only half of seniors who plan on attending college from urban high schools—compared to 91% of those attending suburban schools—obtain a college application from the university they wish to attend; only 18% of urban students—compared to 41% from suburban schools—apply to college by the fall of their senior year of high school (Avery & Kane, 2004).

Another element of college knowledge pertains to an understanding of postsecondary options (Hooker & Brand, 2010). Many high-performing first-generation students are not familiar with the higher education opportunities available to them, and consequently attend two-year colleges or vocational schools close to home or delay enrollment entirely (Roderick et al., 2009). Parents who have not attended college are less able to help their children compare the substantive differences among universities that may seem similar to an inexperienced observer (Fann, Jarsky, & McDonough, 2009). Quality knowledge about options is crucial for students to select an institution that best fits their interests and needs—a choice that contributes significantly to students' likelihood of persistence (Hooker & Brand, 2010). Cultivating early awareness of higher education in the 9th- and 10th-grade years or in middle school provides more time for students to learn about and prepare for various postsecondary possibilities (Knight, 2003).

Misinformation concerning the costs of college attendance and financial aid availability is another barrier to higher education for many students, especially those in low-income, urban school districts (Boden, 2011). Financial aid literacy is associated with socioeconomic status and high school resources (De La Rosa, 2006; Perna, 2008). High achieving students, many of whom are from more advantaged backgrounds, tend to receive the most financial aid information from their schools (Perna, 2008). The students who can benefit most from financial aid are often least likely to have parents who have gone to college and thus rely heavily on the overworked school counselors for guidance (McDonough & Calderone, 2006). As many as 20% of eligible low-income students do not file a Free Application for Federal Student Aid (FAFSA; King, 2004). One way to boost college-going is to support students in developing college knowledge through relationships with adults and peers. I now discuss the roles other individuals (i.e., counselors, mentors, peers) play in students' acquisition of college knowledge.

The People Who Can Support College Knowledge Acquisition

The support and expectations of influential people in students' lives play an important role in postsecondary decision-making (McClafferty & Mc-Donough, 2000). Three interrelated circles influence students' development of college knowledge: (a) familial networks (i.e., siblings, parents, etc.), (b) in-class actors (i.e., teachers), and (c) out-of-class agents (i.e., counselors, mentors, and peers). Given that family members of low-income students are not likely to possess significant college knowledge and teachers are most concerned with imparting academic content, I focus here on individuals in the third category.

High school counselors can have positive influences on students' college preparation, aspirations, goal-setting, and motivation (McDonough & Calderone, 2006). The perceived expectations of school counselors regarding students' college prospects, however, can affect the likelihood that students ask for assistance (Holcomb-McCoy, 2010). Studies have shown that counselors' biases may impact the quality and quantity of information provided to specific groups of students (Hart & Gray, 1992; Terenzini, Cabrera, & Bernal, 2001). Students who are identified early as college-bound tend to be those who are prepared for and enroll in college, while students who are not expected to pursue higher education may not receive the support needed to become college-ready (McDonough & Calderone, 2006). Many counselors are also understaffed and may prioritize non-college-going issues (e.g., discipline), especially in low-performing schools. Most low-income students attend large public high schools where one college counselor is expected to advise anywhere from 1,000 to 5,000 students (De La Rosa, 2006) using a counseling model—one-on-one appointments with students who actively seek assistance—originally designed for middle- and upper-income schools (Stephan, 2013).

College-bound students whose needs are not fully met by their high school's staff can benefit from postsecondary access and mentoring programs (De La Rosa, 2006). Mentors provide students with knowledge of higher education, including how the system works and how to access financial aid opportunities. Research has shown that the positive impact of mentors on college preparation and planning is particularly substantial for students in urban schools (Ahn, 2010; Farmer-Hinton, 2008; Stanton-Salazar, 1997).

In addition to knowledgeable adults such as counselors and mentors, students may receive social and informational postsecondary support from other college-bound peers (Tierney & Venegas, 2006). Schools with trained peer counselors can leverage students' peer networks to provide guidance on applying to college and securing financial aid. Moreover, students who participate in crossed-aged activities such as clubs and sports have opportunities to receive advice from older peers with more knowledge about college preparation (Knight, 2003). Establishing relationships with people outside of class who possess college knowledge—counselors, mentors, and peers—can translate to social capital that may aid low-income students in seeking higher education. I now turn to a discussion of social capital theory, its relation to other forms of capital, and its relevance to the acquisition of college knowledge.

Understanding Social Capital

The theory of social capital (Bourdieu, 1973, 1986; Coleman, 1988) is a useful analytic tool to study low-income, first-generation students' development of college readiness in general and college knowledge in particular (Auerbach, 2004; Noguera, 1999; Perna, 2000; Plank & Jordan, 2001; Tierney & Venegas, 2006). Unlike other forms of capital (i.e., economic, human, cultural), social capital does not reside within an individual but in the network of one's relationships (Coleman, 1988). These relationships can be useful due to the potential resources available through these connections. Social capital relevant to college-going is unequally distributed throughout society (Auerbach, 2004), which helps to explain disparities in college readiness between low-income students and their middle- or upper-income counterparts (Stephan, 2013). Although many have argued that those who are seen as the "fathers" of social capital—Pierre Bourdieu and James Coleman—have different interpretations of the concept (Adler & Kwon, 2002; Dika & Singh, 2002; Stanton-Salazar, 1997), I call upon both theorists to help understand how social capital informs our understanding of college knowledge.

French sociologist Pierre Bourdieu (1973, 1986) asserted that not everyone in a society can employ social capital equally. Bourdieu stressed that intelligence and merit need to combine with other forms of capital (i.e., economic, cultural, social) to be of any tangible benefit. Cultural capital refers to noneconomic advantages (e.g., attitudes, behaviors, credentials, education, and possessions) that can promote social mobility (Bourdieu, 1986; Lamont & Lareau, 1988). Bourdieu posited that the transmission of cultural capital from generation to generation maintains the class hierarchy in society. The assumption is that individuals unintentionally pass on cultural capital, and social structures such as the educational system perpetuate that transfer. The forces of the social structure determine what constitutes dominant cultural capital, possessed primarily by middle- and upper-income individuals, and non-dominant cultural capital, found in low-income communities (Carter, 2003). Because cultural capital can be converted into economic capital (i.e., money and assets), those from non-dominant communities are likely to remain in the same social class regardless of their efforts to change their position in society (Bourdieu, 1986). The social structure prevents those in lower classes from accessing the requisite economic and cultural capital, and constantly shifts the requirements to keep the dominant class in power. To Bourdieu, social capital is a form of oppression, as it perpetuates class divisions.

American sociologist James Coleman (1988) shared Bourdieu's conception that social capital comes from the networks and groups of which one is a member. Yet while Bourdieu emphasized the role of institutionalized relationships and structures, Coleman focused on explaining differences in individual social mobility (Musoba & Baez, 2009). Coleman (1988) stated that "social capital is defined by its function" (p. 302), which is to facilitate activity among individuals within a social structure (i.e., family or community). A focus of Coleman's social capital is the maintenance of strong families and communities where members assist one another.

Coleman's (1988) theory asserts that the purpose of social capital is to create human capital—the skills, knowledge, and abilities embodied in a person. Social capital is used as a proxy for the conditions of the social structure, and human capital is a proxy for agency, the ability to affect one's own outcomes (Musoba & Baez, 2009). Coleman (1988) argued that parents may gain social capital to transfer to their children by participating in the community network. For example, by fostering quality educational opportunities, parents are able to transform social capital into human capital for their children. Children can also develop social capital by interacting with their community.

Coleman (1988) outlined six forms of social capital: (a) obligations and expectations, (b) norms and effective sanctions, (c) authority relations,

(d) information potential, (e) intentional organizations, and (f) appropriable social organizations. Although these forms are interrelated, information potential and appropriable social organizations are especially pertinent to amassing college knowledge. I shall elaborate below on the reasons for their importance, but first I briefly discuss the other forms Coleman identified insofar as they are interconnected.

Coleman's Forms of Social Capital

In a well-functioning community, members who possess particular resources help other members when those resources are needed, and exchange obligations and expectations (Coleman, 1988). For example, community member A assists member B. Member B now has an obligation to reciprocate at a later date, and member A has an expectation that his needs will be met when he requires resources belonging to member B. In order for this process to take place, a certain level of trust must exist between the actors involved in the transaction, instilling confidence that obligations will be repaid. A community's norms, or standards and customs, can promote desirable behavior or inhibit objectionable actions through the threat of effective sanctions. For example, consider a community that rewards high academic achievement and shames those who drop out of school. These norms and sanctions may help to promote educational attainment among youth within this community. Some individuals engage in groups with the intention of deriving a return on their investment. These intentional organizations can be business-oriented for the purpose of earning income or voluntary associations to generate a public good. Lastly, authority relations come into play when community members collectively choose to transfer the rights of control over certain actions to a leader who acts on behalf of the community; this leader then "has access to an extensive network of capital that amplifies the social capital of individual members" (Dynes, 2006, p. 2).

Information potential. Information potential (Coleman, 1988) is particularly pertinent to college-going given that accessing higher education requires specific knowledge (e.g., the application process, academic requirements, financial aid, etc.). Information is valuable to enable appropriate action. The relationships one has within one's network can provide access to information that may not be available otherwise. The quality of social capital, determined by the quantity and characteristics of individuals in one's network, distinguishes people of different socioeconomic groups and in turn has implications for students' access to college knowledge.

Parents with bachelor's degrees and their children are likely to be associated with other college-educated and potentially influential people. By interacting with educated people in their networks, these students can access information potential such as college-going advice, contacts, and strategies. Parents and children from low-income communities, in contrast, typically have fewer educated individuals in their networks. Their relationships with community members may be valuable for a variety of reasons, but may not provide resources germane to college-going. In other words, while low-income communities possess social capital in the form of information potential, the information is unlikely to pertain to college-going.

Appropriable social organizations. In contrast to intentional organizations that produce a specific intended benefit for their members or the public, some groups provide unintended advantages (Coleman, 1988). For example, a softball league is a social organization intended for purely recreational purposes, but members may gain unintended benefits such as networking for business or advice on problems they face. Middle- and upper-income students and parents often belong to appropriable social organizations with other college-educated members where college knowledge is likely to be shared. While low-income parents may be involved in appropriable social organizations that develop social capital, unlike their middle- to upper-income counterparts, the inadvertent benefits of membership are not likely to help their children acquire college knowledge. Many low-income, first-generation college students therefore rely on social capital derived from sources outside of their family's networks (e.g., teachers, counselors, mentors, and peers) to access information about higher education.

Research Design

Participants

I recruited a purposeful sample of 33 high school seniors to participate in the study. Access to the study participants was gained through a college access mentoring program of which all students were members. The

TABLE 4.1. Demographics and academic indicators of sample and school populations

	School A Population	School A Sample	School B Population	School B Sample	School C Population	School C Sample
# of students	1500	14	2500	10	1000	7
% African American	2%	0%	2%	20%	6%	15%
% Hispanic	88%	86%	62%	80%	58%	0%
% Asian	10%	14%	23%	0%	33%	85%
% White	>1%	0%	13%	0%	2%	0%
Average SAT	1170	1422	1454	1581	1325	1440
Average SAT Math	400	464	496	512	452	515
Average SAT Verbal	387	426	476	513	434	438
Average SAT Writing	383	423	482	520	439	463
Average GPA	n/a	3.66	n/a	3.67	n/a	3.66
Cohort Graduation Rate	66.9%	n/a	79.5%	n/a	89.9%	n/a
College-going Rate of Graduates	53.4%	n/a	65.3%	n/a	71.6%	n/a

Source: California Department of Education (2013)

criteria for inclusion were students who: (a) attended a high school in a low-income community and (b) would be first in their families to attend college in the 2013–14 academic year. Two students were excluded from the original sample because they had at least one college-educated parent. A total of 31 participants were included in the analysis. The sample was generated from three urban public high schools in the Los Angeles Unified School District, with student populations of approximately 1,000, 1,500, and 2,500 (California Department of Education, 2013).

Eighty-three percent of the students were 18 years old and 17% were 17 years of age. Fifty-eight percent of the participants in the study were female. Thirty-nine percent of the students had at least one parent who did not attend high school. Sixty-one percent had at least one parent with a high school diploma. Sixty-five percent of the students in the sample were Latina/o, 26% were Asian, and 3% were African American. Fifty-five percent of students spoke English in their homes, and 29% also spoke a second language at home. Nineteen percent of the students were born outside the United States, and 61% of the participants had parents who were foreign-born.

Participants had an average GPA of 3.67, and their average SAT scores surpassed the average scores of their high schools. Table 4.1 presents the racial composition, average GPAs, SAT scores, cohort graduation rates, and college enrollment rates of the entire student population and sample from each of the three school sites. All students had applied to at least three colleges, and many had already been accepted to at least one university at the time of the data collection.

Data Collection and Analysis

I visited each school during the mentoring program's monthly meetings to recruit participants. A raffle for a $50 Amazon gift card was offered as an incentive to participate. I returned to each school to conduct one-on-one face-to-face semi-structured interviews in the college centers of the three high schools. The average length of the interviews was approximately15 minutes. The interviews were audio recorded and transcribed. Participants also completed a biographical questionnaire at the end of their interview.

Data analysis drew on both inductive and deductive strategies to code the interview transcripts. I used the practice of open coding to allow themes to inductively emerge based on the data (Glaser & Strauss, 1967). I also developed codes a priori informed by the social capital framework used in the study (Blumer, 1954). Using Facebook messaging, I posed follow-up questions and conducted member checking with participants regarding my data interpretations to increase the trustworthiness of my conclusions (Creswell, 2007).

Limitations

All participants had voluntarily participated in a mentoring program run by a large private university. Students applied in the spring of their junior year and were accepted based on minimum GPA requirements and self-reported plans to attend college. The findings of the study are thus reflective of the experiences of a particular group of students that may be characteristically different from students who have not sought external college-going resources. The data concerning GPAs, SAT scores, and parent information (i.e., place of birth, highest level of education, occupation) were self-reported, and may affect the trustworthiness of some of the study's findings. Not all students reported on each item in the biographical questionnaire, and approximately 60% of participants who were contacted did not respond to the follow-up questions and member checking on Facebook.

Findings

I present the findings of the study below in three sections. Findings are organized based on the out-of-class agents who were instrumental to participants' development of college knowledge: college counselors, mentors, and peers.

College Counselors and College Knowledge

Nearly 70% of participants remarked that their college counselor was the person from whom they received most of their information regarding higher education. Some students developed stronger relationships with their counselors than others. According to one participant, "[M]y connection to my college counselor was extremely helpful and I noticed that my friends who also had a strong connection to her were also having an easier time applying to college and getting their question solved." Another student emphasized the importance of her relationship with the counselor, acknowledging that not all her peers shared her experience: "[I]t is the connection that I have with her that keeps me informed . . . those who don't go to [the college counselor] often would be missing important information." One participant recognized that her connection to the college counselor made it possible for the counselor "to write a very personalized recommendation letter to send to my colleges, which I'm sure had a large impact on my acceptances." When the students felt familiarity and a degree of comfort with their counselor, they could actively seek and receive college knowledge. Said one participant, "[S]ince [the college counselor] knew who I was, she was always very easy to come to for advice on college decisions and to go to when I had questions about applying to colleges and about financial aid."

Many students who were aware of important college-going information had established positive relationships with their college counselors early in high school. Said one participant:

It was back in ninth grade when I first met my college counselor. . . . It turned out that I had made an impression on her because the next year she even offered me the chance to apply for a scholarship, which [is] only allowed [for] one kid from each school to apply to. Later on, during my junior year, [the college counselor] also awarded me with a Book Award from [a Women's College], and then during my senior year she would award me with another scholarship.

This student recognized the importance of getting to know her college counselor early, expressing that "all of these opportunities were available to me only because I had begun building a personal relationship with my college counselor since my first year of high school."

Volunteering in the college center as a "service worker" enabled some students to obtain information easier and faster. As one participant reflected, "working with [the college counselor] definitely gave me the advantage of asking the questions I have and getting them answered right away." Other students took note of the benefits their peers enjoyed for being service workers. "The college counselor does have many students that help her out and are always with her, even during class time," said one participant.

"I think that she probably does give them personalized attention." Another student mentioned a specific advantage that service workers received—information about scholarships:

> Since [the service workers] are always willing to help her, I have noticed that [the college counselor] constantly lets them know of scholarships that she thinks they are perfect for. Since she gets to know them better she is able to help them more because she knows where their interests lie and what kind of scholarships are related to those interests.

Not all students, however, forged the same kind of connection with their college counselor. Some failed to mention the college counselor when asked from whom they received information about college, and other students expressed a degree of frustration with their college counselor. Said one student, "[S]he's always in a rush and trying to dismiss us ASAP. When this happens to me and I can't go to her for advice or help, I take matters into my own hands and try to find assistance elsewhere." Another participant expressed her dissatisfaction with her counselor, stating that "despite me trying to get something as simple as a transcript, she never stopped to help me. It was always, 'come back later.'" This same student went on to explain that when "students that always spent time with her came in . . . and asked for something more time-consuming than what I needed help with, she would help them regardless."

Even students who were close with their counselors recognized that other students had varied college preparatory experiences. One participant said that "those who described the college center and [the college counselor] as being intimidating, which meant they rarely spoke to her, seemed to have a rougher time when applying and it seemed that they had less college-prep opportunities." A student at a different school advocated for her less academically successful peers, who needed more assistance accessing higher education:

> [The college counselor] has called students [that] have a 3.0 GPA many more times throughout the year than students that have less of a GPA. I think she should also give them some attention. A majority of my friends have less than a 3.0 GPA and they do complain that they have had many problems with the college process because they don't have enough help.

Despite some of their frustrations, students acknowledged the hard work of their counselors. After sharing her unhappiness with her experience with the counselor, one student softened her critique: "[I'm] not discrediting my college counselor though. I believe she is hard working and tries to help everyone, but she does have her preferences." Another acknowledged the reality that "the school has only one college counselor and she is expected to look over 646 seniors and 500 or more juniors. It is really hard for her to meet these requirements, but she still does her best." One student reflected on the need to be proactive to obtain college knowledge: "since there are so many seniors, it is the student's job to keep in contact with the college center. It is the students who remain active at the college center that receive most information."

Mentors and College Knowledge

Mentoring programs—like the one the participants joined—can assist low-income students during the college application process when college counselors are unavailable. "[T]he college counselor was always busy. So I decided that because I had no idea what the college process was like, I had to get help outside of school, so I applied for [the mentoring program]," remarked a senior. Approximately 25% of the participants reported receiving the most college knowledge from their mentor. As one student recalled, "[My mentor] helped me go through the colleges, pick the name, location, what I want to major in, what kind of community it was at . . . she's the one who gave me the most information."

Participants who specifically mentioned their mentors spoke highly of the guidance they received. "My mentor has helped me so much along the college application process and has been there for me and I think that [the mentor] did help me tremendously," said one student. Another explained that she would "contact [her mentor] and ask how do you do this, how do you do that, and ask her what the best websites for scholarships, and she'll reply and help me." One student's remarks further underscore the important contribution mentors can have: "I rely on her a lot . . . more than I should. I don't know if I would have gotten through the process myself because I relied on her a lot, and I still do." In addition to the college-educated adults with whom they associated outside of class such as counselors and mentors, students relied on each other for information about college, which I address below.

Peers and College Knowledge

All students reported that their friends were also applying to college; only two respondents mentioned having any friends who were not college-bound. One student shared: "I hang out with friends that are very college-bound so we are always aware of what to do and we ask each other stuff related to college and because of that, it inspires us to take vigorous classes such as AP classes and study for the SAT and ACT."

Participants who worked in the college center as service workers were able to transmit much of their knowledge to other students. According to one service worker, "As I help [my counselor] prepare different events or information sessions, I learn about applying to college first hand so that I can pass on what I know to my peers."

Participants who befriended older students during their earlier years in high school found these friendships particularly useful for accessing college knowledge. For example, one student explained that "despite having above a 3.5 GPA, I still didn't know I could go to a UC or a Cal State. I always assumed I would go straight to work or to a community college." She went on to describe the influence of her older friends on her ideas about college:

> When I received advice on what path to take regarding college from my friends, my thoughts changed. My friends were seniors and I was a junior. They introduced me to the colleges [that] were available for me. It is because of them that I learned there was more than just community college out there.

The vast majority (more than 80%) of participants were members of sports teams or other student organizations, which provided opportunities to learn from older peers with more knowledge about college preparation. For example, one student-athlete stated:

> I've been a part of sports since my sophomore year. I ran three consecutive seasons on the cross country team, two years in Track & Field, and one year in boys' volleyball. Throughout those years I had known that my teammates were applying to colleges and going to be attending them once they graduated. . . . I will say that as I build strong relationships with my fellow runners, I was interested in going to meetings when people from admissions would

come. The sports, organizations, and my peers helped me to stay on track in a sense.

Other participants reflected on early high school experiences in student organizations where they were able to learn from older students. One recalled, "I remember the seniors while I was in junior year talk about writing personal statements and how long it took to write them and edit them." Another student reported learning the importance of having "other peers read and also revise [your personal statement]" through his participation in a cross-aged club. Some participants continued to learn from older friends who had graduated from their high school and entered college. For example, one student described his involvement with the Academic Decathlon team alumni: "I learned more about college from the previous Decathletes who during their break would come and . . . share their views and knowledge about college life and the process in applying for college." Crossed-aged classes also provided opportunities for sharing college knowledge among peers. As one student explained, "in AP Calculus class in my junior year I had students that were seniors in my period. The seniors during class would talk about applying to college. They would talk about rank, SAT scores. . . ." Whether in or out of class, student interactions led to the sharing of college knowledge.

Discussion

The findings of this study suggest that students attained college knowledge from their peers and the few college-educated adults (i.e., counselors and mentors) with whom they associated outside of the classroom. Specifically, the participants developed college-relevant social capital in the form of information potential and appropriable social organizations, which I now discuss in more detail.

Social Capital via Information Potential

The strong relationships that many participants developed with out-of-class agents represent social capital in the form of information potential. The informational resources—college knowledge—possessed by college counselors and mentors are extremely valuable to college-bound first-generation students. Information about scholarships and other forms of financial aid is most important, especially for low-income students for whom the cost of higher education is a major barrier (Boden, 2011).

The true value of information, as Coleman (1988) has argued, is that it is often a necessary requirement for action. For example, recall the student who received information to apply for a scholarship during 10th grade after she made a good impression on her college counselor. The information itself did not get this student money needed to pay for college; rather, her action of applying for the scholarship made the difference. This opportunity to apply would not have been present, however, without the information derived from the social capital that resided in the student's relationship with the college counselor.

The students who worked in the college center and spent significant time with the college counselors were able to easily acquire information about college-going. Recall one participant's observation that the college counselor informed the service workers who "are always willing to help her" about "scholarships [the counselor] thinks they are perfect for." This anecdote is an example of the exchange of obligations and expectations, another form of social capital, which ultimately facilitated students' acquisition of vital information about scholarships. The trust many students built with counselors provided them a level of attention necessary for obtaining assistance with their applications. Those students who had not developed social capital with their college counselor were not as fortunate, and were burdened with seeking support elsewhere or not receiving assistance at all.

The findings suggest that participants recognized their counselors were overworked and unable to offer sufficient individual support for all students. Even if more students at these schools were savvy enough to seek out the college counselor during their freshman year to develop social capital, the current counselor-to-student ratios would not allow for these opportunities. The traditional model of counseling—one-on-one appointments with students who seek assistance—may not be the most effective to serve a population of mostly first-generation, low-income students (Stephan, 2013). By providing inadequate counseling services, schools only allow for relatively few students (i.e., service workers and their friends) to access college knowledge, thus contributing to the reproduction of social inequality (Bourdieu, 1973). Innovative models are needed to create the conditions under which more students may build social capital in the form of information potential with college counselors (Stephan, 2013).

Participants also seemed to be aware that counselors held different expectations for individual students' college prospects, which impacted the distribution of college knowledge (Holcomb-McCoy, 2010). Recall the student who commented about her friends with GPAs below a 3.0 who "complain that they have had many problems with the college process because they don't have enough help." Another example is the student who was deterred from seeking assistance from the college counselor and "had to take matters into [her] own hands and try to find assistance elsewhere." This finding supports extant research that underscores the role of counselors' expectations and suggests the need to hold all students to high standards (Hart & Gray, 1992; Holcomb-McCoy, 2010; Terenzini et al., 2001). Given insufficient staffing of college counselors, college access and mentoring programs like the one in which the participants took part can provide students with information potential. However, these types of programs have limited capacity and cannot support college planning for all low-income students.

Social Capital via Appropriable Social Organizations

That most participants surrounded themselves with people who were supportive of their college goals is an important aspect of establishing a college-going culture. The peer relationships that participants developed represent significant social capital for first-generation students applying to college. The participants and their college-bound friends supported one another, reminding each other of deadlines and motivating each other to fulfill their goals. While these students joined their friend groups for a variety of reasons, one unintended benefit of their friendship was the exchange of college knowledge. These friend groups can be considered appropriable social organizations (Coleman, 1988).

Other, more formal groups, like sports teams and student clubs, are also appropriable social organizations. With membership in these groups came the unplanned advantage of college-relevant social capital. Such organizations, comprised of students from all grades, provided enhanced potential for acquiring college knowledge than a small group of friends. For three of the four years that a student belongs to an appropriable social organization in high school, he or she has access to older students who may be applying to college. The student who was a member of the track and field, cross country, and volleyball teams, for example, had opportunities to develop social capital and time to absorb college knowledge from his older peers. By fostering extracurricular involvement and crossed-aged interactions, schools can maximize the potential for students to generate college-relevant social capital with one another.

Conclusion

Issues concerning college readiness are increasing in import due to demand for more college-educated workers in today's economy (Howell et al., 2010; Hyslop & Tucker, 2012; Tierney & Garcia, 2010). First-generation, low-income students are at a disadvantage with regard to being ready for college compared to students from middle- or upper-income families with college-educated parents. Most low-income students' parents not only lack disposable income (i.e., economic capital) to pay for college expenses, but also cannot provide the specific types of cultural and social capital that facilitate college-going. Despite these social and economic barriers, however, the participants in this study developed some college knowledge through various forms of school-based social capital. Specifically, those students who established strong relationships with their college counselor and mentor benefited from information potential relevant to higher education. Friend groups and student organizations in which college knowledge was an unintended advantage (appropriable social organizations) also fostered participants' development of social capital.

I have argued that schools have the ability to produce social capital that is positive—providing cultural capital relevant to higher education and creating a college-going culture. It could also be negative—reproducing the social structure by limiting opportunities for underserved students (Noguera, 1999). The work of Bourdieu and Coleman is useful in analyzing how students form and maintain networks that lead to better comprehension of what I have called "college knowledge." I have suggested that without such networks, becoming college-ready is difficult for those students who, because of societal inequalities, are frequently the least ready for higher education.

Future research should explore ways of cultivating school-based social capital that will facilitate students' acquisition of college knowledge. The findings of this study suggest that intentionally connecting younger students with older peers who have more familiarity with preparing for postsecondary education is a strategy that schools can take to maximize students' acquisition of college knowledge. Creating more occasions for low-income students to establish relationships with college-educated individuals, including counselors and volunteer mentors, may support students' secondary-postsecondary transitions. Strategies to enhance college knowledge through the development of school-based social capital are unlikely to replace the many advantages associated with having college-educated parents or adequate access to college counselors. They can, however, help to level the playing field for low-income, first-generation students as they prepare to enter higher education.

References

Adelman, C. (2006). *The toolbox revisted: Paths to degree completion from high school through college.* Washington, DC: U.S. Department of Education.

Adler, P. S., & Kwon, S. (2002). Social capital: Prospects for a new concept. *The Academy of Management Review, 27*(1), 17–40.

Ahn, J. (2010). The role of social network locations in the college access mentoring of urban youth. *Education and Urban Society, 42*(7), 839–859.

Auerbach, S. (2004). Engaging Latino parents in supporting college pathways: Lessons from a college access program. *Journal of Hispanic Higher Education, 3*(2), 125–145.

Avery, C., & Kane, T. J. (2004). Student perceptions of college opportunities. The Boston COACH program. In *College choices: The economics of where to go, when to go, and how to pay for it* (pp. 355–394). Chicago: University of Chicago Press.

Bailey, M. J., & Dynarski, S. M. (2011). *Gains and gaps: Changing inequality in US college entry and completion* (No. w17633). National Bureau of Economic Research. Retrieved from http://users.nber.org/~dynarski/Bailey_Dynarski.pdf

Baker, D. B., Clay, J. N., & Gratama, C. A. (2005). *The essence of college readiness: Implications for students, parents, schools, and researchers.* Bothell, WA: The BERC Group.

Bell, A. D., Rowan-Kenyon, H. T., & Perna, L. W. (2009). College knowledge of 9th and 11th grade students: Variation by school and state context. *Journal of Higher Education, 80*(6), 663–685.

Blumer, H. (1954). What is wrong with social theory? *American Sociological Review*, *19*(1), 3–10.

Boden, K. (2011). Perceived academic preparedness of first-generation Latino college students. *Journal of Hispanic Higher Education*, *10*(2), 96–106.

Bourdieu, P. (1973). Cultural reproduction and social reproduction. In R. Brown (Ed.), *Knowledge, education, and cultural change: Papers in the sociology of education* (pp. 71–112). London: Tavistock Publications Limited.

Bourdieu, P. (1986). The forms of capital. In J. G. Richardson (Ed.), *Handbook of theory and research for the sociology of education* (pp. 241–258). New York: Greenwood Press.

California Department of Education. (2013). *DataQuest (CA Dept of Education)*. Retrieved July 15, 2013, from http://dq.cde.ca.gov/dataquest/

Carter, P. L. (2003). "Black" cultural capital, status positioning, and schooling conflicts for low-income African American youth. *Social Problems*, *50*(1), 136–155.

Coleman, J. S. (1988). Social capital in the creation of human capital. *The American Journal of Sociology*, *94*, S95–S120.

Conley, D. T. (2008). Rethinking college readiness. *New Directions for Higher Education*, *2008*(144), 3–13.

Creswell, J. W. (2007). *Qualitative inquiry and research design: Choosing among five approaches*. Thousand Oaks, CA: SAGE Publications.

DeAngelo, L., & Franke, R. (2011). Completing college: Assessing graduation rates at four-year institutions. Higher Education Research Institute. Retrieved from http://heri.ucla.edu/DARCU/CompletingCollege2011.pdf

De La Rosa, M. L. (2006). Is opportunity knocking?: Low-income students' perceptions of college and financial aid. *American Behavioral Scientist*, *49*(12), 1670–1686.

Dika, S. L., & Singh, K. (2002). Applications of social capital in educational literature: A critical synthesis. *Review of Educational Research*, *72*(1), 31–60.

Dohm, A., & Shniper, L. (2007, November). *Occupational employment projections to 2016. Bureau of Labor Statistics*. Retrieved February 23, 2013, from http://www.bls.gov/opub/mlr/2007/11/art5full.pdf

Dynes, R. R. (2006). Social Capital: Dealing With Community Emergencies. *Homeland Security Affairs*, *2*(2).

Fann, A., Jarsky, K. M., & McDonough, P. M. (2009). Parent involvement in the college planning process: A case study of P-20 collaboration. *Journal of Hispanic Higher Education, 8*(4), 374–393.

Farmer-Hinton, R. L. (2008). Social capital and college planning: Students of color using school networks for support and guidance. *Education & Urban Society, 41*, 127–157.

Glaser, B. G. & Strauss, A. L. (1967). *The discovery of grounded theory: Strategies for qualitative research.* Chicago: Aldine Publishing Company.

Hart, P., & Gray, M. J. (1992). *From gatekeeper to advocate: Transforming the role of the school counselor.* New York: College Entrance Examination Board.

Holcomb-McCoy, C. (2010). Involving low-income parents and parents of color in college readiness activities: An exploratory study. *Professional School Counseling, 14*, 115–124.

Hooker, S., & Brand, B. (2010). College knowledge: A critical component of college and career readiness. *New Directions for Youth Development, 2010*(127), 75–85.

Howell, J. S., Kurlaender, M., & Grodsky, E. (2010). Postsecondary preparation and remediation: Examining the effect of the early assessment program at California State University. *Journal of Policy Analysis and Management, 29*(4), 726–748.

Hyslop, A., & Tucker, B. (2012). *Ready by design: A college and career agenda for California.* Washington, DC: Education Sector. Retrieved from http://www.educationsector.org/sites/default/files/publications/ReadybyDesign-RELEASED.pdf

Johnson, H. (2009). *Educating California: Choices for the future.* San Francisco: Public Policy Institute of California. Retrieved from http://www.ppic.org/main/publication.asp?i=891

Johnson, N. (2012). *The institutional costs of student attrition.* Washington, DC: American Institutes for Research. Retrieved from http://www.deltacostproject.org/sites/default/files/products/Delta-Cost-Attrition-Research-Paper.pdf

King, J. E. (2004). *Missed opportunities: Students who do not apply for financial aid.* Washington, DC: American Council on Education.

Knight, M. (2003). Through urban youth's eyes: Negotiating K-16 policies, practices, and their futures. *Educational Policy, 17*(5), 531–557.

Lamont, M, & Lareau, A. (1988). Cultural capital: Allusions, gaps and glissandos in recent theoretical developments. *Sociological Theory, 6*, 153–168.

McAlister, S., & Mevs, P. (2012). *College readiness: A guide to the field.*

Providence, RI: Annenberg Institute for School Reform at Brown University. Retrieved from http://annenberginstitute.org/sites/default/files/CRIS_Guide.pdf

McClafferty, K., & McDonough, P. (2000, November). Creating a K-16 environment: Reflections on the process of establishing a college culture in secondary schools. Presented at the annual meeting of the Association for the Study of Higher Education, Sacramento, CA.

McDonough, P. M., & Calderone, S. (2006). The meaning of money perceptual differences between college counselors and low-income families about college costs and financial aid. *American Behavioral Scientist*, *49*(12), 1703–1718.

Musoba, G., & Baez, B. (2009). The cultural capital of cultural and social capital: an economy of translations. *Higher Education: Handbook of Theory and Research*, *24*, 151–182.

Noguera, P. (1999). Transforming urban schools through investments in social capital. *In Motion Magazine*. Retrieved from http://www.inmotionmagazine.com/pncap1.html

Obama, B. H. (2009, February 24). *Remarks of President Barack Obama—Address to Joint Session of Congress.* Retrieved from http://www.whitehouse.gov/the_press_office/Remarks-of-President-Barack-Obama-Address-to-Joint-Session-of-Congress/

Perna, L. W. (2000). Differences in the decision to attend college among African Americans, Hispanics, and Whites. *Journal of Higher Education*, *71*(2), 117–141.

Perna, L. W. (2006). Understanding the relationship between information about college prices and financial aid and students' college-related behaviors. *American Behavioral Scientist*, *49*(12), 1620–1635.

Perna, L. W. (2008). Understanding high school students' willingness to borrow to pay college prices. *Research in Higher Education*, *49*(7), 589–606.

Plank, S. B., & Jordan, W. J. (2001). Effects of information, guidance, and actions on postsecondary destinations: A study of talent loss. *American Educational Research Journal*, *38*(4), 947–979.

Porter, A. C., & Polikoff, M. S. (2012). Measuring academic readiness for college. *Educational Policy*, *26*(3), 394–417.

Roderick, M., Nagaoka, J., & Coca, V. (2009). College readiness for all: The challenge for urban high schools. *The Future of Children*, *19*(1), 185–210.

Stanton-Salazar, R. D. (1997). A social capital framework for understanding the socialization of racial minority children and youths. *Harvard Educational Review, 67*(1), 1–39.

Stephan, J. (2013). Social capital and the college enrollment process: How can a school program make a difference? *Teachers College Record, 115*(4), 1–39.

Terenzini, P. T., Cabrera, A. F., & Bernal, E. M. (2001). Swimming against the tide: The poor in American higher education. (College Board Research Report No. 2001-1). Retrieved from http://research.collegeboard.org/sites/default/files/publications/2012/7/researchreport-2001-1-swimming-against-tide-the-poor-american-higher-education.pdf

Tierney, W. G., & Garcia, L. D. (2010). Remediation in higher education: The role of information. *American Behavioral Scientist, 55*(2), 102–120.

Tierney, W. G., & Venegas, K. M. (2006). Fictive kin and social capital: The role of peer groups in applying and paying for college. *American Behavioral Scientist, 49*(12), 1687–1702.

Turner, S. (2005). Going to college and finishing college: Explaining different educational outcomes. In Caroline Hoxby (Ed.), *College choices: The economics of where to go, when to go, and how to pay for it* (pp. 13-56). Chicago: University of Chicago Press.

5

---◀◉▶---

THE EARLY ASSESSMENT PROGRAM

Is Early Notification Enough?

LISA D. GARCIA

The authors featured in this volume conceptualize college readiness as the preparation required to enroll in credit-bearing college courses and persist to degree attainment. As Daniel Almeida suggested in chapter 4, one area of readiness that is often inaccessible to first-generation high school students pertains to college knowledge, which supports students' campus integration. Another challenge we have discussed in this text— and my concern in this chapter—relates to academic preparedness generally and cognitive academic factors specifically, or ensuring that secondary students demonstrate proficiency in main academic subjects.

Postsecondary remedial education, or non-credit-bearing coursework for incoming students who are underprepared in English and math, continues to be a central concern in academic and political circles. Being eligible for college admission but not being ready for college-level coursework— as measured by standardized test scores—is at a minimum counterintuitive (Vandal, 2010). This problem leads some policymakers to ask: Why do four-year institutions admit students who are not qualified to do the work? Why are secondary schools not producing college-ready students? Should all students be encouraged to attend college if many are not ready for continued studies? As other authors in this volume have pointed out,

President Obama pledged that the United States will once again have the highest proportion of college graduates in the world by 2020 (The White House, n.d.). As this nation commits to providing tertiary education for more individuals, many seem underprepared for college-level work; post-secondary developmental needs continue to hold steady amidst continued discussions about remediation's usefulness and efficiency (Aud et al., 2011; Calcagno & Long, 2008; Martorell & McFarlin, 2011; Parsad & Lewis, 2003; Scott-Clayton & Rodriguez, 2012).

Quantitative and qualitative evidence has documented both successes and failures of various remedial programs. Scholars have also examined the timing of these interventions. In particular, they have considered whether students should be evaluated for their college readiness while still matriculating in high school. This type of "early warning" remedial intervention provides students time to "catch up" on those skills required for college-level English and math coursework while still in high school (Venezia & Voloch, 2012). By the end of their senior year, students are ready for placement into the appropriate college-level courses. This intervention potentially reduces remedial enrollment as well as the temporal and monetary costs—to students and institutions—associated with being underprepared for college.

The disconnect between K-12 and postsecondary content is well documented in college preparation and access literature (Adelman, 1998, 2006; Complete College America, 2012; Kirst & Bracco, 2004). The premise that information is good—especially if it arrives in time for students to improve their skills while still in high school—is shared by many administrators and faculty charged with increasing college completion rates. However, some researchers have argued that information about one's preparedness for college coursework alone is not enough to overcome academic deficiencies and be successful in college (Conley, 2010; Tierney & Garcia, 2008, 2011). In other words, an early indicator of under-preparedness for college void of any systematic and meaningful academic preparation does not help students, especially those who are the least prepared, increase their readiness prior to college entrance. Early information by itself is thus insufficient to significantly reduce institutional remediation rates.

While Almeida's previous chapter investigated how urban high school students acquire college knowledge, a non-cognitive area of college readiness, I focus on students' academic preparation in general and cognitive academic performance in particular. Specifically, I examine the California State University (CSU) system's Early Assessment Program (EAP), one of the most prominent and expansive early warning interventions in the country (Lumina Foundation, 2007; McLean, 2012; National Conference of State Legislatures, n.d.). The EAP aims to diminish CSU's remediation rates by identifying students who are not college-ready in English and math while they are still in high school. In the context of this program, whether a student is considered college-ready depends on his or her state standardized test scores, which in turn inform his or her first-year course placement (i.e., remedial or college-level). Thus while college readiness broadly defined involves a range of cognitive and non-cognitive factors, for the purpose of this chapter I focus on readiness as measured by cognitive academic indicators.

I first provide an overview of the EAP including its history, development, and implementation, followed by an examination of the program's results, accomplishments, and criticisms. I suggest that this early warning intervention has fallen short of its goal to better prepare the state's high school students for the academic demands of postsecondary education. Despite added program interventions and overall declines in CSU remediation over the years, I point out that research demonstrating program effectiveness is lacking, and highlight areas in need of future research. I begin by discussing the history of remediation at the CSU.

The CSU and Remediation

Remedial education at the California State University (CSU) is not an anomaly among colleges and universities. Remediation has a long history in American higher education (Boylan, Bonham, & White, 1999). There have always been students who require an intervention—namely extra instruction and/or tutoring resources—in order to prepare for college-level coursework. Today's remedial courses focus on writing, reading, and mathematics and are offered at two-year and four-year institutions (Parsad & Lewis, 2003). Approximately 1.7 million (36%) first-year undergraduate students reported ever taking a remedial course in 2007–08 (Aud et al., 2011); at public institutions, the percentages were 42% at two-year, 39% at four-year non-doctorate (comprehensive), and 24% at four-year doctorate (research) institutions. Remediation in public higher education costs roughly $3 billion a year (Alliance for Excellent Education, 2011). This cost includes the thousands of students (roughly 30% of the total) who gain admission to a college, place into remedial courses, and are so frustrated about not being ready for college-level coursework that they forgo college enrollment altogether (Complete College America, 2012; Jenkins, Smith Jaggars, & Roksa, 2009).

Remedial students who enroll in college also struggle to finish their remedial coursework and eventually transition to college-level courses. At public two-year institutions, nearly four in ten remedial students never complete their remedial courses (Complete College America, 2012). Further, 30% of students who complete their remedial courses do not even attempt their lower-division college-level classes within two years (Jenkins et al., 2009). Remedial students who do persevere and continue their studies have less opportunity to actually finish a certificate or degree from two-year and four-year institutions. Fewer than one in ten graduate from community colleges within three years; about one-third actually complete a bachelor's degrees in six years (Complete College America, 2012). In short, students who are not ready for college-level coursework when they initially enroll in college are at a disadvantage in pursuing and completing their postsecondary goals.

The CSU, as a comprehensive university, is comparable with most of its peers in that at least a third of incoming students require a remedial intervention. In California, remediation is present in all sectors of public higher education. Remediation rates range from a low of 28% at the state's research university—the University of California (UC)—to 85% at the California Community Colleges (CCCs; California Legislative Analyst Office, 2011). CSU remedial students share the same struggles to complete their degrees, contributing to the CSU's stagnant 50% graduation rate within six years for first-time freshmen (CSU, November 2012).

The California State University is one of the nation's largest four-year university systems with 23 campuses and approximately 437,000 students (CSU, 2013); CSU has struggled with remedial education since the inception of the 1960 Master Plan for Higher Education (CDE, 1960; Crouch & McNenny, 2000). As Bryan Rodríguez discussed in chapter 3, the Master Plan ensures that every Californian can access public higher education. Each of the state's three public institutions of higher education—the UC, the CSU, and the CCC—accommodates different segments of the state's student population: the UC enrolls the top 12.5% of high school graduates, the CSU accepts the top 33.3% of graduates, and CCCs are open enrollment. All Californians are ensured access to a postsecondary education regardless of their academic qualifications or whether they are looking to complete a degree, a certificate, or just a few classes.

The Master Plan (CDE, 1960) also delineated the primary missions of each of the three segments—the UC serves as the state's primary research university offering doctoral, master's, and bachelor's degrees; the CSU is a primarily teaching institution offering master's and bachelor's degrees; and the CCCs offer associate's degrees and certificates in both academic and vocational/technical subjects as well as serve students preparing to transfer to the UC or CSU. The Master Plan explicitly stated that the CCCs are responsible for providing remedial education to the state's postsecondary students. Since the UC set admissions criteria that included both a minimum high school GPA in A–G approved courses (i.e., high school curricula that make students eligible for admission to the state's universities) and a minimum score on standardized admissions tests (e.g., ACT and SAT), state educators and policymakers believed that offering remedial coursework at the UC should not be necessary; UC students would be prepared to enroll in college-level coursework as they were the most academically competitive in the state. However, the Master Plan only set a minimum high school GPA with no compulsory standardized admissions testing for CSU enrollment, creating ambiguity as to whether the CSU needed to offer remedial coursework (Crouch & McNenny, 2000).

Since 1964, CSU leaders have openly questioned whether the university should offer remedial coursework (Crouch & McNenny, 2000). Faculty and administrators were divided as to whether such courses were needed on a large scale. The CSU did not officially offer remedial courses and many students were not assessed before starting their studies. Policies regarding assessment and placement varied across campuses. Some campuses designed local English and math assessments to place students into level-appropriate classes (White, 1989). Because there was no consistency in course placement among campuses, a student could be placed in a freshman English course at one campus and a remedial English course at another.

By 1975, the CSU decided that students would at least be assessed for proficiency in English and mathematics. A few years later, the university's placement tests—the English Placement Test (EPT) and Entry Level Mathematics (ELM) Exam—debuted. For the first time in the university's history, a system-wide instrument assessed students' readiness for college-level English and math coursework. Though the placement exams were designed by faculty members, state legislators set the EPT and ELM cut scores (White, 1989). Students were not denied admission to the CSU if they did not pass the exams (White, 1995); those scoring above the cut point were placed into college-level coursework, and those scoring below were enrolled in a series of remedial classes. Neither the testing agencies that oversee the EPT nor individual CSU campuses have conducted validity studies that corroborate cut scores with course placement (CSUS Academic Senate, 2013).

Remediation rates remained stagnant throughout the 1980s and 1990s, and university officials bemoaned the fact that approximately 50% of CSU students were not prepared for college-level English and/or math each year (Crouch & McNenny, 2000). Widespread under-preparedness translated to longer time-to-degree, since remedial students could not yet take credit-bearing courses that fulfilled degree and graduation requirements. The CSU system board of trustees proposed shifting all of its remedial education to the community colleges insofar as so many remedial courses "threaten[ed] the value of a CSU diploma" (Gallego, 1995, p. 3). When the CSU system trustees' plan failed to gain support from the CCCs and other educational leaders, alternatives were considered. One suggestion was to deduct part of the cost of university remedial courses from state aid to state-supported high schools (Kirst, 1997).

In 1996 the CSU board of trustees took a bold step in attempting to reduce the numbers of CSU students with remedial needs; the board adopted the goal of 90% proficiency in English and math for first-time students by the year 2007 (Crouch & McNenny, 2000; Richard, 2007). A year later in 1997, CSU Executive Order 665 (EO 665) solidified the university's stance on testing for placement purposes. Executive Order 665 required that all incoming students be assessed by way of the university's EPT and/or ELM if a student had not met the proficiency requirement as measured by alternative measures (i.e., a qualifying score on ACT, SAT, or AP assessments, or completion of a qualifying course; CSU, 1997). Executive Order 665 also mandated that students complete remedial coursework within a certain time frame—one academic year—from when they entered the university. Students who did not meet this requirement would be disenrolled and required to complete remediation at a community college. By the year 2000, the CSU had a system-wide policy for testing and remediating underprepared students.

Today, CSU students are systematically assessed for college-level proficiency before they start coursework, often even before they are notified of their admission to the university. In the fall of 2013, the CSU enrolled 60,592 first-time freshmen (CSU, n.d. d). Of these first-time freshmen, 19,438 students (32.1%) were placed into remedial English courses and

17,636 (29.1%) into remedial math. These rates, while concerning, represent a decrease in remedial need relative to prior years. Disaggregated data by race and ethnicity reveal that even higher rates of African Americans and Latinos are assigned to remedial coursework. These data are presented in Table 5.1.

Legislators' and university officials' concerns about the financial costs of remediation have escalated over the last decade. In 2004, David Spence, then-CSU system executive vice chancellor, stated that the expenditure could be as much as $30 to $35 million a year (Mills, 2004). A more recent figure places the cost to the university at approximately $30 million annually (CSU, February 2011; CSU, January 18 2013). While this figure comprises only 1.6% of the 2011–12 instructional and 0.66% of the total operating budgets respectively, many stakeholders suggest that taxpayers should not be paying twice for students to learn skills they should have learned in high school, and that these funds are better used elsewhere. Besides the costs to the university, there are also costs to students and families in the form of extra tuition and longer time-to-completion because remedial courses often do not count toward a degree (CSU, n.d. a; Strong American Schools, 2008).

Finally, CSU leaders have been concerned about how high remediation rates affect students' academic performance as they progress in their studies. That students performing well in their high schools—earning at least a B average and graduating in the top one-third of their high school classes—score below proficient on the university's placement tests signals a misalignment between secondary and postsecondary expectations (Mills, 2004). Studies on postsecondary remediation have pointed to mixed results in terms of persistence and completion (Adelman, 1998; Attewell, Lavin, Domina, & Levey, 2006; Breneman & Haarlow, 1998; Calcagno & Long, 2008; Martorell & McFarlin, 2011). Students who arrive at postsecondary education ready to engage in college-level coursework are more likely to persist in and graduate from college on time than their underprepared counterparts. Next I will discuss the CSU's primary approach to preparing high school students for college coursework—the EAP.

The Early Assessment Program (EAP)

By the early 2000s, California State University (CSU) officials recognized that their 2007 90% proficiency goal would not be met, and developed a

TABLE 5.1. CSU regularly admitted first-time freshman English and math remediation rates, total and by ethnicity (1998–2013)

Year	Total frosh	# & % English	# & % Math	Total black frosh	Black # & % English	Black # & % math	Total Latino frosh	Latino # & % English	Latino # & % math
1998	28,327	13,353 (47%)	15,378 (54%)	1,505	1,000 (66.4%)	1,211 (80.0%)	5,850	3,700 (63.2%)	4,226 (72.3%)
1999	31,187	14,500 (46%)	14,841 (48%)	1,584	1,018 (64.3%)	1,175 (74.2%)	6,324	3,952 (62.5%)	4,133 (65.4%)
2000	33,822	15,448 (45.7%)	15,289 (45.2%)	1,744	1,149 (65.9%)	1,274 (73.1%)	6,941	4,209 (60.1%)	4,382 (63.1%)
2001	36,665	16,925 (46.2%)	16,924 (46.2%)	2,028	1,306 (64.4%)	1,511 (74.5%)	7,777	4,887 (62.8%)	5,033 (64.7%)
2002	37,870	18,575 (49.0%)	14,016 (37.0%)	2,138	1,466 (68.6%)	1,389 (65.0%)	7,927	5,214 (65.8%)	4,322 (54.5%)
2003	38,086	18,375 (48.2%)	13,982 (36.7%)	2,121	1,462 (68.9%)	1,351 (63.7%)	8,308	5,301 (63.8%)	4,278 (51.5%)
2004	38,859	18,126 (46.6%)	14,289 (36.8%)	2,245	1,514 (67.4%)	1,456 (64.9%)	9,320	5,906 (63.3%)	4,952 (53.1%)
2005	43,005	19,429 (45.2%)	15,579 (36.2%)	2,598	1,667 (64.2%)	1,629 (62.7%)	10,779	6,575 (61.0%)	5,545 (51.4%)
2006	46,081	20,860 (45.3%)	17,303 (37.5%)	2,865	1,812 (63.2%)	1,871 (65.3%)	12,028	7,351 (61.1%)	6,354 (52.8%)
2007	49,274	22,766 (46.2%)	18,320 (37.2%)	3,042	1,990 (65.4%)	1,945 (63.9%)	13,185	8,185 (62.1%)	6,907 (52.4%)

TABLE 5.1. continued

Year	Total frosh	# & % English	# & % Math	Total black_frosh	Black # & % English	Black # & % math	Total Latino frosh	Latino # & % English	Latino # & % math
2008	50,187	23,579 (47.0%)	18,660 (37.2%)	2,954	1,947 (65.9%)	1,894 (64.1%)	14,341	8,999 (62.8%)	7,499 (52.3%)
2009	50,367	24,732 (49.1%)	18,960 (37.6%)	2,532	1,804 (71.2%)	1,718 (67.9%)	16,676	10,565 (63.4%)	8,637 (51.8%)
2010	47,885	23,602 (49.3%)	16,912 (35.3%)	2,361	1,638 (69.4%)	1,520 (64.4%)	17,126	10,908 (63.7%)	8,464 (49.4%)
2011	54,478	18,371 (33.7%)	18,133 (33.3%)	2,583	1,359 (52.6%)	1,621 (62.8%)	20,584	9,351 (45.4%)	9,334 (45.3%)
2012	55,692	18,690 (33.6%)	17,011 (30.5%)	2,522	1,255 (49.8%)	1,395 (55.3%)	22,408	10,113 (45.1%)	9,247 (41.3%)
2013	60,592	19,438 (32.1%)	17,636 (29.1%)	2,597	1,197 (46.1%)	1,396 (53.8%)	24,962	10,473 (42.0%)	9,688 (38.8%)

Source: CSU Proficiency Rates (n.d.)

comprehensive remedial education program that targeted students' academic shortcomings at the secondary level. In 2004 the CSU Chancellor's Office announced the implementation of the Early Assessment Program (EAP) to reduce the numbers of students requiring English and mathematics remediation. The EAP is a collaborative effort on the part of the CSU, the State Board of Education, and the California Department of Education. The program's goals are broad, spanning students' secondary and postsecondary education. The EAP aims to:

- Align high school and CSU standards so that success in high school means readiness for the CSU
- Give more meaning and force to the state's testing program— the California Standards Tests (CSTs)
- Give high school students an early signal about their college readiness and adequate time to prepare before entering CSU
- Make the senior year a time for more direct and specific preparation for college
- Exempt CSU-ready students from taking the university's placement tests, the ACT, or the SAT, thus reducing testing time for students (CSU, November 14, 2012).

The EAP attempts to better align high school and university standards. The program is voluntary, and participating high school students should ideally gain a better understanding of postsecondary-level academic expectations before matriculating to the CSU. Since implementation in 2004, 70%-80% of eligible students opt to participate in the program each year; more than 3 million have participated in the EAP to date (ETS, n.d.).

The EAP is not a stand-alone test; it is administered alongside the annual state standards testing—the California Standards Tests (CSTs; CSU, June 2011). In California, students take the CSTs each spring from 2nd grade to 11th grade. The CSTs measure students' progress toward achieving California's academic content standards in English, mathematics, science, and history (ETS, 2013). CSTs measure what students should know and be able to do in each grade and subject tested. The EAP is offered only to 11th-graders who are taking the CSTs. The EAP has an English and mathematics component. Students receive a letter in the winter of their junior year (see Figure 5.1) introducing the EAP and encouraging them to participate in the voluntary assessment when they take the mandatory

CSTs in the coming months. Students may also be encouraged to participate by their English and math teachers and academic counselors.

Students participating in the English EAP complete two sections in addition to the regular CSTs—(a) 15 additional multiple-choice questions and (b) a 45-minute essay, responding to a short passage and essay prompt (CSU, February 8 2011). There is no one universal date for testing; the California Department of Education sets a window of time and allows individual school districts to arrange their own dates (CSU, 2010). The English EAP administration is often split into two sessions. Students take the essay portion in late winter or early spring to allow time for human scoring and the extra 15 multiple-choice items when the CSTs are administered in the spring. Students participating in the math EAP complete one extra section in addition to the regular CSTs in Algebra 2 or High School Summative Mathematics—15 additional multiple-choice questions. The math EAP is administered at the same time as the CSTs.

Students are notified of their CST and EAP results during summer before their senior year via an individual STAR (Standardized Testing and Reporting) Results paper score report sent directly to students' homes (see Figure 5.2). Schools also receive copies of students' CSTs and EAP paper score reports. The paper score report directs students to a website for further information about the program and college readiness at the CSU. Prior to the 2012 administration of the English EAP, students were either classified as "Ready for College" or "Not Ready for College." Since 2012, however, students have been classified as "Ready for College," "Ready for College—Conditional," or "Did Not Demonstrate College Readiness on This Assessment" on both the English and math sections.

If students are "ready," they can enroll in college-level English and/or math upon CSU entrance; they only need to maintain their reading, writing, and math skills during their senior year. Even if those students do not end up attending a CSU campus, they have a better idea that they are prepared for college-level coursework. A status of "ready—conditional" means that students have demonstrated readiness for English and/or math at the CSU but will need to take an appropriate English and/or math course in the senior year to ensure that they continue to be ready. Finally, if students are "not ready," then they have several options to demonstrate readiness for college-level English and/or math coursework: they can either take the CSU English Placement Test (EPT) and/or Entry Level Mathematics (ELM) Exam during the spring of their senior year or satisfy the placement requirement with test or course completion.1 If students are unable to demonstrate readiness, the CSU places the students in the appropriate remedial English and/or math course based on their performance on the EPT and/or ELM assessments.

The basic presumption of the EAP is that early notification of under-preparedness—while students are still attending high school—will decrease remedial need at the postsecondary level. Students who do not demonstrate "readiness" on the English and/or math EAP need to further develop their skills before they graduate from high school. Non-ready students can "catch up" during their senior year of high school and prepare to take and pass the CSU placement exams in the spring of their senior year.

The CSU offers recommendations to help students prepare for the EPT and ELM exams. For the EPT, the university encourages students to enroll in a special CSU-developed Expository Reading and Writing Course (ERWC) offered at California high schools (CSU, n.d. c). This senior-year course targets the skills necessary to be successful in reading and writing at the CSU. Approximately 20% of the state's high school English teachers (about 9,600) have been trained to teach the course (Gewertz, 2011). Nearly 400 of California's 1,400 public high schools have fully implemented the ERWC; other high schools use some of its modules. The CSU suggests that students whose high schools do not offer the ERWC course should focus on learning those same skills in their regularly scheduled English courses. Students may also access test preparation materials available on the CSU English Success website (CSU, n.d. a). The CSU recommends that students who are not ready in math focus on learning needed skills in their math courses. Students are also encouraged to use the online test preparation materials to prepare for the ELM available at the CSU Math Success website (www.csumathsuccess.org).

The EAP thus has two goals: more closely aligning high school and college standards, and raising students' awareness of their proficiency for college-level coursework. Now I turn to a discussion of EAP results and research on the program's effectiveness.

EAP's Reception and Results

Several policymakers and scholars have examined the Early Assessment Program's (EAP) design and results since its implementation a decade ago.

Some have lauded the EAP for its effectiveness and innovation in addressing under-preparedness while students are still in high school. Early after the EAP's implementation, then U.S. secretary of education Margaret Spellings (2006) encouraged postsecondary institutions to work more closely with state and local school officials to implement early assessment programs similar to the CSU's EAP. In 2007, the Lumina Foundation stated that the EAP "is playing a huge role in helping [students] realize [their] dream [of earning a college degree]" (Lumina Foundation, 2007, p. 4). Lumina went on to say that the "EAP is expected to have a huge and positive impact on the state's public higher education institutions and the students they serve" (p. 5).

Other high-profile education outlets have endorsed the use of the EAP in reducing remediation rates. The U.S. Department of Education's Institute of Education Sciences (IES) expressed its satisfaction with the program back in 2007, identifying the EAP as one of its "programs, practices, and policies that are effective for improving access to or persistence in postsecondary education" (p. 44). The Campaign for College Opportunity (2007) also cited EAP as a "practice with promise . . . [that is] remarkable" (p. 2) in helping more Californians prepare for college-level coursework and increasing statewide enrollment in postsecondary education.

Despite the praise for the EAP in alerting high school students of their under-preparedness, there are still few evidence-based conclusions about the effectiveness of the EAP as an early warning program. Achieve (2009) convened a group of scholars to examine the EAP assessment. They concluded that the assessment addresses essential college-ready content identified by CSU faculty and is rigorous. However, they were critical of the test development and suggested that the EAP could benefit from targeted improvements. Achieve criticized the English EAP for not requiring students to read the passage in order to answer the multiple-choice items, which would provide a more accurate picture of their ability to derive meaning from college-level material. They also noted that the procedural nature of many multiple-choice math items was problematic. They suggested that test developers create additional selected-response items that "resemble the more cognitively demanding augmentation items, would ensure the assessment of the kinds of higher order skills students need to be prepared for college" (p. 6).

Howell, Kurleander, and Grodsky (2010) examined the EAP at CSU Sacramento and concluded that the assessment provided an early sign of under-preparedness for college. They found statistically significant effects of EAP participation on remedial need; participation in EAP reduced the probability of remediation at CSU Sacramento by 6.1% in English and by 4.1% in math. The researchers also found that students who were not ready for college-level coursework were not discouraged from applying to CSU Sacramento as freshmen; they surmised that the EAP motivated students to increase their academic preparation while still in high school. Howell and colleagues warned, though, that more research was needed to confirm their findings.

One study questioned the lack of data about EAP and the program's true impact on reducing remediation (Gewertz, 2011), positing that the execution of the EAP might not fulfill its promise. Gewertz scrutinized the reduction in English remediation over the last few years. She suggested that the professional development and training associated with the senior-year ERWC (the CSU-developed writing course) was the real reason why students were better prepared for college-level English. She commended the CSU for starting a more nuanced discussion of postsecondary remediation, but urged the university to scrutinize EAP's effectiveness.

The Policy Analysis for California Education (PACE) research center provided a thorough review of the EAP and all relevant studies of the program's effectiveness to date (McLean, 2012). Similar to other researchers, PACE was hesitant to declare the program effective in reducing the numbers of CSU students who placed into remedial coursework. The report outlined recommendations for promoting the usefulness of the program in helping high school students better prepare for college-level coursework.

William Tierney and I have questioned the usefulness of the EAP, especially the English section (Tierney & Garcia, 2008, 2011). We have focused our research and criticisms of the program squarely on its effectiveness helping the students who are least prepared to attend college—low-income, first-generation students who attend high schools with low college preparation rates. The majority of the students in our qualitative studies were unaware of what the EAP was, whether they had participated, and how they could better prepare for college-level coursework at their high schools.

The Need for More Research

Remediation rates for entering CSU freshmen have improved over the years (see Table 5.1). The English remediation rate fluctuated between

TABLE 5.2. 2006–2013 EAP English and math results

Year	# English EAP students tested	English EAP–ready	English–ready conditional	English EAP– not ready	# Math EAP students tested	Math EAP ready	Math EAP–ready conditional	Math– EAP not ready
2006	312,167	48,072 (15%)	NA	264,095 (85%)	137,067	16,120 (12%)	58,822 (43%)	62,125 (45%)
2007	342,348	55,206 (16%)	NA	282,775 (83%)	141,648	17,173 (12%)	60,697 (43%)	63,710 (45%)
2008	352,943	60,392 (17%)	NA	288,599 (82%)	147,885	19,442 (13%)	62,660 (42%)	65,718 (44%)
2009	366,949	59,381 (16%)	NA	303,998 (83%)	169,478	22,247 (13%)	74,467 (44%)	72,688 (43%)
2010	378,870	77,826 (21%)	NA	297,630 (79%)	178,667	26,056 (14%)	75,502 (42%)	77,053 (43%)
2011	383,060	85,732 (23%)	NA	293,673 (77%)	190,946	29,526 (15%)	81,856 (43%)	79,507 (42%)
2012	383,565	87,086 (23%)	58,057 (15%)	237,459 (62%)	203,972	30,430 (15%)	92,850 (46%)	80,639 (40%)
2013	384,722	87,318 (23%)	56,552 (15%)	240,367 (63%)	212,386	30,781 (14%)	97,378 (46%)	84,623 (40%)

Source: CSU (n.d. b)

45% and 50% from the late 1990s through 2010; in 2011, the rate dropped significantly to 33% and remained steady in the following years. The freshman math remediation rate has steadily decreased since 1998, adjusting from 54% to about 30% in 2013. While the remediation rates for first-time CSU freshmen have decreased over time, the passage rates for the CSU EAP have remained relatively steady since 2006, when the first class of participating students (who were high school juniors in 2004) entered the CSU (see Table 5.2). There have been slight increases in the percentage of those students who are "ready" for the rigors of CSU coursework (15%-23% in English and 12%-14% in math).

The increases in CSU proficiency rates may have resulted from students' awareness of their proficiency status earlier via the EAP intervention. Students who start their senior year of high school knowing that they are underprepared may find the motivation and resources to improve their English and math skills. For the math EAP, between 42% and 46% of students each year have been "ready—conditional" for college-level math coursework. These seniors simply need to take and pass their college preparatory math class to avoid remediation at the CSU. The recent addition of the English EAP "Ready for College—Conditional" status with the spring 2012 administration creates similar options for students with underdeveloped reading and writing skills. Since 2012, the 15% of students who have been given "ready—conditional" status each year have had the chance to avoid remediation by passing a college preparatory senior-year course. Students may have also benefitted from the CSU-developed Expository Reading and Writing Course (ERWC) option, which prepares students to pass the English Placement Test (Hafner, Joseph, & McCormick, 2010).

However, the research base has not yet established clear evidence linking the EAP to system-wide decreases in remediation rates. The only analysis that shows that the EAP reduced the probability of students placing into remedial coursework (by 6.1% in English and by 4.1% in math) focused on a single CSU campus—Sacramento (Howell et al., 2010). Further research is needed to determine whether EAP participation has positioned students to be more successful in college coursework and persist to graduation.

There are other possible reasons why English and math remediation rates have decreased over the years. English rates may have declined sharply in 2011 because the EPT cut score was lowered from 151 to 147, classifying thousands of students as "ready" who would have previously been placed in remedial English (CSU, June 2010). Similar to English remediation rates, CSU math remediation rates may have declined starting a decade ago as the university's ELM assessment was overhauled—the assessment was redesigned and the grading scale changed at this time—with implementation starting in spring 2002 (CSU, 2002). Lowering remediation assessment cut scores, offering the CSU-developed ERWC, and adding the English "ready—conditional" status likely all contributed to the downturn in CSU remediation rates over the years. Research has yet to parse out how much of the decline in remedial need may be attributed to assessment reform and how much may be associated with the EAP intervention.

Further, the lowering of the English Placement Test (EPT) cut score (from 151 to 147) effective for freshmen enrolling in fall 2011 may have enabled more students to avoid remedial classification (CSU, June 2010), but how these students are performing in college-level courses (e.g., passage rates, instructor observations, persistence) remains unclear. Efforts to transition students into college-level coursework faster may allow students to begin earning college credits sooner. However, research is needed to examine whether students scoring between 151 and 147, who are now deemed college-ready due to the cut-score change, are receiving sufficient support to persist without remedial intervention.

The CSU has funded and implemented the EAP for a decade. The university has modified the program, adjusting scoring thresholds on the EAP and expanding ways by which students can become college-ready. CSU continues to train English teachers to teach the ERWC senior preparatory course. Further, access to the ERWC has broadened since the class was included on the A–G course list, which is used to determine admission eligibility for the University of California (UC) and the CSU (CSU, n.d. c). The expansion of ERWC curriculum to middle schools is also under way (CSU Center for Advancement of Reading, 2011/2012). CSU officials have also developed their more comprehensive Early Start Program (ESP), a summer remedial intervention discussed by Julia Duncheon in the subsequent chapter. Amidst these reforms, the EAP has remained a cornerstone of their college readiness initiative (CSU, January 8 2013). Researchers appear to agree that the EAP is useful for identifying students who lack college-ready English and math skills. However, research that has examined the EAP suggests that the program can be improved to increase its overall effectiveness.

Conclusion

The CSU's Early Assessment Program is the nation's largest early warning remediation program. The EAP is the first step of a more comprehensive remediation program the university has been implementing since 2012—the Early Start Program. As of this writing, the EAP is still a separate program with its own website and materials. It is feasible that this will change in the future as the CSU merges the different components of its remediation program—the EAP, the ERWC, the CSU Success websites, the EPT and ELM, and the Early Start Program—into one, unified conglomerate of a single, multifaceted early warning remediation program. The university has not indicated that the EAP will be replaced by another assessment.

For most of the state's high school students, the EAP is the first indicator that their future college and university admissions offers are not necessarily a predictor of being ready to engage in college-level coursework. As I have discussed in this chapter, early notification of unpreparedness alone is not enough to get students ready for college during their high school senior year. The CSU, in conjunction with secondary schools, has worked to improve the preparatory options available to students who learn they are not ready for college (e.g., developing and expanding access to the ERWC course). Such developments represent efforts to move beyond simply providing students with information regarding their readiness. While the CSU has made improvements to the EAP, future research is needed to demonstrate the effectiveness of the program. Given that information alone is not enough, strengthening the potential impact of this program requires delivering meaningful academic interventions that address students' academic shortcomings long before their last year in high school.

Note

1. For English, students may either earn a high enough test score (i.e., 500< on the critical reading section of the SAT Reasoning Test, 22< on the ACT English Test, or a score of 3< on either the AP Language and Composition or AP Composition and Literature exams) or transfer to CSU the credits for a college course that satisfies the CSU General Education requirement in English Composition (with a grade of C or better). For math, students may either earn a high enough test score (i.e., 550< on the mathematics section of the SAT Reasoning

Test, 550< on a SAT mathematics subject test [level 1 or level 2], 23< on the ACT mathematics test, or a score of 3< on an AP Calculus or Statistics exam), or transfer to CSU the credits for a college course that satisfies the CSU General Education requirement in quantitative reasoning (with a grade of C or better).

References

Achieve, Inc. (2009, October). *An analysis of the Early Assessment Program (EAP) assessments for algebra II, summative high school mathematics, and English*. Washington, DC: Author. Retrieved form http://www.stanford.edu/group/pace/PUBLICATIONS/CDP/AchieveFINALEAPReportOct2009.pdf

Adelman, C. (1998). The kiss of death? An alternative view of college remediation. *National Crosstalk, 6*(3), 11.

Adelman, C. (2006). *The toolbox revisited: Paths to degree completion from high school through college*. Washington, DC: U.S. Department of Education.

Alliance for Excellent Education. (2011, May). *Saving now and saving later: How high school reform can reduce the nation's wasted remediation dollars [Issue brief]*. Washington, DC: Author.

Attewell, R., Lavin, D., Domina, T., & Levey, T. (2006). New evidence on college remediation. *The Journal of Higher Education, 77*, 886–924.

Aud, S., Hussar, G., Kena, G., Bianco, K., Frohlich, L., Kemp, J., & Tahan, K. (2011). *The condition of education, 2011 (NCES 2011-033)*. Washington, DC: National Center for Education Statistics, U.S. Department of Education.

Boylan, H. R., Bonham, B. S., & White, S. R. (1999, Winter). Developmental and remedial education in postsecondary education. *New Directions for Higher Education*, (108), 87–101.

Breneman, D. W., & Haarlow, W. N. (1998). Remedial education: Costs and consequences. In *Fordham Report: Volume 2*(9). *Remediation in higher education: A symposium* (pp. 1–50). Washington, DC: Thomas B. Fordham Foundation.

Calcagno, J. C., & Long, B. T. (2008, April). *The impact of postsecondary remediation using a regression discontinuity approach: Addressing endogenous sorting and noncompliance*. [NCPR Working Paper]. New York: National Center for Postsecondary Research.

California Department of Education (CDE). (1960). *A Master Plan for*

Higher Education in California: 1960-1975. Sacramento, CA: California Department of Education.

California Legislative Analyst Office. (2011, March). Higher education: Answers to frequently asked questions. Are entering freshmen Prepared for college-level work? Retrieved from http://www.lao.ca.gov/sections/higher_ed/FAQs/Higher_Education_Issue_02.pdf

California State University (CSU). (1997). Determination of competence in English and mathematics—Executive Order 665 [Memo]. Retrieved from http://www.calstate.edu/EO/EO-665.pdf

California State University (CSU). (2002). *Entry Level Mathematics (ELM) problem book.* Long Beach, CA: Author. Retrieved from http://www.calstate.edu/SAS/elmproblembook01_02.pdf

California State University (CSU). (2010). Early Assessment Program and Early Start Program [Presentation]. Retrieved from www.calstate.edu/sas/conferences/2010/EAP_Early%20Start%202010.pptx

California State University (CSU). (2010, June 11). The Early Start Program—Executive Order No. 1048 [Memorandum]. Retrieved from http://www.calstate.edu/eo/EO-1048.pdf

California State University (CSU). (2011, February 8). California State University's Early Start Program frequently asked questions. Retrieved from http://www.calstate.edu/air/documents/Early-Start-FAQ-February-2011.pdf

California State University (CSU). (2011, June 30). EAP augmentation of STAR standards. Retrieved from http://www.calstate.edu/eap/augmentation.shtml

California State University (CSU). (2012, November). First-time full-time freshmen degree-seeking FTF graduation and continuation rates. Retrieved from http://www.asd.calstate.edu/csrde/index.shtml#ftf

California State University (CSU). (2012, November 14). About the Early Assessment Program. Retrieved from http://www.calstate.edu/eap/about.shtml

California State University (CSU). (2013, January 8). Early Start Initiative. Retrieved from http://www.calstate.edu/acadaff/EarlyStart/

California State University (CSU). (2013, January 18). Final Budget and Actual Summaries. Retrieved from http://www.calstate.edu/budget/final-budget-summaries/

California State University (CSU). (2013). *The California State University fact book, 2013.* Long Beach, CA: Author. Retrieved from http://www.calstate.edu/pa/2013Facts/documents/facts2013.pdf

California State University (CSU). (n.d. a). Early Assessment Program. Retrieved from http://www.calstate.edu/eap/

California State University (CSU). (n. d. b). Early Assessment Program: Testing and results. Retrieved from http://www.calstate.edu/eap/testing_and_results.shtml

California State University (CSU). (n.d. c). Expository Reading and Writing Course. Retrieved from http://www.calstate.edu/eap/english course/

California State University (CSU). (n.d. d). Final regularly admitted first-time freshmen remediation system-wide. Long Beach, CA: Author. Retrieved from http://www.asd.calstate.edu/remediation/12/Rem_Sys_fall2012.htm

California State University (CSU) Center for Advancement of Reading. (2011/2012, Winter). ERWC for grades 7-11. *CAR Quarterly, 4*(2), 3. Retrieved from http://www.calstate.edu/car/documents/CQuarterly_Win2011_Vol4_Iss2-acc.pdf

California State University, Sacramento (CSUS) Academic Senate. (2013, March 7). *Faculty senate meeting.* Sacramento, CA: Author.

California State University (CSU) Proficiency Rates (n.d.). "First time freshmen remediation systemwide." Retrieved from: http://www.asd.calstate.edu/remediation/12/Rem_Sys_fall2012.htm

Campaign for College Opportunity. (2007). *Practices with promise: A collection of working solutions for college opportunity (Executive Summary).* Oakland, CA: Author.

Complete College America. (2012). *Remediation: Higher education's bridge to nowhere.* Washington, DC: Author.

Conley, D. T. (2010, September). *Replacing remediation with readiness [NCPR Working Paper].* Paper presented at the NCPR Developmental Education Conference: What Policies and Practices Work for Students? Teachers College, Columbia University, New York.

Crouch, M. K., & McNenny, G. (2000). Looking back, looking forward: California grapples with "remediation." *Journal of Basic Writing, 19*(2), 44–71.

Educational Testing Service (ETS). (2013). California Standards Tests (CSTs). Retrieved from http://www.startest.org/cst.html

Educational Testing Service (ETS). (n.d.). Early Assessment Program (EAP) for college readiness. Retrieved from http://eap2012.ets.org/

Gallego, A. P. (1995). Another look at the remedial role. *Community College Times, 7*(17), 3.

Gewertz, C. (2011, January 20). Success of college-readiness intervention hard to gauge. *Education Week*. Retrieved from http://www.edweek. org/ew/articles/2011/01/20/18eap_ep.h30.html

Hafner, A., Joseph, R., & McCormick, J. (2010). College readiness for all: Assessing the impact of English professional development on teaching practice and student learning. *Journal of Urban Learning, Teaching, and Research, 6*, 15–30.

Howell, J. S., Kurlaender, M., & Grodsky, E. (2010). Postsecondary preparation and remediation: Examining the effect of the Early Assessment Program at California State University. *Journal of Policy Analysis and Management, 29*, 726–748.

Institute of Education Sciences. (2007). *Education research grants (Request for applications no. IES-NCER-2008-01)*. Washington, DC: Institute of Education Sciences, U.S. Department of Education.

Jenkins, D., Smith Jaggars, S., & Roksa, J. (2009, November). *Promoting gatekeeper course success among community college students needing remediation: Findings and recommendations from a Virginia study*. New York: Community College Research Center, Teachers College, Columbia University.

Kirst, M. W. (1997). Exam confusion: Admissions and placement tests lack standardization. *National Crosstalk, 5*(1), 3.

Kirst, M. W., & Bracco, K. R. (2004). Bridging the great divide: How the K–12 and postsecondary split hurts students, and what can be done about it. In M. W. Kirst & A. Venezia (Eds.), *From high school to college: Improving opportunities for success in postsecondary education* (pp. 1–30). San Francisco: Jossey-Bass.

Lumina Foundation. (2007, Winter). A changing picture: California effort focuses on early intervention and high school-college alignment. *Focus*, 2–7.

Martorell, P., & McFarlin, I. (2011). Help or hindrance? The effects of college remediation on academic and labor market outcomes. *Review of Economics and Statistics, 93*, 436–454.

McLean, H. (2012). *California's Early Assessment Program: Its effectiveness and the obstacles to successful program implementation*. Stanford, CA: Policy Analysis for California Education. Retrieved from http://www.stanford.edu/group/pace/PUBLICATIONS/PACE_EAP_March_2012.pdf

Mills, K. (2004). Preparing for success in college: California State

University is working closely with high schools to improve English and math skills. *National Crosstalk, 12*(4), 6–7.

National Conference of State Legislatures. (n.d.). Improving college completion: Reforming remedial education. Retrieved from http://www.ncsl.org/issues-research/educ/improving-college-completion-reforming-remedial.aspx

Parsad, B., & Lewis, L. (2003). *Remedial education at degree-granting postsecondary institutions in fall 2000 (NCES Publication No. NCES 2004–010)*. Washington, DC: National Center for Education Statistics, U.S. Department of Education.

Richard, G. W. (2007). California State University remediation policies and practices: Overview and prospects [Agenda Item 3]. Retrieved form http://www.calstate.edu/AcadProg/DvlpMathEnglish/documents/EdPol_A-Item3_09182007-acc.pdf

Scott-Clayton, J., & Rodriguez, O. (2012). *Development, discouragement, or Diversion? New evidence on the effects of college remediation [NBER Working Paper 18328]*. Cambridge, MA: National Bureau of Economic Research. Retrieved from http://www.nber.org/papers/w18457

Spellings, M. (2006). Speech presented at the U.S. University Presidents Summit on International Education on January 6, 2006, in Washington, DC.

Strong American Schools. (2008). *Diploma to nowhere*. Washington, DC: Author. Retrieved from http://www.deltacostproject.org/resources/pdf/DiplomaToNowhere.pdf

Tierney, W. G., & Garcia, L. D. (2008). Preparing underprepared students for college: Remedial education and early assessment programs. *The Journal of At-Risk Issues, 14*(2), 1–7.

Tierney, W. G., & Garcia, L. D. (2011). Remediation in higher education: The role of information. *American Behavioral Scientist, 55*, 102–120.

Vandal, B. (2010). *Getting past go: Rebuilding the remedial education bridge to college success*. Denver, CO: Education Commission of the States.

Venezia, A., & Voloch, D. (2012). Using college placement exams as early signals of college readiness: An examination of California's early assessment program and New York's at home in college program. *New Directions for Higher Education, 2012*(158), 71–79.

White, E. M. (1989). *Developing successful college writing programs*. Portland, MA: Calendar Islands.

White, E. M. (1995). The importance of placement and basic studies:

Helping students succeed under the new elitism. *Journal of Basic Writing, 14*(2), 75–84.

The White House. (n.d.). Issues: Education—support for higher ed. Retrieved from http://www.whitehouse.gov/issues/education/higher-education

Figure 5.1. Early Assessment Program letter to 11th-grade students

CALIFORNIA DEPARTMENT OF EDUCATION
TOM TORLAKSON, State Superintendent of Public Instruction
1430 N Street, Suite 5602
Sacramento, CA 95814-5901
916-319-0800

THE CALIFORNIA STATE UNIVERSITY
TIMOTHY P. WHITE , Chancellor
401 Golden Shore
Long Beach, CA 90802-4210
562-951-4000

CALIFORNIA COMMUNITY COLLEGES
BRICE W. HARRIS, Chancellor
1102 Q Street
Sacramento, CA 95811-6549
916-322-4005

February 2014

Dear Grade Eleven Student:

2014 EARLY ASSESSMENT PROGRAM

In a short time, you will have the option to take the California Standards Tests (CSTs) for English Language Arts and Algebra II or Summative High School Math. These optional assessments are part of the Early Assessment Program (EAP).

The EAP lets you know whether you are ready for college-level coursework in English and mathematics at the end of your junior year of high school. If you have difficulty with one or both of the exams, this early signal gives you an opportunity to improve your skills during your senior year before you enter a California State University (CSU) campus or a participating California Community College (CCC). Whether you plan to attend the CSU or a community college, taking steps to prepare for college before you graduate is important to your future success. You will receive your EAP results on your Student Report in late summer of 2014. A significant benefit of the EAP is that students who have demonstrated proficiency for college-level coursework on the basis of their EAP results are exempt from taking the CSU and participating CCC placement tests for English and mathematics and move directly into college-level classes upon enrollment.

If you would like the CSU or participating CCC to receive your English and/or mathematics EAP results, please **fill in the "bubble" in the "EAP Readiness for College English—EAP Augmentation" and/or "EAP Readiness for College Mathematics—EAP Augmentation" section on your STAR answer sheets to authorize the release of your results. We strongly encourage you to release your results.** If you choose not to release your results and later decide you would like the CSU or a CCC to receive your English and mathematics EAP results, you will be asked to provide a copy of your EAP results to the CSU or participating CCC.

You can access Web-based English and math college prep interactive tutorials to assist you in improving your skills while still in high school. To learn more about the EAP tutorials, please visit the CSU Success Web site at http://www.csusuccess.org. You can also find information about the EAP, your results, and how to get ready for college on the EAP Web site at http://www.collegeeap.org/.

Figure 5.1. continued

February 2014
Page 2

If you have questions regarding the EAP, please talk with your English and mathematics teachers, high school counselor, or career center director or send an e-mail to the CSU Student Academic Support Office at eapmail@calstate.edu.

Sincerely,

Tom Torlakson
State Superintendent of Public Instruction
California Department of Education

Timothy P. White
Chancellor
The California State University

Brice W. Harris
Chancellor
California Community Colleges

TT/TW/BH:pa

Retrieved June 30, 2013 from http://www.calstate.edu/eap/letters.shtml

Figure 5.2. EAP results as shown on the 11th Grade CST Score Report

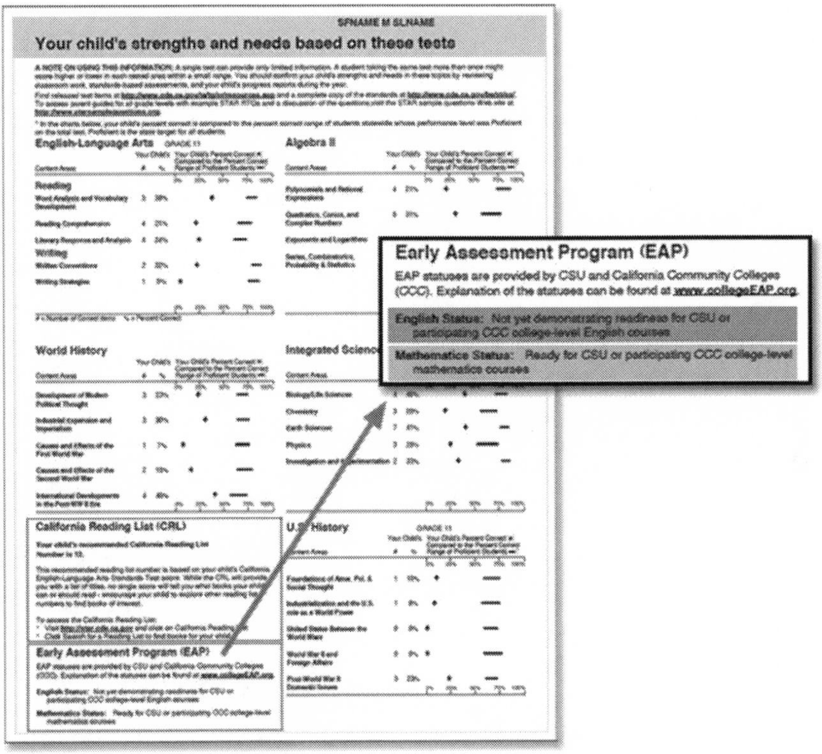

Retrieved from: http://www.csusuccess.org/esw_stu_report_img

6

<hr />

MAKING SENSE OF CONTESTED TERRAIN

Writing Remediation, Faculty Perspectives,
and the Challenge of Implementation

JULIA C. DUNCHEON

High rates of enrollment in postsecondary remediation have prompted growing concern from educational stakeholders, as Lisa Garcia
discussed in the preceding chapter. Remedial or developmental education
refers to non-credit-bearing coursework designed for students who enter
underprepared in English and/or math. As we have noted, college readiness is the preparation needed to enroll in credit-bearing college courses
and persist to graduation. Placement into remediation therefore implies
that students are not college-ready—at least according to the cognitive
indicators (i.e., test scores) typically used to assess students' proficiency.
Nationally, about 50% of students entering two-year colleges and 20% of
students entering four-year institutions are assigned to remediation, and
low-income students of color are overrepresented in these courses (Complete College America, 2012). Remediation is associated with greater
likelihood of attrition, increased time-to-degree, and high costs (Strong
American Schools, 2008).

Under-preparedness in literacy poses particular challenges because
writing serves as the primary form of evaluation in most college courses;

of the students that enroll in remedial English, only 17% obtain a degree (Adelman, 2006). Because literacy learning is complex and inherently political (Rose, 1989), consensus around how to improve outcomes for developmental English students is lacking (Huot, 1996; White, 2005). This study examines college readiness through a focus on writing remediation. Though remedial placement is commonly based on cognitive indicators, this chapter uncovers ways in which writing at the college level also entails non-cognitive competencies and has implications for campus integration. In other words, inquiry into literacy development offers insight into the many facets of college readiness.

The challenges associated with remediation generally and writing remediation specifically have prompted myriad reforms to enhance the success of underprepared students (Goen-Salter, 2008). Garcia discussed one such intervention—the Early Assessment Program—in the prior chapter. The policy literature on remediation has focused on program effectiveness, innovation, and the challenges of assessment and placement (Bettinger, Boatman, & Long, 2013). A growing body of scholarship has begun to explore students' experiences in developmental coursework (Green, 2011). While extant research offers critical insight into the remediation policy context, faculty voices have received little attention (Saxon & Boylan, 2010). Given that faculty run developmental programs and work directly with students, discerning faculty perspectives on remedial education policy is crucial to better understand the problem of under-preparedness and improve student outcomes.

One way to address this gap is to examine policy implementation, as faculty members are responsible for enacting remediation reforms. Implementation research also illuminates the intricacies of change processes and helps to explain policy outcomes (Honig, 2006; Lipsky, 1980; Mills, 1998). Scholars have analyzed policy implementation through the construct of sense-making (Weick, 1995), which attempts to understand how local actors make sense of and respond to the reforms they are charged with enacting (Spillane, Reiser, & Reimer, 2002). The assumption is that the meanings inherent in policy messages are not straightforward and must be constructed by those on the ground; how implementers respond to a reform depends on how they interpret it (Coburn, 2005). Focusing on the sense-making of English faculty members who play a central role in developmental education but are often overlooked in policy discourse may therefore offer insight into the challenges associated with remediation reform.

This study employs a sense-making framework to examine the implementation of the English Early Start Program, a recent remediation policy adopted by the California State University (CSU) system. As previously mentioned, the CSU is the largest and most diverse state university system, serving approximately 437,000 students across 23 campuses ("The California State University," n.d.). Academically underprepared students comprise more than one-third of entering freshmen ("CSU Proficiency Rates," n. d.), and rates have remained relatively stagnant despite numerous reform efforts (King et al., 2011). In contrast to community colleges that typically have open enrollment (Perin, 2006), bachelor's degree-granting institutions such as the CSU set more selective admissions standards (Gumport & Bastedo, 2001). Policies targeting remediation in four-year universities are thus especially controversial and warrant investigation (Parker et al., 2010).

The Early Start Program represents the newest reform implemented by the CSU to address students' remedial needs, and builds on prior reforms such as the Early Assessment Program Garcia reviewed in chapter 5. Early Start requires admitted students who have not demonstrated college-level proficiency to begin remediation during the summer prior to their first semester (EO1048, 2010). The policy generated widespread resistance, especially from English faculty (ASCSU, 2009; Yamada, 2010), but the system proceeded with implementation in 2012. Research on the enactment of this policy has not yet been conducted. The current inquiry investigates English Early Start implementation through the lens of faculty's sense-making. The purpose is to contribute new perspective on remediation policy by uncovering the voices of faculty. Investigation into the perspectives of ground-level stakeholders is critical to better understand the policy landscape, identify challenges to effective reform, and improve policy design (Kegan, & Lahey, 2009). This research is especially important given that remediation occupies highly contested terrain in higher education (Parker, Bustillos, & Behringer, 2010) and improving students' literacy skills is crucial to facilitate college completion (Adelman, 2006).

I offer two caveats. First, my data collection process led me to engage with multiple actors across the system, including both policy designers and implementers. Our interactions led me to believe that stakeholders at all levels of the system are working diligently to improve educational outcomes for CSU students. Though I focus on the perspectives and experiences of faculty members, my purpose here is not to problematize the policy or criticize those who created it. Rather, I am more concerned about the sense-making of faculty members because while they play a central role in delivering developmental education programs, faculty voices are largely absent from remediation policy scholarship (Saxon & Boylan, 2013). Second, obviously, multiple actors have knowledge that has the potential to enhance our understanding of remediation policy. CSU students who have taken Early Start courses and counselors who have helped administer the program in particular may offer valuable insight. Although exploring the perceptions of all relevant stakeholders would have been advantageous, such an undertaking would have been a volume rather than a chapter. Inquiry into the experiences of non-faculty stakeholders offers a fruitful avenue for future research.

The Remediation Policy Context: Contested Terrain

Policy development begins with defining a particular policy problem (Kingdon, 1995). Problem definitions reflect agendas, values, and meaning constructions that are inherently subjective (Bacchi, 2000; Bleiklie, 2000). Problem framing, in turn, creates the milieu within which local actors make sense of new reforms (Coburn, 2006). Thus I discuss the context around remediation in general and writing remediation in particular to situate the inquiry.

Remediation in General

As Almeida noted in chapter 2, policymakers, administrators, and faculty have wrestled with questions of how to address the needs of underprepared students and even whether remediation has a place in postsecondary institutions since the founding of Harvard in 1636 (Jehangir, 2002). Opponents argue that remedial education lowers standards and threatens educational quality in higher education (Fain, 2012; Mac Donald, 1998). They emphasize research associating remedial enrollment with higher rates of attrition and increased time-to-degree (Complete College America, 2012). Many stakeholders lament that taxpayers are paying twice for students to acquire skills they should have learned in high school (Alliance for Excellent Education, 2008), with the institutional cost of remedial services projected to reach as high as $2.89 billion annually (Strong American Schools, 2008). These concerns have prompted policies at the state level that aim to reduce or eliminate remediation in four-year institutions, often by restricting remedial education to community colleges (Gumport & Bastedo, 2001; Mazzeo, 2002; Parker & Richardson, 2005).

Advocates suggest that developmental education furthers democratic goals by expanding access (Lazarick, 1997; Soliday, 2002). They point out that research on remediation's effectiveness has been inconclusive, with some studies findings positive effects (Bettinger & Long, 2009; Bahr, 2010). Remediation may expand access to higher education for the least prepared students (Goudas & Boylan, 2012). Scholars have pointed out that students who enter college underprepared are likely to struggle regardless of whether they enroll in remediation (Calcagno & Long, 2008; Deil-Amen, 2011). Despite the high costs of funding remedial programs, these figures comprise only a fraction—roughly 1%—of total spending on higher education (Handel & Williams, 2011). Remediation thus occupies a contested space in higher education, straddling the tension between excellence and access (Goen-Salter, 2008).

Writing Remediation

In the field of composition studies, writing development is conveyed as a nuanced process shaped by cognitive, social, and cultural factors (Durst, 1990; Juzwik et al., 2006; Nystrand, 2006). Writing remediation is difficult to legislate because the nature of literacy education is so complex and, as scholars have pointed out (Rose, 1985, 1989; Soliday, 1996), inherently political. Reforms aimed at reading and writing instruction tend to spark controversy, revealing tension between policymakers and practitioners (Coburn, 2006; Crouch & McNenny, 2001). Part of the problem stems from the fact that pedagogical concerns are often excluded from remedial policy development, while composition scholars and instructors often focus exclusively on pedagogy, "ignoring basic writing's complex history and the ways it interacts with vested institutional, economic, and political interests" (Goen-Salter, 2008, p. 83).

Composition scholars have asserted that policies targeting literacy remediation for removal embody the assumptions that reading and writing skills should have been mastered in K-12 schooling (Goen & Gillotte-Tropp, 2003) and can be remediated in a lockstep fashion (Rose, 2009). Many suggest that students from diverse linguistic backgrounds are often framed from a deficit perspective, assumed to be deficient and require fixing (Colyar & Stich, 2011; Gutierrez, Morales, & Martinez, 2009; Rose, 1985). The traditional remediation model, which isolates underprepared students in non-credit-bearing, prerequisite classes until they demonstrate competency, reflects a deficit approach (Soliday, 1996). Some scholars and practitioners have advocated for mainstreaming models that place struggling students into college-level classes and provide additional support to eliminate the stigma of remediation and enhance student outcomes (Adams, 2010; Jenkins, Speroni, Belfield, Jaggars, & Edgecombe, 2010).

Another challenge that poses particular problems for literacy remediation reform is assessment (Bailey, 2008; Relles & Tierney, 2013). The dominant "single sample" assessment model requires that students complete a timed writing sample and places them by evaluating their scores relative to a designated cut point (Breland, Bridgeman, & Fowles, 1999; Michael & Shaffer, 1979). The use of wide-scale placement tests provides an efficient and cost-effective way to evaluate large numbers of incoming students (Grubb et al., 2011). However, common assessment models have been found to misplace students and penalize non-mainstream English speakers (Huot & Schendel, 2010; Scott-Clayton, 2012). Composition faculty have advocated for a portfolio model to provide a formative assessment of a student's writing ability (Elbow & Belanoff, 1986), but there has been little movement toward reforming existing placement mechanisms at the state or institutional level (Grubb et al., 2011).

Remediation generally and writing remediation specifically occupy contested terrain in higher education and have implications for how we conceptualize college readiness, identify college-ready students, and support those who are underprepared (Bettinger et al., 2013). Notably, composition scholars' work on developmental education remains largely disconnected from remediation policy research (Goen-Salter, 2008). Without attention to the perspectives of all relevant stakeholders, researchers and legislators lack a comprehensive view of the problem to support policymaking (Kegan & Lahey, 2009). Below I outline the policy under investigation, the CSU Early Start Program, followed by a discussion of the theory I call upon to examine English and composition faculty's sense-making.

The Policy

Executive Order 1048 (EO1048, 2010) created the Early Start Program, requiring students designated for remediation to begin coursework during the summer prior to their first semester. The mandate specified that students would be identified based on their English Placement Test (EPT) score, the exam used for system-wide placement, if not exempted by alternative measures of proficiency (i.e., meeting proficiency benchmarks on the English and math portions of the SAT or ACT; earning passing scores on relevant AP exams). Eligible students could meet their Early Start requirement at any CSU campus, but the edict specified that "if [students] have not started to address a deficiency in either mathematics and/or English, they will not be permitted to enroll at the CSU campus of their admission" (EO1048, 2010, p. 1). The Chancellor's Office set parameters for the minimum number of credits campuses must offer—one unit, or 15 hours of coursework—though campuses were encouraged to offer full three-unit courses (CSU, 2011). The cost was fixed at $182 per unit with financial aid available to students who qualify. Campuses had autonomy to design course curricula and formats (i.e., online or face-to-face) congruent with their program's goals.

The Chancellor's Office expressed various motivations for the program. One problem was that past CSU policies had failed to significantly reduce remedial need, which cost the system roughly $30 million annually (Farar, 2011). The CSU board of trustees' 1995 goal to decrease remediation rates to 10% by 2007 had not been realized (Carter, 2007). Executive Order No. 665 (EO665), issued in 1997, mandated incoming students to complete their remedial coursework within one calendar year or be subject to disenrollment from the CSU. The edict was intended to accelerate students' progress toward degree completion by ensuring that students attended to their remediation sooner. Executive Order 665 spurred some criticism for limiting access; roughly 3,000 students are required to leave the CSU system annually (King et al., 2011).

Meanwhile, many English departments have designed innovative approaches to remedial assessment and instructional delivery. Some campuses replaced traditional placement exams with a directed-self-placement (DSP) model (Royer & Gilles, 2003). Students learn about different course options, evaluate their pre-college literacy experiences, and choose which writing course will best meet their needs. Other campuses eliminated pre-baccalaureate remedial courses and adopted a "stretch" model, which enrolls underprepared students in a yearlong, credit-bearing composition course taught by the same professor (Lalicker, 1999). All stretch coursework is college-level, but students have more time to develop their skills. This model reflects faculty interest in avoiding remedial labeling and has been shown to improve student outcomes relative to traditional remediation (Goen-Salter, 2008; Jenkins et al., 2010).

Nevertheless, system-wide remediation rates as measured by the placement exams remained relatively stagnant, motivating CSU administrators to design the Early Start Program. Existing programs such as Summer Bridge, which "provide students [. . .] with time to learn the ropes of college and to make the kinds of progress necessary to reach college-readiness" (Carter, 2007, p. 10), served as models for the policy. A chancellor's memorandum indicated Early Start was designed "to facilitate a student's graduation" by allowing students to start—and ideally complete—their remedial coursework over the summer. CSU administrators hoped the policy would not only increase student retention and progress, but also "reduce institutional and student cost" (Farar, 2013). Next, I discuss the conceptual framework undergirding the present study.

Conceptual Framework:
Cognition, Sense-Making, and Policy Implementation

Implementation studies have historically adopted institutional or rational approaches, whereby policymaking assumes a hierarchal, coherent, and linear process (McLaughlin, 1987; Schofield, 2004). From these perspectives, a policy articulates a course of actions to address an educational problem (Harman, 1984), and a system of rewards and sanctions is imposed on local actors to achieve stated objectives (Browbrow & Dryzek, 1987). Traditional frameworks assume that policy problems are uncontested and policy messages are straightforward (Trowler, 2002). Policies in practice that fail to meet legislators' intentions are attributed to flawed policy design, insufficient institutional capacity, or implementer misunderstanding or noncompliance (Firestone, 1989; McLaughlin, 1990; Van Meter & Van Horn, 1975).

More recent scholarship has advanced interpretive frameworks that acknowledge the complexity and ambiguity of policymaking (Coburn, 2005; Honig, 2006; Weick, 1995). The interpretive paradigm holds that realities are socially constructed and acknowledges the subjectivity of knowledge and experience (Denzin & Lincoln, 2001). From this view, educational policy directives are not merely instrumental but expressive (Yanow, 1996); policy meanings cannot be taken for granted (Spillane, 2000). Investigation into policy implementation thus requires attention to how stakeholders make sense of a given reform (Coburn, 2001).

This study employs a cognitive framework to examine Early Start implementation through a focus on English faculty's sense-making. A cognitive perspective suggests that how implementers make sense of a policy is crucial to comprehend its translation to practice (Spillane, 2000), which in turn helps to understand policy contexts, explain policy outcomes, and improve policy designs. The construct of sense-making derives from organizational theory and refers to "the making of sense" (Weick, 1995, p. 4). Weick (1995) posited that sense-making is an active process whereby people "generate what they interpret" (p. 13) by integrating new information with their existing schemas. Sense-making is shaped by the interaction of various internal and external factors (Mills, 1998; Yanow, 1996). People act based on the interpretations they construct (Coburn, 2006; Spillane, 2004). Therefore, a cognitive lens seeks insight into policy implementation by focusing on the sense-making of local actors (Spillane, 2000).

The cognitive framework for policy implementation developed by Spillane et al. (2002) suggests that sense-making occurs through the interplay of three key constructs: (a) policy signals, (b) individual cognition, and (c) situated cognition. First, local actors' sense-making is influenced by policy signals, or the external representations used to articulate policy goals (Spillane et al., 2002). These representations include the language, objects, and actions associated with a particular reform and its implementing organizations (Mills, 1998; Yanow, 1996), and provide the tools with which local actors construct meaning. Notably, these signals are value-laden, reflecting the concerns and interpretations of policy designers. Second, sense-making is influenced by individual cognition, or one's prior knowledge, beliefs, experiences, values, and emotions pertaining to a policy issue. Actors' understandings of a policy are necessarily constituted "in terms of what is already known and believed" (Spillane et al., 2002, p. 395). Third, situated cognition, or an individual's social context, influences sense-making and action (Spillane et al., 2002). Situated cognition refers to the "complex web of organizational structures, professional affiliations, social networks, and traditions" (p. 404). Sense-making occurs in relation to one's communities, organizations, and relationships.

Notably, these three constructs do not operate in isolation; sense-making occurs through their interaction. Extending from this frame, a distributed perspective on cognition foregrounds the situation (i.e., social context) as the central unit of analysis (Spillane, Reiser, & Gomez, 2006). This frame posits that "sense-making practice is distributed in the interactive web of actors, artifacts, and situation" (Spillane et al., 2006, p. 60). The environment is not merely the setting in which individual cognition occurs; cognitive practice is constituted by the social contexts and interactions in which individuals are embedded.

The distributed perspective on cognition is particularly useful to investigate how English faculty made sense of and enacted the Early Start Program. I assume that sense-making occurs through the interplay of policy representations, preexisting cognitive schemas, and situation (Spillane et al., 2002). However, because faculty members belong to a particular discipline (i.e., English and composition studies) and work on campuses with unique histories, philosophies, and programs, I focus on how faculty's social context shaped their approach to implementation. While it is well documented that practitioners and policymakers often have unique perspectives on educational problems (Cohen, Moffitt, & Goldin, 2007), knowing how and why faculty members make sense of remediation initiatives is crucial to garner a more holistic view of the policy problem and improve reform efforts.

Prior Research

Two implementation studies focus on remediation policy and offer insight into the present inquiry. Focusing on three community colleges, Shaw (1997) found that each college responded to system-wide policy in ways that reflected their local ideology around developmental education. Thus she argued that state-level political and ideological values do not directly translate to individual institutions. Mills (1998) adopted an interpretive lens to investigate the implementation of a reform in Oklahoma that mandated non-credit-bearing remedial coursework for underprepared students. Findings revealed that local cultures, values, and interests shaped the policy in practice. As such, the enacted policy did not necessarily align with the original aim of the policy designers. Similar to Shaw (1997), Mills (1998) concluded that despite the top-down nature of policymaking in public higher education systems, policy meanings "cannot be determined or dictated from above" (p. 694).

Rationale

The present study contributes to existing scholarship in three primary ways. As I have suggested, the literature on remediation reveals little emphasis on faculty perspectives (Saxon & Boylan, 2010). Policymakers' growing interest in reforming remediation has created opportunities for improvement. Yet many practitioners and researchers of developmental education feel, according to Saxon and Boylan, that they "are being marginalized and dictated to in an effort to find a quick fix to the 'remedial education problem'" (p. 35). This study highlights the experiences of faculty who are directly involved with developmental programs and students.

Second, most of the scholarship on remediation focuses on community colleges, which provide the majority of remedial education (Deil-Amen, 2010; Perin, 2006). Yet public four-year institutions play an integral role in expanding access for underrepresented students, and the place of remediation in these universities is highly contested. By exploring the Early Start Program in the CSUs, this inquiry expands the literature base on remediation in four-year institutions.

The third contribution of this study pertains to implementation research specifically. In general, implementation studies of remediation reforms are few. Moreover, the cognitive frame has not yet been applied to remedial policy implementation. The studies of remedial policy implementation described above draw attention to implementers' interpretations and the role of local contexts and cultures (Mills, 1998; Shaw, 1997). However, the construct of sense-making extends beyond interpretation to consider how actors come to interpret. As Spillane et al. (2002) assert, "if implementation scholarship is to move beyond simply documenting that policies [. . .] evolve during implementation, it must [. . .] unpack how and why policy evolves as it does" (p. 419). By employing a cognitive frame, this study helps to explain why local actors behave in certain ways and thus may inform policy design efforts.

In sum, I am suggesting that faculty perspectives, remedial education in four-year institutions, and local actors' sense-making warrant inquiry to strengthen extant scholarship on remediation reform. I argue that incorporating the views of ground-level stakeholders may enhance understanding of this policy problem and improve policy development.

Research Design

This qualitative inquiry utilized case study methodology to uncover rich and detailed descriptions of how faculty members' sense-making of the English Early Start policy shaped implementation (Lichtman, 2006;

Stake, 2005). This case study is descriptive, drawing from theory to describe the characteristics of a phenomenon (Yin, 1993), and instrumental, or designed to provide insight into the complexities of writing remediation reform (Stake, 2005).

Sample

Sampling in qualitative research is purposeful to maximize the collection of data that will offer insights into the particular research question (Creswell, 2007). A brief overview of CSU governance is useful to explain how I approached sampling. The 23 CSU campuses are governed by a chancellor and a board of trustees who adopt policies and manage fiscal and human resources ("Rules Governing the Board," 2012). Campus presidents and administrators are responsible for implementing CSU mandates, though campuses have historically exercised a fair amount of autonomy (Klompien, 2012). Professional organizations such as the English Council facilitate cross-campus collaboration and advocacy on behalf of faculty.

Although the 23 CSU campuses have unique approaches to writing remediation, first-year composition programs fall into four general categories: (a) traditional models, (b) developmental phases of mainstreaming models (i.e. stretch program and/or DSP), (c) fully implemented stretch models, and (d) fully implemented stretch and directed-self-placement (DSP). According to the CSU English Council website, 12 campuses have fully implemented the stretch model, DSP, or both, and all but three campuses are in the process of developing these programs. I selected a representative sample of 12 campuses, distributed across each category of remedial programming, for in-depth data collection1 (see Table 6.1).

The implementation of Early Start was a complex undertaking that enlisted multiple actors and departments at each CSU campus. From the 12 selected campuses and the Chancellor's Office, I drew a sample of 27 participants to represent the range of stakeholders involved in implementation. First, the associate vice presidents of Academic Affairs were designated the point people for Early Start implementation on each campus (CSU EO1048, 2010). Administration of Early Start fell under the purview of Extended Studies, Extended Education, or Continuing Education, (the name varies across campuses), because the coursework is offered outside the regular academic calendar. The Admissions, Enrollment, and Testing offices played a role in managing students' test scores, course assignments,

TABLE 6.1. Campuses, remedial programs, and participants

Remedial program	Traditional	Developmental phase	Fully implemented stretch	Fully implemented stretch + DSP
Number of campuses (N = 12)	3	3	2	4

and grades. Finally, English and math faculty were responsible for developing curriculum and providing instructors.

After preliminary interviews with key players in the Chancellor's Office and on select campuses, snowball sampling (Lincoln & Guba, 1985) was employed to acquire additional contacts that played a prominent role in Early Start implementation. While I focused on faculty's sense-making of the program's English component, individuals responsible for administering Early Start provided additional insights into campus contexts and the implementation process.

Data Collection

Data collection took place over a five-month period, beginning in the spring semester of 2013 following the first summer of implementation. This time frame allowed for investigation into participants' experiences with initial implementation as well as their preparation for the program's second year. Data were drawn from interviews and extensive document analysis (Creswell, 2007; Hatch, 2002; Stake, 2005). Twenty-seven formal, semi-structured interviews were conducted in person, by phone, or by email, ranging from 30 to 90 minutes. Participants were relatively evenly distributed across campuses and included: three principal policy designers from the Chancellor's Office, five high-level campus administrators, four employees in administrative departments (e.g., offices of Admissions, Enrollment, Testing, and Department of Extended Ed, Continuing Ed, etc.), seven English or Composition department chairs, and eight composition faculty members or instructors. The breakdown of participants' roles is shown in Table 6.2.

TABLE 6.2. Participants' roles

Participants' roles	Chancellor's office policy designers	Campus-level administrators	Administrative employees	English or composition administrators	English/composition faculty
Number of participants (N = 27)	3	5	4	7	8

Four interview protocols were developed based on the participant's role—policy designer, campus administrator, administrative employee, and English or composition faculty. The same interview protocol was used for all modes of communication to ensure consistency.

In addition, document analysis was conducted based on a wide range of sources. Legislative documents related to the Early Start policy and web-based information on CSU student demographics and remediation rates provided background context. Early Start student resources from the CSU website offered insight into program logistics and curriculum. Faculty participants shared materials relevant to first-year composition programs in general and Early Start in particular. Early Start documents included plans for program structure and curriculum. Finally, correspondence among faculty members and upper level administrators was used to better understand local actors' sense-making and consequent approaches to implementation.

Data Analysis

Data analysis began during the data collection process to ensure sufficient data to substantiate findings (Hatch, 2002). Various strategies were employed to ensure trustworthiness (e.g., triangulation, member checks). Document data, particularly program design documents and web-based program information, were used to triangulate interview data. Coding and categorizing were completed via an iterative process involving close review of documents, interview transcriptions, journal entries, and memos

(Bogdan & Biklen, 2003). The constant comparative method (Glaser & Strauss, 1967) was used to identify emerging patterns and themes across data sources and to generate findings (Anfara, Brown, & Mangione, 2002).

Findings

Data analysis suggests that faculty members generally opposed the Early Start mandate and their sense-making was shaped by two principal influences: their professional roles and campus contexts. First, faculty members constructed similar meanings of Early Start policy symbols through their professional roles, or shared expertise in the teaching and learning of literacy. Yet participants' sense-making was also shaped in varying ways by their unique campus contexts. Their shared opposition to the program motivated outright resistance to implementation initially. Yet once they learned they had no choice but to comply, participants adapted the program as best they could to fit their local needs. I present data in two broad sections: (a) sense-making and (b) implementation. An overview of findings is shown below in Figure 6.1.

FIGURE 6.1. English faculty sense-making and implementation of the Early Start Program

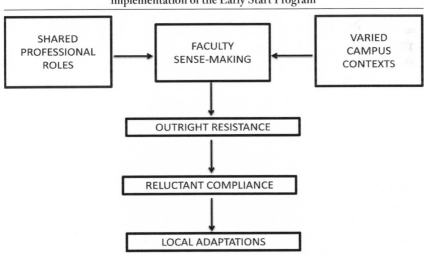

Faculty Sense-Making

Shared professional roles. Faculty made sense of the Early Start policy through the perspective of their roles as teachers and experts in the field of composition studies. Their two common concerns about Early Start are discussed below.

Stigmatizing underprepared students. First, participants perceived that their constructions of underprepared students were at odds with those embodied in CSU policies such as Early Start. Many critiqued the construct of a "remedial" student. One professor explained, "[T]hose aware of the history of writing instruction understand that no generation of students has come to the university prepared to write at the university." Said another faculty member, "teachers have always taught classes with students of varied skill levels." Another professor challenged the notion that students labeled "remedial" by the English Placement Test (EPT) are incapable of completing college-level work: "That's just not the case in my experience when I see these students in classes. They might need more time than we might think they need, but . . . they haven't had the opportunity to do the things we really want them to do." Faculty members tended to portray students as entering college with varied literacy skills.

However, faculty members perceived that the Early Start Program reflected deficit thinking about underprepared students. As one professor explained, in the instance of Early Start, "I think remediation functions as a way to say we can fix something. We're going to fix student writing. We're going to get all these people who are designated as remedial [and] get them to do something that says they're not remedial anymore." Many faculty members felt that by requiring only a particular group of students to take summer school, Early Start framed underprepared students in problematic ways. Said one professor, "[CSU administrators] still believe that students are coming in deficient. Rather than coming in different." Participants thus problematized Early Start for stigmatizing underprepared students—who are mostly low-income and of color. As one faculty member explained, Early Start "is sort of indiscriminately leveled at people who are poor or linguistically non-mainstream."

Creating poor conditions for literacy learning. Faculty members' expertise of composition studies also shaped their sense-making of Early Start. They emphasized that learning to read and write was a "process" that required certain conditions such as time and quality feedback. One faculty member explained, "The only thing that really works with novice writers is if they get to spend more time writing and talking to somebody about their writing." Yet participants perceived that Early Start did not create these conditions. As one professor stated, "all of the research shows that [literacy] skills develop slowly and over time and with lots of instruction and interaction, exactly what Early Start doesn't provide." Many acknowledged that Early Start could be effective in math, but maintained that, in the words of one campus administrator, policymakers "shouldn't treat Math and English equally." As one participant said, "it's possible to wake up one morning, not know what the quadratic formula is, and the next morning you do know it. There's a light switch in math. There's no light switch in English."

Faculty thus tended to interpret the Early Start policy as an attempted "quick fix" or "inoculation approach" that was misaligned with the needs of underprepared writers. The program's one-unit minimum requirement represented an important policy signal. As one faculty member explained, "[the Chancellor's Office] is asking us to move a group of students from one area into another area based on a one-credit summer course, 15 hours of work, but all our experience says that student writing doesn't improve in 15 hours." Another participant echoed this sentiment: "there's no time within a one-credit Early Start structure to do much of anything meaningful." Others suggested that a one-unit course "doesn't do anything," "isn't going to change a lifetime of language practices," or "is a waste of students' time." In sum, faculty's professional roles led them to develop two shared concerns regarding Early Start: one pertaining to student labeling and the other pertaining to writing pedagogy.

Varied campus contexts. While faculty members constructed similar meanings of Early Start through the lens of their professional roles, participants' sense-making also varied based on their specific campus contexts. As discussed above, CSU campuses have developed distinct first-year writing programs and serve unique student populations. As one faculty member explained, "What college readiness means is different on different campuses."

One campus, for instance, had designed its own version of a mandatory summer remediation program years before the Early Start policy. The Early Start mandate encountered little to no resistance from actors on this campus, for whom a summer program was already the norm. As one participant shared, "we got used to having a mandated Early Start. The CSU mandate for us is kind of irrelevant." Participants acknowledged, however, that their experience was unique to their campus; said one professor, "our campus made its own choices and then went its own way." The other campuses in the sample fell into one of three categories: traditional, stretch, or directed-self-placement (DSP), with some campuses using both stretch and DSP. These contexts shaped faculty's sense-making of Early Start in particular ways.

Traditional. Participants working on campuses with traditional remedial programs insisted that Early Start was unnecessary because their developmental students already moved through their course sequence successfully. Said one faculty member, "I can expect every quarter, about 90% of our [remedial] students to receive credit for the course and then move on. If our students are succeeding and they're passing, then why do we have Early Start?" Another participant cited research showing the effectiveness of the program on her campus: "the [students] who did those remedial courses end up better prepared than the ones who just tested into the higher levels of English." Because faculty members perceived that students were already benefitting from their existing programs, they did not perceive the need for Early Start.

Stretch. For participants working on stretch campuses that no longer offer remedial courses, the Early Start mandate represented both a philosophical and practical conflict. These faculty members emphasized that "we don't believe in remediation" or "we don't see any of our students as remedial." Participants used phrases such as: "quote-unquote remediate," "the so-called remedial courses," and "what the administrators were calling remedial concerns." One explained: "we think students who have earned a high school diploma are ready to come in and take college-level courses and not be stigmatized and ushered into separate paths."

Actors on stretch campuses thus perceived the Early Start Program as attempting to remedy a problem they did not have. In the words of one participant, "we don't have a remediation problem because none of our students are remedial." One faculty member opined, "the point of Early Start is to reduce the amount of remediation that students need, [but] all our courses are university level composition." Another participant stated, "We don't even have remedial classes that [students] need to get out of." Faculty running stretch programs did not see the relevance of the Early Start Program for their local context. They further worried that by making their students take summer remediation, Early Start undermined their local philosophies because, in the words of one participant, "it created a remedial course we don't have."

DSP. The sense-making of faculty members on campuses that assign students to first year writing courses using directed-self-placement (DSP) was shaped by their views of the English Placement Test (EPT). DSP allows students to place themselves based on evaluation of their prior writing experiences and information about course offerings. Faculty members on these campuses cited problems with the EPT. In the words of one professor, "[an EPT score] is fairly meaningless in terms of how students will do in an actual course where you do actual writing." Many pointed out that faculty developed the test in the 1970s for local use and diagnostic purposes rather than system-wide placement. Others suggested that test administration had been, as one participant said, "taken over by a big testing company." Professors in these departments had designed DSP mechanisms to reduce the role of test scores in course placement.

These actors problematized the Early Start Program for assigning students to summer coursework based on their EPT score. As one faculty member explained, "[DSP] campuses are trying to say, 'Look, EPT is just one small bit of evidence. We're trying to get away from using the EPT as the sole determining [placement] factor and here you [the chancellor] are telling us that's what we have to do.'" Many participants worried that Early Start would send contradictory messages to students. One faculty member said, "All the materials from our campus say, 'We do not use your EPT scores. You will get to choose which freshman course you want.' Now at the same time, the Chancellor's Office said, 'If your EPT score is too low, you must take a remedial course called Early Start.'" Participants perceived the mandate as undermining their alternative placement mechanisms and even expanding the role of the EPT; by creating a precondition to enrollment for students scoring below the cut point, according to one faculty member, "the Early Start Program has turned [the EPT] into a default admissions test."

Implementation Process

From resistance to compliance. Faculty's view that Early Start undermined their professional experience and knowledge shaped their engagement in the implementation process. As one participant explained, "the conversation in English Council seemed to be focused on whether to resist or embrace this mandate." English faculty initially refused to comply. One professor explained, "the [English and] composition faculty had decided to not participate, to not design an Early Start English course or to get involved in any way." In the words of another participant, "[we] were essentially saying 'we're not going to do it. We refuse to do it.'"

However, two factors motivated faculty members to participate in implementation. On the one hand, participants felt that they needed to support their campus administrators. As one participant shared, "for a couple of months, we argued back and forth, but [our campus administrator] felt she had an obligation to carry out this law." On the other hand, faculty members were told that if they would not design an Early Start program, someone else would. One professor explained that when his department initially declined to take part, "the school said, 'Okay, we'll turn [Early Start] over to Pearson.' And then [our composition director] said, 'Wait wait, wait, okay, we'll do it.'" Faculty members on other campuses recounted similar pressures. According to one participant, "our choices were to let somebody completely unskilled and untrained in reading and writing instruction be at the helm of this particular project, or for us to design what we thought was the least objectionable thing we could do."

At that point, English faculty reluctantly engaged in the implementation process. As one professor explained, "I did my job as the writing program director. I developed an Early Start Program because that's my job. But I complained about it the whole time to anybody who would listen, because that's also a part of my job is to do what's best for the students." Thus, while local stakeholders ultimately complied with the mandate, in the words of one campus administrator, "there was a lot of concern and a lot of push back and a lot of whining too."

Local adaptations. Variation across campuses shaped participants' sensemaking and in turn their approach to implementation. Faculty created course structures and curricula that best fit their department's goals and practices, with some fulfilling only the minimum, one-unit requirement, and others developing more extensive courses. Many English faculty members refused to create three-unit courses based on principle. As one participant explained, "we were minimally compliant. We all thought it was a terrible idea and I was able to convince the higher-ups to keep things as small as possible. So we ran a whole bunch of these little one-unit classes." Another participant described a similar approach: "I think [our one-unit] online course is a way of trying to spend as little money as we can on our campus on something that we don't necessarily believe is good or effective." Campuses running stretch programs tended to develop only one-unit courses since they had no remedial courses for students to finish early; said one participant, "we weren't going to re-create the remedial structure that we had gotten rid of."

Other departments tried to use the mandate as an opportunity to reform their programs in desirable ways. One faculty member explained that although her campus did not have remedial courses, she designed the three-unit course as a way to offer students additional literacy support. Several campuses capitalized on the mandate to pilot stretch or DSP models. One participant recounted how his campus used "the Early Start push for redesign as a vehicle" to implement a stretch model. Another professor said, "We decided if we were doing [Early Start], it would be a good way to begin to pilot some materials for our directed-self-placement program." Many departments thus developed curriculum that introduced students to different course options and guided them in choosing their composition course. In the words of one faculty member, "it's kind of lemonade out of lemons. It's kind of the idea that you take what's given to you and you develop something positive out of it. That's what we did." Thus, while faculty members generally felt that the policy was problematic, they worked to adapt Early Start in ways that best fit with their local programs and goals.

Discussion

Increased need for college graduates and concern for widespread underpreparedness have sparked a flurry of remediation reforms over the past two decades (Parker et al., 2010). Writing remediation is inherently political and represents particularly contested terrain for policy development (Goen-Salter, 2008; Soliday, 1996), but the voices of faculty members have been largely excluded from policy research on remedial education (Saxon & Boylan, 2013). This study employed the construct of sense-making to investigate the implementation of the CSU Early Start Program, focusing on why and how English faculty responded to the policy. Data analysis indicated that faculty interpretations of the needs of developmental English students differed extensively from those embodied in the CSU mandate. While this divide between administrators and practitioners is unsurprising (Cohen et al., 2007), I am arguing that acknowledging faculty perspectives is necessary to better understand the challenges associated with remedial education in four-year institutions and improve reform efforts.

Findings showed that faculty members' professional roles and campus contexts influenced their sense-making of Early Start in different ways. Their shared roles as teachers and literacy experts led them to construct similar meanings of the policy, which fueled their outright resistance to implementation. That faculty members' professional roles shaped their sense-making is consistent with existing literature. Spillane et al. (2002) suggested that professional specializations, or memberships in professional communities, facilitate participants' development of shared "norms, knowledge, perspectives, commitments, and often a language or vocabulary" (p. 409). These professional discourses shape how individuals see themselves, engage with their work, and make sense of reforms (Clark, 1983; Van Maanen & Barley, 1984).

Faculty's shared experience as literacy instructors led them to reject the construct of the remedial student and in turn view Early Start as discriminatory. This finding speaks to existing composition research that problematizes how underprepared students are framed via policymaking (Gutierrez et al., 2009; Soliday, 1996). Composition scholars have suggested that many remediation policies embody the assumption that students from non-mainstream literacy backgrounds are deficient (Goen & Gillotte-Tropp, 2003). Many faculty members rejected practices that separate and label students who are in different stages of literacy development. Thus participants suggested that by requiring a particular group of students to complete summer coursework, Early Start stigmatized those who had been underserved by the K-12 system.

Faculty's concern for remedial labeling was exacerbated by their perception that the treatment was flawed. Policy signals played an important role in faculty's meaning-making (Spillane et al., 2002). Faculty interpreted the parameters of the policy, especially the one-unit, 15-hour minimum, as failing to create conditions that facilitate writing improvement. This concern grew stronger in light of faculty's interpretations of the policy objectives. The stated goal—to allow students' acceleration through or movement out of remediation—led participants to feel that CSU administrators were setting unrealistic expectations for literacy teaching and learning. Faculty perceived the policy's parameters as misaligned with its goals, echoing Mills' (1998) assertion that policy meanings "cannot be determined or dictated from above" (p. 694).

Participants' pedagogical opposition to the program underscores the particular challenges associated with reforming literacy remediation (Rose,

1985, 2011; Soliday, 1996). Spillane, Reiser, and Gomez (2006) have argued that policy messages are understood through social practices but these practices vary across disciplines within the same organization; English teachers tend to participate in these practices more actively than math teachers. That English faculty strongly opposed Early Start while math faculty did not speaks to this claim. The English Council served as an important space for faculty's engagement in collective sense-making around Early Start policy signals and allowed them to show unified resistance to the mandate.

This study also sheds light on the tensions that arise between policymakers and practitioners around literacy remediation. Existing literature suggests that policy development tends to ignore the pedagogical and curricular aspects of composition (Goen-Salter, 2008; Saxon & Boylan, 2010). Most faculty members perceived that the Early Start policy embodied this problem. Given their view that the mandate stigmatized underrepresented groups, faculty also saw themselves as protecting and defending students from marginalization by the Chancellor's Office. Notably, whether the CSU administrators intended to frame students in problematic ways mattered little for faculty's sense-making; faculty responded to Early Start based on their interpretation that the policy reinforced deficit thinking. The sense-making framework is useful in this regard—the question is not whether one party or the other is right or wrong, but rather how stakeholders come to understand and act on the meanings embedded in a particular reform (Spillane et al., 2002). That faculty interpreted this program as harming rather than helping students is important because it represents a barrier to reform and suggests the need for better communication among policy designers and local actors around literacy remediation.

Given participants' rejection of the policy, their response to implementation might aptly be characterized as reluctant compliance. They participated only because they perceived they had no choice. This finding is reflective of the challenge of top-down policymaking in large public systems. Simply because implementers comply with a mandate does not mean they embrace the policy in the manner desired by legislators (Mills, 1998; Shaw, 1997). Faculty's motivations for complying, however, are significant. Participants did not wish to defy their campus administrators who were obligated to implement Early Start. Faculty's compliance also speaks to their dedication to students, as they recognized that allowing an external organization with minimal literacy expertise to design the curriculum might not meet students' learning needs. In this respect, despite the controversy spurred by the Early Start policy, the story reveals the deep commitment of these stakeholders to student success.

While faculty's professional roles shaped their sense-making in similar ways, variation stemmed from participants' unique campus contexts. Participants interpreted the program in relation to their local needs, philosophies, and goals (Mills, 1998; Shaw, 1997). Those on campuses with traditional remedial courses cited the success of their programs as a reason why Early Start was unwarranted. Those on stretch campuses viewed the policy as aiming to fix a problem that their campuses had already solved. Those using directed-self-placement to assign students to first-year coursework problematized the mandate for identifying underprepared students based on the English Placement Test (EPT). Finally, where mandatory summer remediation was already provided, the policy motivated little to no resistance because it did not require significant local change. This variation highlights the importance of institutional culture, or an organization's "expression of shared norms and values" (Harris, 2007, p. 4), in shaping policy and practice (Kezar & Eckel, 2002; Mills & Hyle, 2001; Tierney, 1988).

The philosophy undergirding the Early Start mandate—that if students have the opportunity to start remedial coursework sooner, they may finish faster—makes logical sense. However, the problem the policy aimed to fix (i.e., non-credit-bearing remedial coursework impeding student progress) and the strategy for identifying underprepared students (i.e., low scores on the EPT) were not congruent with the established practices of many campuses. Although the policy design allowed for local autonomy and adaptation with curriculum development, this flexibility did not affect many participants' concern that the ultimate goal of the policy was unachievable given their program structures. Thus policy scholars have argued for considering local institutional context in policy development (Harris, 2007; Mills, 1998).

Given varying local demands, some departments complied with the policy only minimally and a few created more comprehensive courses. Many devised ways to use Early Start to achieve their local goals such as piloting a directed-self-placement model, making, as one participant said, "lemonade out of lemons." Thus some faculty expressed they were able to create something positive out of the policy despite their philosophical disagreement. While the fact that implementers adapt policies to meet their local needs has been well documented (McLaughlin, 2006; Schneider & Ingram, 1990; Yanow, 1996), the sense-making framework offers insight into how and why this takes place (Spillane et al., 2006). Faculty members' approaches to implementation cannot be characterized as motivated by either their roles or contexts alone. Participants strove to reconcile their professional motivations for resisting the policy with the needs of their specific writing programs. This study suggests that professional expertise interacts with local organizational cultures and practices in complex ways to shape implementers' actions.

More fundamentally, this inquiry underscores the importance of including faculty voices in remediation policy research. How faculty members make sense of developmental education shapes how they respond to reform, and their views often differ from those of policymakers (Cohen et al., 2007). Faculty members possess disciplinary expertise and local insight into students' under-preparedness that cannot be obtained from 30,000 feet in the air. I am not suggesting that faculty members are right and policymakers are wrong. Rather, I am suggesting that the nuances and challenges of remediation cannot be fully understood without examining both points of view. For example, most policy research relies on remediation rates reported by higher education systems and derived from wide-scale placement tests. Roughly 34% of CSU students required English remediation in fall 2012 according to the EPT (CSU Analytic Studies, 2013). This statistic implies that about one-third of CSU freshmen are taking non-credit-bearing remedial courses, not progressing toward a degree. Yet this study revealed that more than half of CSU English departments do not use the EPT and/or do not offer traditional remediation; the experiences of underprepared CSU students are actually quite varied. Faculty perspectives support a more nuanced understanding of the remedial education landscape and, in turn, improved policy design.

Future Directions

This study highlights several areas for future research. First, more research into faculty perspectives on developmental education is needed to help clarify the policy context. Given the persistent divide between policy and practice (Goen & Gillotte-Tropp, 2003), inquiry into faculty's experiences may also facilitate greater collaboration among administrators and faculty and improved policy design. In addition, this study focused on the sense-making of local actors, but this framework can also be employed to examine how policy designers make sense of reforms. Investigation into the factors that shape administrators' sense-making would be useful to better understand how and why remediation policies are constructed in particular ways and with particular parameters for local implementation. At the same time, implementation research has tended to focus on either policy designers or implementers (McLaughlin, 2006). While this scholarship has yielded important findings, studies involving actors at all levels may provide a more complete picture of how policymaking unfolds and why challenges arise.

This study explored the implementation of CSU's Early Start Program through the lens of faculty sense-making to uncover ground-level perspectives on the challenges of remedial writing reform. I have suggested that faculty's professional roles and campus contexts shaped their meaning-making and motivated responses to the policy that were both unified and varied. That faculty constructed unique meanings of developmental education is not surprising but warrants attention nonetheless. Identifying the perspectives of all relevant stakeholders may generate a more comprehensive understanding of student under-preparedness and college readiness, and in turn support improved reform efforts.

References

Academic Senate of the California State University (ASCSU). (2009). Opposition to Impending Implementation of Mandatory Early Start Programs. Resolution (AS-2895-09/APEP/AA). Approved May 2009. Retrieved from http://www.calstate.edu/Acadsen/Records/Resolutions/2008-2009/2895.shtml

Adams, P. (2010). *Creative ways to deal with remedial/developmental education. Persistence in high school and college: Tools to increase persistence and degree attainment.* Princeton, NJ: Princeton University Press.

Adelman, C. (2006). *The toolbox revisited: Paths to degree completion from high school through college.* Washington, DC: U.S. Department of Education.

Alliance for Excellent Education. (2008). *Paying Double: Inadequate High Schools and Community College Remediation.* Washington, DC: Author.

Anfara, V. A. Jr., Brown, K. M., & Mangione, T. L. (2002). Qualitative analysis on stage: Making the research process more public. *Educational Researcher, October* (2002), 28–38.

Bacchi, C. (2000). Policy as discourse: What does it mean? Where does it get us? *Discourse: Studies in the cultural politics of education, 21*(1), 45–57.

Bahr, P. R. (2010). Revisiting the efficacy of postsecondary remediation: The moderating effects of depth/breadth of deficiency. *The Review of Higher Education, 33*(2), 177–205.

Bailey, T. (2008). Challenge and opportunity: Rethinking the role and function of developmental education in community college (CCRC Working Paper No. 14). Community College Research Center, Teachers College, Columbia University. Retrieved from http://ccrc. tc.columbia.edu/Publication.asp?uid=658

Bettinger, E. P., Boatman, A., & Long, B. T. (2013). Student supports: Developmental education and other academic programs. *The Future of Children, 23*(1), 93–115.

Bettinger, E. P., & Long, B. T. (2009). Addressing the needs of underprepared students in higher education: Does college remediation work? *Journal of Human Resources, 44*(3), 736–771.

Bleiklie, I. (2000). Policy regimes and policy making. In M. Kogan, M. Bauer, I Bleiklie, and M. Henkel (eds.), *Transforming higher education: A comparative study* (pp. 53–87). London: Jessica Kingsley.

Bogdan, R. C., & Biklen, S. K. (2003). *Qualitative research for education: An introduction to theories and methods* (4th ed.). Boston: Allyn & Bacon.

Breland, H., Bridgeman, B., & Fowles, M. (1999). Writing assessment in admission to higher education: Review and framework. *College Board Report No. 99-3* (pp. 1–44). Princeton, NJ: Educational Testing Service.

Browbrow, D. B., & Dryzek, J. S. (1987). *Policy analysis by design.* Pittsburgh, PA: University of Pittsburgh Press.

Calcagno, J. C., & Long, B. T. (2008) *The impact of postsecondary remediation using a regression discontinuity approach: Addressing endogenous sorting and noncompliance (NCPR Working Paper).* New York: National Center for Postsecondary Research.

California State University (CSU). (2011). CMS Early Start Program phase 1 objectives: Frequently Asked Questions. Retrieved from http://www. google.com/url?sa=t&rct=j&q=&esrc=s&source=web&cd=1&cad=r-ja&ved=0CDUQFjAA&url=http%3A%2F%2Fwww.calstate.edu%-2FacadAff%2FEarlyStart%2Fdocs%2FEarly_Start_FAQ-8172011. pdf&ei=ePodUYX8E4SLjAKi2oGACg&usg=AFQjCNE3RtQs7hx-cgG9VM8afVem07I4_9g&sig2=lUqoeEwShD3re9362ztfpw

"The California State University." (n.d.). California State University: Working for California. Website. Retrieved 15 April 2013 from http:// www.calstate.edu

California State University (CSU) Analytic Studies. (2013). CSU Freshman

Remediation System-wide. Retrieved 2 September 2013 from http://www.asd.calstate.edu/remediation/12/Rem_Sys_fall2012.htm

California State University (CSU) English Council. (April 2010). *CSU English Council Position Statement: Mandatory Early Start.* Retrieved from http://csuenglishcouncil.wordpress.com/2010/04/21/psmandatoryearlystart2010/

California State University (CSU) English Council. (April 2011). *Statement on Early Start Program.* Adopted 15 April 2011. Retrieved from http://www.google.com/url?sa=t&rct=j&q=&esrc=s&source=web&cd=4&ved=0CEUQFjAD&url=http%3A%2F%2Fwww.csulb.edu%2Fdivisions%2Faa%2Fgrad_undergrad%2Fsenate%2Fdocuments%2FCSUEnglishCouncilonEarlyStartProgram.pdf&ei=QdIdUZL5AcH7igK_vIGQDQ&usg=AFQjCNFIfglJfQnYdBCXK8bgAkhBnyRc2g&sig2=d2kuzfEtS6Dl8ifH5TVTVQ

California State University (CSU) Exec. Order No. 1048. (EO1048) (2010). Retrieved from http://www.calstate.edu/eo/EO-1048.html

Carter, H. L. (2007, September 19). Minutes of meeting of Committee on Educational Policy. Long Beach, CA: Trustees of the California State University. Retrieved from http://wenku.baidu.com/view/97803f49c850ad02de804121.html?from=related

Clark, B. (1983). *The higher education system: Academic organization in cross-national perspective.* Berkeley, CA: University of California Press.

Coburn, C. E. (2001). Collective sensemaking about reading: How teachers mediate reading policy in their professional communities. *Educational Evaluation and Policy Analysis, 23,* 145–170.

Coburn, C. E. (2005). Shaping teacher sensemaking: School leaders and the enactment of reading policy. *Educational Policy, 19*(3), 476–509.

Coburn, C. E. (2006). Framing the problem of reading instruction: Using frame analysis to uncover microprocesses of policy implementation. *American Educational Research Journal, 43,* 343–379.

Cohen, D. K., Moffitt, S. L., & Goldin, S. (2007). Policy and practice: The dilemma. *American Journal of Education, 113*(4), 515–548.

Colyar, J. E., & Stich, A. E. (2011). Discourses of remediation: Low-income students and academic identities. *American Behavioral Scientist, 55*(2) 121–141.

Complete College America. (2012). *Remediation: Higher Education's Bridge to Nowhere.* Washington, DC: Author.

Creswell, J. W. (2007). Qualitative inquiry and research design: Choosing among five traditions. Thousand Oaks, CA: Sage.

Crisco, V. (2002). Conflicting expectations: The politics of developmental education in California. In Higbee, J. L., Lundell, D. B., Duranczyk, I. M. (Eds.). *Developmental education: Policy and practice* (pp. 45–54). Auburn, CA: National Association for Developmental Education.

Crouch, M. K., & McNenny, G. (2000). Looking back, looking forward: California grapples with "remediation." *Journal of Basic Writing, 19*(2), 44–71.

Deil-Amen, R. (2011). Beyond remedial dichotomies: Are 'underprepared' college students a marginalized minority? *New Directions for Community Colleges, 155,* 59–71.

Duncan, G. J., & Murnane, R. J. (Eds.) (2011). *Whither opportunity? Rising inequality, schools, and children's life chances.* New York: Russell Sage.

Durst, R. K. (2006). Writing at the postsecondary level. In Smagorinsky, P. (Ed.). *Research on composition: Multiple perspectives on two decades of change.* New York: Teachers College Press.

Elbow, P., & Belanoff, P. (1986). Portfolios as a substitute for proficiency examinations. *College Composition and Communication, 37*(3), 336–339.

Fain, P. (2012, June 19). Overkill on remediation? *Inside Higher Ed.* Retrieved 19 September 2013 from http://www.insidehighered.com/news/2012/06/19/complete-college-america-declares-war-remediation

Farar, D. S. (2011, January 24-25). Minutes of meeting of Committee on Educational Policy. Long Beach, CA: Trustees of the California State University. Retrieved from https://www.google.com/url?sa=t&rct=j&q=&esrc=s&source=web&cd=3&ved=0CEMQFjAC&url=https%3A%2F%2Fwww.calstate.edu%2Fbot%2Fagendas%2Fmar11%2FEdPol.pdf&ei=gdcdUfKzJKmuigLunYGQBg&usg=AFQjCNGXmIgNeJP6HpYoFt0o4J32iWkvBw&sig2=F-8ZAqluxYfw4MQhxIl5KGQ

Farar, D. S. (2013, November 13). Minutes of meeting of Committee on Educational Policy. Long Beach, CA: Trustees of the California State University. Retrieved from http://www.google.com/url?sa=t&rct=j&q=&esrc=s&source=web&cd=3&ved=0CEAQFjAC&url=http%3A%2F%2Fwww.calstate.edu%2FBOT%2Fagendas%2Fjan13%2FEdPol.pdf&ei=8NYdUaPpDqnuiQKtwYHoCg&usg=AFQjCNE4I_GXCFYd1tew89X8ouoiDMZwDg&sig2=hFtDIzYory_U6vubgHeYrw

Firestone, W. A. (1989). Using reform: Conceptualizing district initiative. *Educational Evaluation and Policy Analysis, 11*(2), 151–164.

Glaser, B., & Strauss, A. (1967). *The discovery of grounded theory: Strategies for qualitative research.* Chicago: Aldine.

Goen-Salter, S. (2008). Critiquing the need to eliminate remediation: Lessons from San Francisco State. *Journal of Basic Writing, 27*(2), 81–105.

Goen, S., & Gillotte-Tropp, H. (2003). Integrating Reading and Writing: A Response to the Basic Writing "Crisis." *Journal of Basic Writing, 22*(2), 90–113.

Goudas, A. M., & Boylan, H. R. (2012). Addressing flawed research in developmental education. *Journal of Developmental Education, 36*(1), 2–13.

Green, L. A. (2011). College students' perceptions of the impact of developmental courses on their academic performance and persistence. Research in Developmental Education 24(1), 1–4.

Grubb, W. N., Boner, E., Frankel, K., Parker, L., Patterson, D., Gabriner, R., Hope, L., Shorring, E., Smith, B., Taylor, R., Walton, I., & Wilson, S. (2011). Assessment and alignment: The dynamic aspects of developmental education. [Working Paper #7]. Stanford, CA: Policy Analysis for California Education (PACE).

Gumport, P. J., & Bastedo, M. N. (2001). Academic stratification and endemic conflict: Remedial education policy at CUNY. *The Review of Higher Education, 24*(4), 333–349.

Gutierrez, K. D., Morales, P. Z., & Martinez, D. C. (2009). Re-mediating literacy: Culture, difference, and learning for students from non dominant communities. *Review of Research in Education, 33*, 212–245.

Handel, S. J., & Williams, R. A. (2011). Reimagining remediation. *Change: The Magazine of Higher Learning, 43*(2), 28–33.

Harman, G. (1984). Conceptual and theoretical issues. In J. R. Hough (Ed.). *Educational policy: An international survey* (pp. 13–29). London: Croom Helm.

Harris, M. S. (2007). From policy design to campus: Implementation of a tuition decentralization policy. *Education Policy Analysis Archives, 15*(16), 1–18.

Hatch, A. (2002). *Doing qualitative research in education settings.* Albany, NY: State University of New York Press.

Honig, M. (2006). Complexity and policy implementation: Challenges and opportunities for the field. In M. Honig (Ed.). *New Directions in Education Policy Implementation: Confronting Complexity* (pp. 1–23). Albany, NY: State University of New York Press.

Huot, B. (1996). Toward a new theory of writing assessment. *College Composition and Communication, 47*(4), 549–566.

Huot, B., & Schendel, E. (2010). Reflecting on assessment: Validity inquiry as ethical inquiry. *Journal of Teaching Writing, 17*(1 & 2), 37.

Jehangir, R. R. (2002). Higher education for whom? The battle to include developmental education at the four-year university. In Higbee, J. L., Lundell, D. B., Duranczyk, I. M. (Eds.). *Developmental education: Policy and practice* (pp. 17–34). Auburn, CA: National Association for Developmental Education.

Jenkins, D., Speroni, C., Belfield, C., Jaggars, S. S., & Edgecombe, N. (2010). A model for accelerating academic success of community college remedial English students: Is the accelerated learning program (ALP) effective and affordable? New York: Community College Research Center.

Juzwik, M. M., Curcic, S., Wolbers, K., Moxley, K. D., Dimling, L. M., & Shankland, R. K. (2006). Writing Into the 21st Century : An Overview of Research on Writing, 1999–2004. *Written Communication, 23*(4), 451–476. doi:10.1177/0741088306291619

Kegan, R., & Lahey, L. L. (2009). Immunity to change: How to overcome it and unlock the potential in yourself and your organization. Boston: Harvard Business Press.

Kezar, A., & Eckel, P. D. (2002). The effect of institutional culture on change strategies in higher education: Universal principles or culturally responsive concepts? *Journal of Higher Education, 73*(4), 435–460.

King, K. R., McEnvoy, A., & Teixeira, S. (2011). *Remediation as a civil rights issue in the California State University system.* Los Angeles: The Civil Rights Project.

Kingdon, J. (1984). *Agendas, alternatives, and public policies.* New York: Harper Collins College.

Klompien, K. J. (2012). "Speaking truth to power": A history of the California State University English Council. (Doctoral dissertation). Retrieved from Indiana University of Pennsylvania DSpace. http://hdl.handle.net/2069/1877.

Lalicker, W. B. (1999). A basic introduction to basic writing program structures: A baseline and five alternatives. *BWe: Basic Writing e-Journal, 1*(6).

Lazarick, L. (1997). Back to the basics: Remedial education. *Community College Journal, 68*(2), 11–15.

Lichtman, M. (200X). *Qualitative research in education: A user's guide.* Thousand Oaks, CA: Sage.

Lincoln, Y. S., & Guba, E. G. (1985). *Naturalistic inquiry.* Newbury Park, CA: Sage Publications.

Lipsky, M. (1980). *Street level bureaucracy: Dilemmas of the individual in public services.* Beverly Hills, CA: Sage.

Mac Donald, H. (1998, Winter). CUNY Could be great again. *City Journal.*

Marlink, J., & Wahleithner, J. (2011). *Improving students' academic writing: Building a bridge to success.* California Writing Project: National Writing Project Local Sites Research Initiative.

Mazzeo, C. (2002). Stakes for students: Agenda-setting and remedial education. *Review of Higher Education, 26*(1), 19–39.

McLaughlin, M. W. (1987). Learning from experience: Lessons from policy implementation. *Educational Evaluation and Policy Analysis, 9*(2), 171–178.

McLaughlin, M. W. (2006). Implementation Research in Education: Lessons Learned, Lingering Questions, New Opportunities. In M. Honig (Ed.). *New Directions in Education Policy Implementation,* (209–229). Albany, NY: State University of New York Press.

Michael, W., & Shaffer, P. (1979). A comparison of the validity of the test of standard written English (tswe) and of the California state university and colleges English placement test (csuc-ept) in the prediction of grades in a basic English composition course and of overall freshman-year grade point average. *Educational and Psychological Measurement, 39*(1), 131.

Mills, M. (1998). From coordinating board to campus: Implementation of a policy mandate on remedial education. *The Journal of Higher Education, 69*(6), 672-697.

Mills, M. R., & Hyle, A. E. (2001). No rookies on rookies: Compliance and opportunism in policy implementation. *Journal of Higher Education, 72*(4), 453–477.

Nystrand, M. (2006). The social and historical context of writing research. In C. A MacArthur, S. Graham, & J. Fitzgerald (Eds.), *Handbook of writing research,* (pp. 11–27). New York: Guilford.

Parker, T. L. (2007). Ending college remediation: Consequences for access and opportunity. *ASHE Lumina Policy Brief, 2,* (October 2007).

Parker, T. L., & Richardson, R. C. (2005). Ending remediation at CUNY: Implications for access and excellence. *Journal of Educational Research and Policy Studies, 5*(2), 1–22.

Parker, T. L., Bustillos, L. T., & Behringer, L. B. (2010). Remedial and developmental education policy at a crossroads. Boston: Getting Past Go & Policy Research on Preparation Access and Remedial Education (PRePARE). Retrieved from http://www.gettingpastgo.org/docs/Literature-Review-GPG.pdf

Perin, D. (2006). Can community colleges protect both access and standards? The problem of remediation. *Teachers College Record, 108*(3), 339–373.

Relles, S. R., & Tierney, W. G. (2013). The Challenge of Writing Remediation: Can Composition Research Inform Higher Education Policy? *Teachers College Record, 115*, 1–45.

Rose, M. (1985). The language of exclusion. *College English 47*(8), 341–59.

Rose, M. (1989). The politics of remediation. In *Lives on the boundary: The struggles and achievements of America's underprepared* (pp. 167–204). New York: Free Press.

Rose, M. (2011). Rethinking Remedial Education and the Academic-Vocational Divide. *Mind, Culture, and Activity, 19*(1), 1–16.

Royer, D., & Gilles, R. (2003) Introduction. Directed Self-Placement: Principles and Practices. Daniel Royer and Roger Gilles, eds. Cresskill, NJ: Hampton.

"Rules governing the Board of Trustees of the California State University." (2012). Revised 25 January 2012. Retrieved from http://www.calstate.edu/bot/documents/rules_of_procedure.pdf

Saxon, D. P., & Boylan, H. R. (2010). Editorial: What are we going to do about it? *Journal of Developmental Education, 34*(2), 36–37.

Schneider, A. & Ingram, H. (1997). *Policy Design for Democracy*. Lawrence, KS: University Press.

Schofield, J. (2004). A model of learned implementation. *Public Administration, 82*(2), 283–308.

Scott-Clayton, J. (2012). *Do high-stakes placement exams predict college success? (CCRC Working Paper No. 41)*. New York: Community College Research Center, Teachers College, Columbia University.

Shaw, K. M. (1997). Remedial education as ideological battleground: Emerging remedial education policies in the community college. *Educational Evaluation and Policy Analysis, 19*(3), 284–296.

Soliday, M. (1996). From the margins to the mainstream: Reconceiving remediation. *College Composition and Communication, 47*(1), 85–100.

Soliday, M. (2002). *The politics of remediation*. Pittsburgh, PA: The University of Pittsburgh Press.

Spillane, J. P. (2000). Cognition and policy implementation: District policymakers and the reform of mathematics education. *Cognition and Instruction, 18*(2), 141–179.

Spillane, J. P., Reiser, B. J., & Reimer, T. (2002). Policy implementation and cognition: Reframing and refocusing implementation research. *Review of Educational Research, 72*, 387–431.

Spillane, J. P., Reiser, B. J., & Gomez, L. M. (2006). Policy implementation and cognition: The role of human, social, and distributed cognition in framing policy implementation. In M. Honig (Ed.). *New Directions in Education Policy Implementation,* (pp. 47–64). Albany, NY: State University of New York Press.

Stake, R. E. (2005). Qualitative case studies. In Denzin, N. K. & Lincoln, Y. S. (Eds.), *The handbook of qualitative research, 3rd ed,* (pp. 443-465). Thousand Oaks, CA: Sage.

Strong American Schools. (2008). *Diploma to nowhere.* Washington, DC: Author.

Trowler, P. R. (2002). Introduction: Higher education policy, institutional change. In P. R. Trowler (Ed.). *Higher education policy and institutional change* (pp. 1-23). Philadelphia: The Society for Research into Higher Education and Open University Press.

Walpole, M. B. (2007). Economically and educationally challenged students in higher education: Access to outcomes. ASHE Higher Education Report, Vol. 33, No. 3. San Francisco: Jossey-Bass.

White, E. M. (1995). The importance of placement and basic studies: Helping students succeed under the new elitism. *Journal of Basic Writing, 14*(2), 75–84.

"The California State University." (n.d.). Webpage: http://www.calstate. edu/. Retrieved 13 June 2013.

Tierney, W. G. (1988). Organizational culture in higher education. *Journal of Higher Education, 59*(1), 2–21.

Van Maanen, J., & Barley, S. (1984). Occupational communities: Culture and control in organizations. *Research in Organizational Behavior, 6,* 287–365.

Van Meter, D. S., & Van Horn, C. E. (1975). The policy implementation process: A conceptual framework. *Administration and Society, 6*(4), 445–488.

Weick, K. E. (1995). *Sensemaking in organizations.* Thousand Oaks, CA: Sage.

Yamada, T. (2010). Restructuring the California State University: A call to action. *Thought and Action, (Fall 2010)*, 91–106.

Yanow, D. (1996). *How does a policy mean: Interpreting policy and organizational actions.* Washington, DC: George Washington University Press.

Yin, R. K. (2009). *Case study research: Design and methods, 4th ed.* Thousand Oaks, CA: Sage Publications.

Note

1. Participants on campuses running stretch and DSP frequently asserted that their campus did not have remediation. While I categorize the four approaches as remedial programs for the purpose of this paper, it is important to note that campuses with mainstreamed models fully reject the label of "remediation."

7

---◀◦▶---

ON THE PATH TO COMPLETION

Exploring How Higher Education Policy
Influences the Least Ready College Students

BRYAN ADÁN RODRÍGUEZ

Higher education policy changes to financial aid and course enrollment reflect a shift in priority from college access to college completion (Kantrowitz, 2012). Amid increasing budgetary constraints, community colleges in California and across the country are being forced to do more with less. Although the state has recently provided additional monies to the community college sector, the 112-campus system has less financial support today than in years past. From 2008 to 2014, the California Community College system lost 12% of its state funding, or $809 million according to the Chancellor's Office, and student enrollment dropped from 2.9 to 2.4 million students.

The negative impact of low completion rates on the federal education budget, economy, and American competitiveness has motivated the growing emphasis on college completion. As Julia Duncheon outlined in chapter 1, entities such as the Lumina Foundation, the Gates Foundation, MDRC, and the American Association of Community Colleges have promoted a college completion agenda. Lisa Garcia and Duncheon's chapters in part II examined policies designed to decrease remedial need—and thereby enhance completion rates—in four-year universities. Policymakers have also adopted reforms to address poor completion rates in community colleges, which are the focus of the current investigation. The shift from access to completion is evident in the following three policy changes:

- The establishment of a minimum graduation rate threshold of 20% for institutions to remain eligible for Pell Grant funding (Department of Education, 2012)
- Congress' approval to reduce student eligibility of Pell Grant funding from nine years to six years (Department of Education, 2012)
- The governing board of California's community colleges approval of system-wide registration policies that favor students who are focused on earning a degree or transferring to a four-year college and have completed orientation and assessment tests (Association of Community College Trustees, 2012)

These reforms aim to enhance college completion by incentivizing institutions to graduate students in a timely manner. Yet these changes also have implications for students who enter postsecondary institutions. For example, the implementation of minimum college completion rates for Pell Grant eligibility may motivate postsecondary institutions to become more selective in the admissions process. Community college students must now have a high school diploma or high school equivalency degree (Shapiro et al., 2012). It is plausible that variables traditionally correlated with college completion, such as high school GPA and admissions test scores, may become increasingly used to exclude students from entering two-year institutions. One wonders how these reforms may affect students at risk of not completing college.

Permit me to remind the reader of our broad definition of college readiness: college readiness is the preparation a student needs to enroll in credit-bearing (i.e., non-remedial) courses in a postsecondary institution and persist to graduation. Prior chapters have examined college readiness through the lens of high school students' experiences and remediation reform efforts in the California State University system. Here I focus on California's community college sector in light of the policy shift from an emphasis on access to completion. How academically underprepared two-year college students perceive their chances of persistence given recent policy developments has not yet been studied, but may offer insight into the potential impact of these reforms on students at risk of non-completion.

This study describes the experiences of students who I defined in part I as the "least ready" community college students who will be affected by new restrictions on financial aid and course enrollment. As I discussed in chapter 3, the least ready students are defined as those who place into lower level remedial courses (i.e., three levels below transfer). I selected participants based on traditional cognitive college readiness indicators (i.e., remedial placement as determined by standardized test scores). Focusing on students' perceptions of financial aid and course enrollment policy enabled me to examine how non-cognitive factors (i.e., campus integration) influence persistence. As I mentioned in part I, I use the term "least ready" to reflect a contemporary policy dilemma regarding how to support community college students who are said to be significantly academically underprepared. That these students are least ready speaks to inequitable college preparatory opportunities rather than a flaw inherent in the student. Further, along with Duncheon, I could have done a case study that involved several different constituencies—faculty, legislators who are considering restricting access to these students, and the like. What I have attempted here, however, is to come to terms with the group that will be most impacted by policies aimed at restricting access.

The chapter proceeds as follows. I first offer background on three specific reforms that have affected community colleges. Next, I outline the research design used to investigate the perspectives of the least prepared students. I then present the findings and close with an analysis and directions for future research.

Background and Policy Context

This inquiry considered three reforms: (a) the establishment of a 20% minimum graduation rate threshold for institutions to remain eligible for Pell Grant funding, (b) the reduction of student eligibility for Pell Grant funding from nine years to six years, and (c) registration policies in the California Community College system that favor students who are focused on earning a degree or transferring to a four-year college and have completed orientation and assessment tests. These policies target the problem of low college completion and shape the financial and educational experiences of the least ready students in significant ways.

Pell Grant Eligibility Tied to a Minimum Graduation Rate of 20%

More than half of all students who enter a postsecondary institution do not obtain a degree or certificate within eight years of enrollment (Department of Education, 2012). Aiming to incentivize degree completion, Congress approved a plan in 2012 establishing a 20% minimum graduation rate benchmark for institutions to maintain Pell Grant funding eligibility.

In California, an estimated 54% of degree-seeking community college students receive a certificate or degree, or transfer to a four-year institution (California Community Colleges Student Task Force, 2012). This rate is lower for African American and Latina/o students, 42% and 43% respectively. Of the students who enter one level below transfer level in math, 46.2% receive a certificate or degree or transfer. Of the students who enter community college four levels below transfer level, only 25.5% receive a certificate or degree or transfer. Only 41% of students seeking to transfer to four-year institutions are successful. The success rates of African American and Latina/o students are significantly lower than the overall average; approximately 34% of African American and 31% of Latina/o students transfer.

Although the new eligibility benchmark for Pell Grant funding motivates institutions to enhance student completion rates, it may also cause postsecondary schools to become more selective in the admissions process. As Kantrowitz (2012) states, "one of the easiest ways to increase graduation rates is to exclude high-risk students" (p. 1). For example, Pell Grant eligibility now requires recipients to have a high school diploma or high school equivalency degree (Shapiro et al., 2012). Underprepared students who are more likely to drop out of college than their college-ready counterparts may experience diminished access to postsecondary institutions as a result of the Pell Grant change. Although estimates vary, roughly 100,000 to 150,000 students may be affected by the new policy (Adams, 2012). By emphasizing graduation rates, the college completion agenda may sacrifice college access for vulnerable populations without necessarily improving students' postsecondary outcomes.

Student Pell Grant Eligibility Reduced from Nine Years to Six Years

In addition to Pell Grant reforms that target institutions, changes to the Pell Grant have influenced students directly. Traditionally, Pell Grant funding has been offered to qualified students for up to nine years or 18 full-time semesters. As of July 1, 2012, however, maximum Pell Grant eligibility was reduced for students at all postsecondary institutions to 12 full-time semesters (six years) of funding. The reduction in funding eligibility retroactively impacts students who currently receive the Pell Grant and have exceeded 12 semesters. The maximum is applied proportionally to their enrollment for students who are less than full-time. As a result of this policy change, an estimated 63,000 recipients did not receive an average award of $3,905 during the 2012–13 academic year (Association of Community College Trustees, 2012).

Although the eligibility reduction is designed to reduce the overall costs of the Pell Grant award, it may negatively affect students with limited knowledge of how to navigate the system or students whose life circumstances cause them to take longer to complete their degree. More than 9 million students rely on Pell Grants to complete college. Research demonstrates that need-based grant aid increases college enrollment among low- and middle-income students as well as reduces the likelihood of dropping out of college (TICAS, 2013). An estimated 80% of all Pell Grant recipients are first-generation college students (Pell Institute, 2013). Pell Grant aid is particularly important for students of color. Nearly half of African American undergraduates and an estimated 40% of Latina/o undergraduates depend on Pell Grants to attend college (TICAS, 2013). Although comprising 24% of all Pell Grant recipients, African American students make up 41% of recipients working toward a college degree after six years (TICAS, 2011). Consequently, students who are likely to face particular challenges under the new eligibility policy include those who are low-income, of color, first-generation, working full-time and/or enrolled part-time, and single parents.

Priority Course Registration Granted to Students Meeting Specified Requirements

The number of courses offered to students in community colleges has declined significantly within recent years. From the 2007–08 to 2011–12 school years, the number of available course sections decreased 21%, from 420,000 to 334,000 (Bohn, Reyes, & Johnson, 2013). Although Proposition 30 funding has enabled community colleges to recuperate a portion of course offerings, limited seating continues to plague community colleges in California.

The California Community College system responded to the problem of limited space by instituting new registration policies. Beginning in fall 2014, the colleges granted priority enrollment to students who meet specified criteria or have fulfilled particular requirements. The following general categories of students receive priority registration for course enrollment:

- New students who have completed college orientation and academic assessment, and who have set up a formal academic or vocational education plan
- Returning students in good academic standing with no more than 100 credits (60 credits are needed for transfer to a university as a junior; California Community Colleges Student Success Initiative, 2013).

Students planning to acquire such necessary skills as learning English will also receive registration priority. Within these categories, first priority is granted to active-duty military, veterans, and current and former foster youth who are new and fully matriculated or continuing in good standing. Former and current foster youth were granted priority under California Assembly Bill 194, which took effect January 1, 2012 (Skyler, 2012). Next in line are new and continuing low-income students and students with disabilities (i.e., those in the Extended Opportunity Programs and Services and Disabled Student Programs and Services) in good academic standing, who were granted priority registration under Title V regulations. The question of which student groups are granted priority has garnered much controversy. However, consistent with the policy shift toward completion, these reforms place greater emphasis on first-time students who demonstrate plans to finish a two-year degree or certificate or transfer to a four-year school. The system's 112 campuses are working to inform current students of the new rules and give those on academic probation an opportunity to improve their grades.

Supporters of the priority enrollment measure argue that the new policy will free up spaces for students on-track to degree completion. Then-chancellor of the Community Colleges Board of Governors, Jack Scott, stated:

> In the past, community colleges have been able to serve everyone and students could accrue a large number of units or do poorly in all of their courses and still receive priority registration. Now

that colleges have had to cut back on the courses they can offer, those students were taking up seats in classrooms and crowding out newer students focused on job training, degree attainment or transfer. (California Community College Chancellor's Office, 2012).

This new policy thus ensures that students who have a clear academic or vocational plan will be able to make progress. According to the California Community Colleges Student Task Force (2012), the new plan also offers "an educational roadmap to indicate appropriate courses and available support services" that will guide students toward identifying a program of study (p. 7).

Although the priority registration policy may benefit some traditionally high-risk students, such as those who qualify for Extended Opportunity Program and Services (EOP&S), it may also have negative consequences. Those students who are first-generation or come from low-income backgrounds and do not receive priority enrollment may be at a disadvantage compared to others. First-generation and low-income college students often have limited college knowledge, which leaves them ill prepared to navigate the process of constructing a postsecondary academic or vocational plan. These student groups may be less likely to be on-track to graduate or transfer compared to their more privileged peers, or may potentially be less likely to complete the orientation and assessment tests required to obtain priority registration. Yet because this policy is relatively new and understudied, how it will impact the educational trajectories of all community college students remains unclear.

Research Design

Method

I have drawn on a variety of qualitative methods to explore the educational and life experiences of 25 underprepared students enrolled in community college. Data collection spanned a period of five weeks and involved survey questionnaires, one-on-one semi-structured interviews, document analysis, and field notes.

I utilized survey questionnaires to collect demographic data on the students in the sample; student-reported data from the surveys were used to triangulate data reported in participant interviews. Participants were contacted to complete a 30-minute interview regarding their experiences as community college students. I then conducted one-on-one semi-structured interviews with each participant in person or by phone. Interviews were designed to capture in-depth qualitative data regarding students' perceptions of their academic experiences, future educational plans, and the costs and benefits of higher education. Audio from the interviews was recorded and transcribed. I conducted document analysis based on press releases, policy memos, and legislative documents that offered information regarding policy changes. Thematic analysis was used to identify common themes and patterns across the data.

I employed a number of qualitative research techniques to ensure the reliability and trustworthiness of the study. Member checks were performed through follow-up conversations with participants after their interviews to ensure the accuracy of the data and to test the meaning making of the researcher (Yanow & Schwartz-Shea, 2006). I also used peer review during data analysis to obtain feedback regarding my interpretations.

Sample

Data were collected from a sample of 25 community college students. The participants in the study were recruited from three community colleges in California. The 25 students in the sample fit my definition of the least ready students and were at risk of being affected by the three policy changes previously mentioned. All of the participants identified as low-income, first-generation, and/or of color, and all were enrolled in remedial courses. Students were either on an academic/transfer track or a non-transfer/terminal program track. The racial/ethnic distribution of the sample was as follows: 74% Latina/o; 21% African American; 5% Asian. Fifty-three percent of the population identified as women and 47% were men. The age range of the sample population was 18 to 34, and the median age for the sample was 25.

Data Presentation

This study explored how, if at all, changes in financial aid and course availability shape students' expectations of degree completion, which has not yet been explored in prior research. Findings underscore the crucial role that community college plays in the academic and career path of a student population that has traditionally had limited access to higher education. I present data around three central themes: (a) aspirations of the least ready, (b) perceptions of financial aid, and (c) perceptions of course availability.

Aspirations of the Least Ready

The data reveal that participants held high aspirations for their futures, despite their academic under-preparedness for college-level coursework. Most of the students in the sample reported that completing community college was a critical step toward improving their life opportunities in general and career trajectories in particular. As one student summarized, "Without an education, you're not going to go very far."

Students often referred to community college as their best option, suggesting that their non-school alternatives were limited. For some students, taking college courses enabled them to do something productive. "If I was not enrolled in community college," said one participant, "I would be just at home—just up to no good." Another student admitted that he would probably "be at home watching TV." A young man commented on the value of community college in preparing him for furthering his education: "I'm glad I'm getting this experience, so when I hopefully get to a university, I'll be more mature and my head will be on straight."

Most participants recognized that social mobility was difficult to attain without a postsecondary degree. One student who returned to school after working in retail compared himself to his peers who had gone straight to college: "I see classmates from high school and they're doing better [than me] because they've gone off to colleges and universities and they're actually doing stuff—and making more money than me too."

For participants, completing a postsecondary degree was the only way to avoid unemployment or working in low-skilled, service-sector jobs. A young woman pointed out that if she were not in community college, "I would probably still be working in retail or something like that, you know?" Other students offered similar reflections. According to one student, "I would be working at a fast-food restaurant to provide for my son—I'm a dad." Another individual in the study referred to "McDonald's or Burger King" as her only job option with just a high school diploma. One person explained his motivation to attend community college as follows: "I decided to enroll in school because my parents motivated me, they really pressured me. . . . Besides [going to college], there aren't that many opportunities out there [for me]."

Participants thus viewed community college as a pathway to achieving their future academic and career goals. Many planned to transfer to a four-year school. As one student explained, "Five years from now, I hope I can be at a Cal State getting my bachelor's degree." Another commented, "I feel like [community] college is a stepping-stone. . . . You can't just go out and get a good job; I got to have that education because I hope to get a bachelor's [degree]."

Many participants specified career objectives that they hoped would be attainable through earning a certificate or transferring. One person said, "Five years from now, I hope I can graduate from a Cal State and become a forensic scientist." Another emphasized the importance of education for his career path, stating, "I hope one day to get a Master's degree. Community college is going to help me get a better job—it's going to be my stability in the future. Hopefully I can be a teacher working in a high school, teaching psychology."

A different participant commented that before she started community college, "I was working at a retail store and I had just had a baby. That's when I decided to go back to school. Working in a retail store is not what I want to do—I want to be a nurse." One student shared, "I would like to be a crime scene investigator, like they do on the [television] shows, like CSI."

Another student expressed desire to eventually work in the criminal justice system. One participant pointed out that college offered benefits beyond social mobility: "Going to college, outside of the financial benefits, is a sense of achievement. I get to pass it along to the next generation."

Overall, those in the study recognized the value of postsecondary education generally and community college particularly as critical for determining their future career path. Yet despite their high aspirations, some reported worrying about their prospects for degree completion. As one participant explained, "My [community college] experience has been productive. The biggest challenge for me has just been trying to manage my time to complete my degree, that's been hard."

Students reported a variety of obstacles that made degree attainment difficult to reach, which I discuss in the subsequent sections.

Perceptions of Financial Aid

Participants reported that their ability to access postsecondary education depended on the availability of financial aid. However, students also referenced additional financial burdens—despite the support of financial aid—that made progressing toward a degree difficult.

Individuals were asked about their thoughts on financial aid and completing their degree at community college. All in the sample stressed that financial aid was crucial in their pursuit of postsecondary education. One said, "Having financial aid helps me with the costs [of college], so I don't have to worry about working overtime at work and I can just focus more on my classes." Another shared, "One of things that worries me about college is financial debt. If I don't get [financial aid], I ain't going to school." A different student shared a similar sentiment: "Getting financial aid is basically the only way I can [attend community college]. I mean, I work, too, but I live at home with my mom and have to help her out with money. So, having [financial] aid makes it all possible."

Participants' reliance on financial aid was evident when they emphasized that they had no alternative method for affording a college education. As one student said: "I've received financial aid for like three years, and it's helped me a lot, but if my financial aid got pulled, there's no way I would be able to go to school—like no way. I would probably have to go work for a year or something like that, and then maybe come back [to school]." Another shared that he would drop out without financial aid. "Honestly," said a different participant, "the only reason I've been able to go to school is [because of] financial aid. . . . My parents can't really help [with the cost of college]. I wouldn't be doing this without it."

Though participants stressed that attending college would not have been possible without financial aid, financial burdens still impeded academic progress for many. One young man explained that he had to leave school for a while because his financial aid was insufficient: "Covering the costs of college has been a challenge, and that's why I originally dropped out of [community college]. I received financial aid and fee waivers, but I still didn't have enough money for outside costs."

Others discussed the difficulty of balancing school and employment, since many had to work part-time or full-time jobs to supplement their financial aid. As one student-worker explained, "It's like I tell my little brother, 'we're from a low-income family, it's going to be difficult to pay for college—especially now.' We go to school and we have to work—it's tougher for us." Many shared a similar sentiment, suggesting that they did not have the luxury of focusing solely on school because college affordability remained a central concern.

Familial obligations also presented significant hurdles on the path to degree completion. A woman in the study explained, "The biggest challenge for me has been being a single mother, not knowing where my son is going to be while I'm in school, how I'm going to support him when I'm in school, that's what's taken most of my time as a student." While she admitted that "if I didn't have financial aid, [attending school] probably wouldn't be possible," her responsibilities as a parent led her to feel that "my situation isn't really as simple like it is for some other students."

Another parent who had been attending community college off and on for six years offered, "I think I'll get my degree in about two to three more years. [I left school] because [. . .] I was working and I didn't have time for school. Being a single mother, I had to work and go to school." In these ways, the additional pressures many students faced, such as the need to care for children, often made progressing toward a degree difficult. Participants continued to confront financial hardship despite benefiting from the financial aid they received.

Perceptions of Course Availability

The availability of courses played a significant role in these community college students' academic experience. Many of the participants had access to priority enrollment, but those who had to follow typical enrollment protocol faced additional obstacles. Regardless of their enrollment status, all of the students reflected on the stress caused by limited seating.

A majority of students reported having priority enrollment at their school, which enabled them to find classes for their course of study more easily. Students with priority enrollment included military veterans, students participating in the Extended Opportunity Programs & Services (EOP&S), or student-athletes. These participants expressed awareness that they were fortunate to have priority status. As one person explained, "Finding classes has been good because I joined a program called EOP&S, so I get priority in finding all of my classes. But I see a lot of students who are not in the [EOP&S] program who struggle."

Another said that completing his degree would be challenging academically but was made easier because of priority registration. He commented, "Even though I know not all students have priority enrollment, it's helped me be able to take the classes I need to graduate."

According to another participant, "Since I'm a student-athlete, I receive priority enrollment at my school. First [priority] goes to the veterans, then the student-athletes—getting classes is easy for me."

Although certain opportunities available to students (e.g., priority enrollment) facilitated faster progress toward a degree, students pointed out that they had to actively take advantage of them. One participant commented, "There are programs like EOP&S that help you get priority for classes, and like financial aid, if you don't take advantage of, it will prolong how long you're in school." Participants that had priority registration thus recognized that they had an advantage relative to students who did not, but also took initiative to reap potential benefits.

Ten people in the study reported increased difficulty enrolling in the courses necessary for degree completion because they were not granted priority registration. As one student explained, "One of the biggest challenges for me has been finding classes. It's been really difficult. English and math classes, when I've tried finding them, they're already filled." Some felt pressure to change majors because they could not enroll in the classes they initially wanted. As this participant discussed: "The classes I've needed are in chemistry or in biology and those classes have been filled up, and I can't take them. I was interested in trying to do something in science, but now I might have to pursue a degree in criminal justice instead."

Eight anticipated they might need longer than six years—the maximum numbers of years a student may receive the federal Pell Grant—to complete their degree or transfer to a four-year college due to difficulty enrolling in courses. "I've had trouble finding classes—it will probably add a year to getting my degree," shared a student. Someone else said, "At first, I thought I was just going to be at [community college] for just two years . . . but finding classes is difficult, especially today. . . . I'll be lucky to get out of [community college] in six years." He added, "I'm not sure how I'm going to pay for school after [six years]."

Participants' perception that more time would be needed to secure required classes thus fueled further concern about the cost of college. The inability to secure classes they wanted led many students to question what they were doing in postsecondary education. A student shared, "I feel like, I work so hard in class and studying but then it's like, 'oh well, we don't have space for you anymore.' So how am I supposed to get a degree then?" For students who did not benefit from priority enrollment, numerous additional obstacles arose in their path to completion.

Analyzing the Experiences of the Least Ready

The findings underscore the role that community college plays in the academic and career path of a student population who have traditionally had limited access to higher education. The analysis synthesized around three central themes: (a) aspirations of the least ready, (b) perceptions of financial aid, and (c) perceptions of course availability. These interrelated themes offer insight into how the current educational environment has shaped the academic and vocational experiences of community college students.

Aspirations of the Least Ready

Findings suggest that these underprepared students recognized the importance of community college in furthering their academic and vocational goals. Most students recognized that career options for individuals without a postsecondary degree were generally limited to low-wage, service-sector employment such as fast-food restaurant work or retail customer service—positions that many in the study already held. They feared that a life of blue-collar work awaited them if they were not able to complete college.

Despite fearing the alternative, a number of students remained uncertain that they would be able to complete college. Their insecurities regarding their prospects for degree completion echo extant research on postsecondary attainment, which suggests the likelihood of graduation or transfer is slim for the least ready students (EdSource, 2010). According to EdSource, 76% of the least ready math students fail to complete their degree or transfer. Similarly, more than 80% of the least ready English students neither transfer nor complete their degree within seven years (EdSource, 2010). Such statistics are indicative of an aspirations-attainment gap (Roderick, Nagaoka, & Coca, 2009); while many students aspire to obtain a postsecondary degree, research suggests that only about one in four of the least ready students will ultimately do so (EdSource, 2010). Consistent with this literature, findings offer further evidence that underprepared students recognize the importance of higher education. Nearly all of the participants held high aspirations to pursue four-year degrees. Yet they also expressed concern that completing their degrees would require overcoming a myriad of obstacles. Their insecurities were largely shaped by their perception that affording the cost of college and enrolling in required courses were ongoing challenges.

Perceptions of Financial Aid

The availability of financial aid has changed significantly within the past five years. The least ready students in this study were low-income and relied heavily on financial aid to attend school. Participants reported that financial aid enabled them to stay in school, but often it was not enough. Many had to maintain employment in addition to grappling with their academic coursework—a task that was already challenging given their low levels of preparation. Some were forced to leave school for periods of time to support themselves, their family, or their future studies. Nearly every student in the sample said that attending school without financial aid was inconceivable given the rising tuition costs and living expenses.

Participants' experiences speak to existing research that problematizes the high costs of remediation for students. Research has shown that because many remedial courses are non-credit-bearing, underprepared students often take longer to graduate than their college-ready counterparts (EdSource, 2010). This predicament costs students not only time but also money; many of the participants had spent multiple semesters using financial aid to take remedial courses without receiving credit toward a degree. Placing into lower levels of remedial coursework is thus particularly detrimental given that the least ready students disproportionately come from low-income backgrounds.

With stagnating financial aid, increasing college costs, and restrictions to the federal Pell Grant, the least ready are at risk of leaving college. Prior research has suggested that changes to financial aid policies (i.e., reductions to the Pell Grant) may alter perceptions of college affordability among current postsecondary students as well as students entering community college (Baum, McPherson, & Steele, 2008). Limited opportunities (both real and perceived) may potentially cause students to become pessimistic about the affordability of postsecondary schooling—a concern that is confirmed by this study's findings. College cost thus represents one of the largest obstacles for low-income students. For those who are significantly underprepared and confined to low levels of remediation, financial challenges are even greater. Policies that reduce financial aid availability leave these students even more vulnerable.

Perceptions of Course Availability

Course availability across the California Community College system has also been restricted (Bohn et al., 2013). Findings suggest that the restrictions on course availability may take a toll on the least ready students. Nearly all participants stated that enrolling in courses required for degree completion was difficult. Ten students reported experiencing particular difficulty because they were unable to secure a form of priority enrollment. These students faced delays in the completion of their program of study. Some students suggested that not being able to secure certain courses would add a semester or one year to their time-to-degree, and in some instances, longer than one year. Although a few students who had experienced difficulties with course enrollment were unsure if they would experience delays in completion, roughly one-third of the participants expected to attend community college longer than six years. A small number of students reported having difficulty pursuing certain majors due to limited course sections.

The lack of course availability also caused some participants to take longer in beginning remedial course sequences. Given that many remedial subjects are often taught sequentially, the implications for students who place into lower-level courses can be severe (Stigler, Givvin, & Thompson, 2010). Remedial math and English sequences can take up to two years to complete before students may enroll in credit-bearing courses. Research suggests that those students who delay enrolling in remedial course sequences such as math or writing may be less likely to pass the course sequence (EdSource, 2010).

Delays in degree completion may affect not only students' educational paths but also their career trajectories and earnings. Prolonged enrollment may result in forgone earnings while in school, reduced wages during their training period, and fewer years of Pell Grant eligibility beyond community college (DesJardins & Toutkoushian, 2005). These problems were exemplified in the experiences of many participants.

Certain opportunities available to students lessened the burden of decreased course availability and priority registration policies. Students who identified as student-athletes or participated in the EOP&S program were granted priority enrollment. However, not all students were able to take advantage of programs such as EOP&S because they did not qualify due to part-time enrollment or were not aware of the opportunity. This finding reflects prior research on college knowledge, which suggests that many low-income, first-generation students do not know how to navigate the system of higher education (Hooker & Brand, 2010).

A lack of familiarity with postsecondary requirements and programs contributes to the low likelihood that the least ready students will be on-track to graduate or transfer compared to the general student population (EdSource, 2010). For these reasons, policies that offer priority registration to students who can identify a solid academic or vocational plan may be detrimental to underprepared students who are unfamiliar with postsecondary requirements.

Conclusion

This study offered a glimpse into the experiences of academically underprepared students attending community college. I have suggested that higher education policy changes that emphasize completion over access—including new restrictions on financial aid and community college course enrollment—have compromised the educational trajectories of the least ready college students. In many ways, the themes presented reveal the vulnerability that this demographic of students faces. Policies that create additional hurdles for underprepared community college students undermine the ideal of open-access institutions, whereby every individual has an opportunity to pursue a postsecondary degree.

What are the implications of restricting access to higher education for society in general and the least ready students in particular? Is a public policy agenda that may prevent some students from starting and others from finishing aligned with the idea that any high school graduate should be able to pursue a postsecondary credential? What are the consequences for students who are either unable to begin or complete a degree or certificate? Although institutions have tightened requirements in the face of constrained fiscal resources, policies that favor completion over access create additional barriers for the most vulnerable and least ready students. Improving higher education, the nation's economy, and the future prospects for underserved student populations requires striking a careful balance between access and completion.

References

Association of Community College Trustees. (2012). *Pell Grant eligibility changes*. Washington, DC: Author. Retrieved from http://www.acct. org/files/legacy/pdf/pell%20eligibility%20changes%20in%20omnibus.pdf.

Baum, S., McPherson, M., & Steele, P. (2008). *The effectiveness of student aid policies: What the research tells us*. New York: College Board. Retrieved from http://professionals.collegeboard.com/profdownload/rethinking-stu-aid-effectiveness-of-stu-aid-policies.pdf

Bohn, S., Reyes, B., & Johnson, H. (2013). *The impact of budget cuts on California's community colleges*. San Francisco: Public Policy Institute of California. Retrieved from http://www.ppic.org/main/publication. asp?i=1048

California Community Colleges Chancellor's Office. (2013). California Community Colleges Chancellor Brice W. Harris says fall enrollment numbers heading up after years of decline [Press release]. Sacramento, CA: Author. Retrieved from http://californiacommunitycolleges.ccc-co.edu/Newsroom/PressReleases.aspx

California Community Colleges Student Task Force. (2012). *Advancing student success in the California community colleges*. Sacramento, CA: Author. Retrieved from californiacommunitycolleges.cccco.edu/Portals/0/StudentSuccessTaskForce/REPORT_SSTF_FINAL_122911. pdf

California Community Colleges Student Success Initiative. (2013). *California Community Colleges student success initiative implementation* [PowerPoint slides]. Sacramento, CA: Author. Retrieved from http:// www.californiacommunitycolleges.cccco.edu/PolicyInAction/StudentSuccessInitiative.aspx

DesJardins, S. L., & Toutkoushian, R. K. (2005). Are students really rational?: The development of rational thought and its application to student choice. *Higher Education: Handbook of Theory and Research, 20*, 191–240.

Department of Education. (2012). *Student financial assistance*. Washington, DC: Author. Retrieved from http://www2.ed.gov/about/overview/budget/budget13/justifications/p-sfa.pdf

EdSource. (2010). *Course-taking patterns, policies, and practices in developmental education in the California Community Colleges*. Mountain View, CA: Author.

Adams, C. (2012). Budget deal ushers in new Pell Grant eligibility rules. *Education Week, 31*(15), 18.

Hooker, S., & Brand, B. (2010). College knowledge: A critical component of college and career readiness. *New Directions for Youth Development, 2010*(127), 75–85.

Kantrowitz, M. (2012). *The college completion agenda may sacrifice college access for low-income, minority and other at-risk students.* FinAid, LLC. Retrieved from http://www.fastweb.com/nfs/fastweb/static/PDFs/The_Completion_Agenda.pdf

Pell Institute (2013). *Reflections on Pell: Championing social justice through 40 years of educational opportunity.* Washington, DC: Author. Retrieved from http://www.pellinstitute.org/downloads/publications-Reflections_on_Pell_June_2013.pdf

Roderick, M., Nagaoka, J., & Coca, V. (2009). College readiness for all: The challenge for urban high schools. *The Future of Children, 19*(1), 185–210.

Shapiro, D., Dundar, A., Chen, J., Ziskin, M., Park, E., Torres, V., & Chiang, Y. (2012). *Completing college: A national view of student attainment rates.* Indiana, IL: National Student Clearinghouse Research Center.

Skyler, J. (2012). New CA law gives priority course registration to foster youth attending college. *National Center for Youth Law, 30*(3), 1–3.

Stigler, W., Givvin, K. B., & Thompson, B. J. (2010). What community college developmental mathematics students understand about mathematics. *MathAMATYC Educator, 1*(3), 4–17.

The Institute for College Access and Success (TICAS). (2011). *House fy2012 spending bill eliminates Pell Grants for more than 100,000 students next year.* Washington, DC: Author. Retrieved from http://www.ticas.org/files/pub/Pell_Appropriations_Dec_2011_NR.pdf

The Institute for College Access and Success (TICAS). (2013). *Pell Grants help keep college affordable for millions of Americans.* Washington, DC: Author. Retrieved from www.ticas.org/files/pub/Overall_Pell_one-pager_FINAL_03-15-13.pdf

Yanow, D., & Schwartz-Shea, P. (2006). *Interpretation and method: Empirical research methods and the interpretive turn.* New York: M. E. Sharpe, Inc.

Part III

CONCLUSION

8

◄○►

THE WAY FORWARD

Looking Back

WILLIAM G. TIERNEY

Academics have a somewhat deserved reputation for making seemingly simple and straightforward ideas into complex thoughts that defy explanation. As we constructed this book I worried that we were also succumbing to the temptation of over-academicizing college readiness. Shouldn't determining if someone is ready for college be known when he or she graduates from high school? What is so difficult about knowing whether a student is prepared to take a college class?

I graduated from a public high school in an upper-middle-class neighborhood in New York in the 1970s. The school at the time had made it onto the list of one of the 100 best public schools in America. We all went to college, and by "college" I mean a four-year institution. My friends and I talked a lot about where we might apply, what our "safety" school was, and which was our "dream" school. Although I did not realize it at the time, our conversations revolved around where we would go to college—not if we would go to college. Most of our brothers, sisters, neighbors, and even parents had gone to college.

I would wager that we all were ready for college. Graduation from Horace Greeley High School implied college readiness. The shock that we faced when we went to college was typical freshman angst—what was our roommate like, what would we do on the weekend, what was the meaning of life. Classes were not easy, but they were not that much different from what we experienced at Greeley High. The material was simply the next step in our learning experience and we had very little trouble negotiating the milieu of the college campus. Everyone looked like us, and, to a certain extent, acted like us.

As Daniel Almeida noted in part I, the idea of "college readiness" was not much discussed up until about a generation ago. To be sure, even at Harvard College the faculty worried about a student's ability, but the issue was less a systemic problem of students arriving from high school en masse unprepared. It was seen more as something that could be handled on a case-by-case basis. Certainly up until the late 20th century college readiness was neither a state nor federal concern. And as Bryan Rodríguez noted in his chapter, the "least ready" were never really part of the academic equation. Of course they were not ready for college; they were not supposed to participate in higher education. If they did, it was a two-year institution where their aspirations of higher degrees were "cooled out," to use Burton Clark's (1960) famous phrase.

The least ready were students who went to community college and did not transfer to a four-year institution. Policy discussions in state houses did not revolve around whether to fund students who needed to take the equivalent of English 101 numerous times simply to be ready for college-level writing. Until the creation of land-grant institutions at the time of the Civil War, college-going was reserved largely for the children of the wealthy or those who wanted religious instruction. Even after public land grants democratized institutions there was a clear divide between the haves and have-nots. And the least ready have always been the have-nots.

How, then, did we arrive at a situation where the topic of college readiness is arguably one of the most important issues facing education in the 21st century? Some will argue that the problem is relatively simple. If the "least ready" and "not ready" did not aspire to college and state policies did not condone such aspirations, then the problem would be resolved. The assumption here is that if only those who attend the Horace Greeley High Schools of the 21st century were to go to college then the problem would disappear. In some respects, there is a degree of truth to such an assertion. Assume that we eliminated all of the community colleges, all of the weakest four-year institutions, all of remedial education, and allowed students to vie for the remaining seats based on blind reviewed test scores. If one subscribes to such a notion of merit then the likelihood is that college readiness would no longer be an issue.

Some, such as Richard Vedder (2012), would not be adamantly opposed to a modified version of this solution. He and others (Vedder, Robe, & Denhart, 2013) have suggested that the country is educating too many students for the jobs that are needed. By using census data he has pointed out that many college graduates are working in jobs that do not require a college degree. A 2010 investigation of census data, for example, reveals that out of 41.7 million employed college graduates, 37% hold jobs that only require a high school degree (Vedder et al., 2013). From this perspective, the country has jobseekers that cannot find employment because better educated—not better qualified—workers have taken their positions. The discussion should be less about college readiness and more about career readiness argue these critics.

Two problems arise with such an assumption. On the one hand, in a country that prides itself on the democratic ideal of merit, one needs to look not merely at individuals who graduate from Horace Greeley High School and the like, but who these students are. One need not subscribe to Marxism to acknowledge that where children live and what schools they attend play a major role in the sort of education they receive and whether they will be ready for college. If the citizenry believe in a democratic ideal that all men and women are equal, then all children need to be provided equal opportunity. In an environment where we know that college graduates earn greater than a million dollars more than high school graduates over a lifetime (Tierney & Hentschke, 2007) there will be a desire to gain a college degree.

Further, there is considerable counter-evidence that suggests that a college degree is not simply useful for an individual's earnings but also for the person-power needs of the country. As we touched on in part I, President Obama, the Gates and Lumina Foundations, and numerous think tanks have issued calls for increasing college enrollment and decreasing the time it takes a student to graduate (Academy for Educational Development, 2008; Bill & Melinda Gates Foundation, 2010; McAlister & Mevs, 2012; White House, n.d.). Further, whereas the United States has an urgent need for more individuals who hold degrees in science, technology, engineering, and math (STEM), it has an oversupply of individuals with other sorts of degrees. Those with other degrees may well have assumed

positions for which they are overqualified, but they are unqualified for positions that require a bachelor's degree with a particular skill set. Thus the
workforce demands more college graduates with different degrees.

It seems clear that the country needs more students who are ready for
college, but as the chapters in part II demonstrate, what is meant by college
readiness, how to evaluate whether one is college-ready, and what to do to
increase college readiness is by no means clear. Julia Duncheon showed not
only how difficult it is to define the term, but also that different actors have
different interpretations of what should be meant by college readiness and
what should be done if a student is not ready.

We employed a state-level analysis in order to highlight how different
actions take place that may not be inconsistent with one another but are at
best orthogonal. By way of up-close and intimate data, Almeida has shown
us how students lack networks that support the development of social (and
cultural) capital; the result is that students are not college-ready. Lisa Garcia and Duncheon highlighted two statewide strategies that have garnered
a great deal of nationwide attention but apparently little demonstrable results. Rodríguez raised the sobering question about how to think about
those who, regardless of all strategies, are likely to remain unready—even
more so today than yesterday because of increasingly restrictive state and
federal policies.

We considered state-level policies insofar as institutions are not free-
floating entities and able to do whatever they want. How high schools in
Mississippi prepare students for college will differ from how New Jersey or
California engages in the same tasks. High schools within a state may well
vary, but they are guided by state restrictions and policies. Our purpose
also was not to discuss yet again the alphabet soup of college-preparation
programs—AVID, MESA, Upward Bound, Posse, and the like. We ap-
preciate the challenges these stand-alone programs face and have written
about them in the past (Tierney & Hagedorn, 2002). Although analyses
of best practices are always useful to investigate, our purpose here has been
different.

What we have tried to suggest is that individual policies and actions defy any singular instrumental action that a school might make that
will turn a majority of students from not-college-ready to college-ready.
Schools are nested within a state structure that determines the meaning
of college readiness. To a certain degree, who is able to attend college and
who is not gets played out via these policies and actions. Our intent has not
been to offer a despairing analysis that suggests college readiness is such an

obscure construct it defies measurability or successful strategies. However, we have tried to point out the difficulty involved in improving the readiness for college for America's children.

I also wish to raise one additional concern about how the country and the states might deal with college readiness, and that has to do with the pace of change. Just as in 1970 no one was talking about if America's students were college-ready, in 1990 no one was suggesting that Massive Open Online Courses or "MOOCs" might solve many, if not all, of our educational problems (Ng & Koller, 2013). In 2000 no one worried that because of "disruptive technology" (Christensen, Horn, Caldera, & Soares, 2011) the very future of colleges and universities might be threatened. Simply stated, the pace of technological inventions has been increasing so rapidly that predicting what paths to choose for the future in terms of educational strategies is becoming more, rather than less, complex. Whereas Facebook was all the rage as a potential learning tool only five years ago, today inventors are looking at Facebook as yesterday's tool and have moved on to apps. Who can predict what will be invented tomorrow that will make apps look old-fashioned? Although teaching and learning stayed relatively similar for most of a century, anyone who predicts what the schools and colleges of tomorrow will look like is on a fool's errand.

Permit me to offer an alternative scenario that relates to my comments above about assuming that only students who graduate from the Horace Greeley High Schools of the world should go to university. What if we were to look into the future and see these four outcomes in 2025:

Fewer students participate in postsecondary education: Assume that the absolute number of students who enter two- and four-year institutions has declined by 20%. The numbers have declined because of federal and state policies, rather than that consumers have gravitated to some other educational medium (such as MOOCs).

Fewer students hold a postsecondary degree: Even with fewer students the potential exists that overall college completion increases. Assume the opposite. In 2025 the country has 20% fewer A.A. and B.A. graduates, and for good measure, there are fewer transfer students from community colleges to four-year institutions.

More students are in debt: Even with fewer participants and fewer graduates it is entirely possible that those who enter and graduate from a two-year or four-year institution do so more efficiently and encumber less debt. In this scenario, however, the opposite has occurred. Of those who do graduate their debt is greater than the students graduating today by 20%.

And because the college completion rate has not increased, the debt of the non-completers also has increased.

Fewer students are career-ready: Finally, even with a smaller cohort who enters college, graduates, and assumes more debt, it might be possible that those who actually graduate are better prepared for their careers. If they are, and the jobs are high paying, then their debt levels might go down rapidly, and possibly productivity will go up. But what if students are less qualified for future employment than they are today? What if employers determine that 20% fewer college graduates are ready to assume careers than exists today?

I am hard pressed to believe that anyone would view this future scenario as optimistic. Further, such a scenario is likely to have fewer first-generation students and students of color with college degrees. The portrait suggests greater wage inequality between the poor and the wealthy. Rather than a more democratic America, the likelihood exists for a country that is less equal and less fair than today. If we do not want such a scenario then what do we need to do? We know that from the Organization for Economic Co-Operation and Development (OECD) Survey of Adults Skills and Readiness, and several other studies, that the United States is lagging behind other industrialized countries (Soares & Perna, 2014).

We also know multiple changes are on the horizon that will impact college readiness. Increasingly sophisticated software will enable us to re-think what a "course" and "credit hour" mean so that students are no longer tied to "seat time." Advances in learning sciences will enable us to teach different kinds of students based on their need rather than the one-size-fits-all model that currently exists. Blended learning will enable a college degree to occur more quickly than the standard format that is now pervasive in our institutions. Nevertheless, even vigorous critics of open admissions would not argue that significantly fewer students attending and graduating from college or incurring more debt and being less qualified would be to the country's advantage.

We also need to acknowledge that a "magic bullet" is not likely to happen. No one is going to invent a tool that will enable everyone to be college-ready. Accordingly, if we are in agreement that, at a minimum, we want students better prepared entering college so that they will graduate in a shorter period of time and be better prepared for the job market, what should we do based on the previous chapters? Four themes warrant examination.

The import of state coordination: An artifact of the 20th century was that a broad divide grew between secondary and postsecondary education. The relationship between the two was sporadic and marked by miscommunication. What needs to happen in the 21st century is much greater synthesis and coordination. It should not be left up to institutions, or systems, or individual faculties to determine who is ready or not ready. Clearly, based on the data there are varying interpretations of a student's ability to do college-level writing and math depending on the position from where one sits and the assumptions one holds.

Further, as Duncheon has pointed out, what one means by "college-ready" or "in need of remediation" varies even within a postsecondary system. A lack of data also complicates the matter insofar as it is not entirely clear what the consequences are when certain students circumvent remedial classwork and instead take regular classes. As Rodríguez observed in part II, making the rules for course-taking more rigorous places at risk some students who actually may benefit from taking classes more than once.

All of these issues speak to a greater need for coordination by the state. I do not mean that institutions need massive amounts of new regulations, but the guessing game as to what accounts for college readiness is not helpful to institutions or students. State policies, when functioning appropriately, can act like a flight controller who aims to minimize risk and maximize on-flight departures and arrivals. California, and too many other states, lacks this sort of coordination. The point is no longer that a higher education coordinating council operates in one sphere and K-12 operates in another. Instead, we need to explore new ways to work across sectors specifically with regard to college readiness so that students and parents are aware of what is needed to attend college. In addition, teachers and faculty need to communicate in a systematic manner that enables greater cohesion rather than what occurs now, where everyone acts in a manner in which he or she sees fit.

Clearer academic attainment goals need to be developed: Garcia's article pointed out how information, however well intended, is not enough to ensure that more students understand whether they are reading, writing, and doing math at college level. Apparently, the teachers and counselors are also frequently misinformed or have an alternative interpretation of readiness. Once students arrive on a college campus, according to Duncheon, there is a disparity between whether a student is qualified to take a college-level writing class and/or what should happen if the student is not yet ready.

Although the Common Core has certainly been controversial (Applebee, 2013; Wiggins, 2011) and not without its detractors (Burke & Marshall, 2010; Ravitch & Mathis, 2010), the overall goal is in keeping with part of what I am suggesting here. Just as I have suggested that the state needs to coordinate activity in a way that enables a concerted effort, there also needs to be clearer expectations of what we want from students and teachers, schools and postsecondary institutions. Such a point is particularly germane with regard to those who Rodríguez has defined as the "least ready," or those in the sample of Almeida's study who were largely the first in their family to contemplate going to college. Lack of clarity about educational expectations is most harmful not to those who are clearly college-ready but to those who do not know what to expect. Just as a teacher should have clear goals in a class about what a student needs to do to achieve a satisfactory course grade, we can also expect the same when it comes to clarifying what the state, schools, and postsecondary institutions mean by college readiness. Based on the data in part II, the portrait is much more heterogeneous than need be.

Non-cognitive variables need to be better understood and utilized: There has been an overreliance on the interpretation of test scores to determine if a student is ready for college. Granted, the interpretations are various and confusing, but the assumption is that if one scores high on a test then he or she is ready for college, and that is not necessarily the case. Almeida pointed out how many first-generation students lack the social capital first to figure out how to get into college and then to have the wherewithal to develop networks once in college. Rodríguez's work highlighted such points even more so, as these students are not entirely clear on what a college education provides or the support structures that exist to enable success.

David Conley's (2008) and my own work (Tierney, Bailey, Constantine, Finkelstein, & Hurd, 2009) is useful but insufficient if we want to increase college readiness. Up until now we have been gaining knowledge about what students need to know—note-taking skills, time management, financial literacy, and the like—but we are particularly unclear how much a student needs to know in a particular domain (e.g., how financially literate does one need to be) and who is responsible for providing the information. If we are to make significant headway in improving college readiness, then we need to have much more rigorous evaluative measures that pertain to the non-cognitive variables that lead to retention in college.

Greater thought needs to be given to the 40%: A concern about college readiness also should surface an awareness about the not-ready, or never-ready: those who are likely to go no further than graduation from high school. Although the assumption of all of the authors in this volume has been that the country needs to increase college-going in order to ensure economic and social prosperity, no one has maintained that every single ninth-grader needs to graduate from high school and then move on to a postsecondary institution, much less a four-year college or university.

Most projections of jobs in the next 15 or 20 years suggest that about 40% of those jobs will not require any postsecondary education (Carnevale, Smith, & Strohl, 2010). While such analyses certainly suggest that we need to see dramatic increases in the number of students who go to and graduate from college, no one seriously recommends that everyone should go to college. The costs would be enormous and there are not enough jobs that require a postsecondary credential. To be sure, the rationale for this book has been that the state and country need to pay greater attention to the college readiness of students as well as how well prepared they are to begin their careers once they graduate. However, attention also needs to be focused on the career readiness of this other 40%.

College and career readiness are not the same thing. Students are likely to take different curricula, have different goals, and a different track in high school. But it is increasingly difficult to speak of one without the other. How an institution chooses to track one student toward college and another toward a service career is fraught with difficult notions of class (Tierney, forthcoming). My assumption is that as we get more sophisticated with regard to how to think about college readiness, we also will need to take into account what is meant by career readiness and clarify who is responsible for making various decisions and carrying them out.

Of necessity, the way forward needs to look back. Certainly we want to look at policies and programs that have worked or failed, and gauge how they might be useful for the future. As importantly, college readiness speaks to the American idea about what the citizenry wants with regard to education. I have written elsewhere (Tierney, 1991, 2006) about the challenges of meritocracy and education. The country has long argued about what the community is obliged to do for the individual and what the individual ought to do for him- or herself. One possibility within an individualized framework is to ensure that only those who score a grade on a particular test will be deemed college-ready and be able to enter the halls of the academy. The authors of this book have opted for a different scenario that obliges the larger community to create policies that might enable those who are not college-ready to do so. In suggesting this idea our assumption has been threefold. First, the country will be more economically productive if more students attend college. Second, individuals will be able to earn more with a college degree. And third, the country will be enabling individuals to fulfill their potential in a way that speaks to the essential ideas of what the country has aspired to become since its founding.

References

Academy for Educational Development. (2008). *Partnerships for college access and success: A technical assistance, toolkit and resource guide.* Washington, DC: Academy for Educational Development.

Applebee, A. N. (2013). Common Core State Standards: The promise and the peril in a national palimpsest. *English Journal, 103*(1), 25–33.

Bill & Melinda Gates Foundation. (2010, September 7). *Four cities receive $12 million to improve college graduation rates.* Retrieved from www.gatesfoundation.org/press-releases/Pages/ communities-learning-in-partnership-grants- announced-100927.aspx

Burke, L. M., & Marshall, J. A. (2010, May 21). Why national standards won't fix American education: misalignment of power and incentives. *Backgrounder* (No. 2413). Washington, DC: The Heritage Foundation.

Carnevale, A. P., Smith, N., & Strohl, J. (2010). *Help wanted: Projections of jobs and education requirements through 2018.* Washington, DC: Georgetown University Center on Education and the Workforce.

Christensen, C. M., Horn, M. B., Caldera, L., & Soares, L. (2011). *Disrupting college: How disruptive innovation can deliver quality and affordability to postsecondary education.* Mountain View, CA: Innosight Institute.

Clark, B. R. (1960). The "cooling-out" function in higher education. *American Journal of Sociology, 65*(6), 569–576.

Conley, D. T. (2008). *College knowledge: What it really takes for students to succeed and what we can do to get them ready.* San Francisco: Jossey-Bass.

McAlister, S., & Mevs, P. (2012). *College readiness: A guide to the field.* Providence, RI: Annenberg Institute for School Reform at Brown University.

Ng, A., & Koller, D. (2013, August). *The online revolution: education for everyone.* In Proceedings of the 19th ACM SIGKDD International Conference on Knowledge Discovery and Data Mining. Chicago: ACM.

Ravitch, D. & Mathis, W. (2010). *Review of "College- and career-ready students."* Boulder, CO: National Education Policy Center. Retrieved from http://nepc.colorado.edu/publication/college-and-career

Soares, L., & Perna, L. W. (2014). *Readiness for the learning economy insights from OECD's survey of adult skills on workforce readiness and preparation.* Washington, DC: American Council on Education.

Tierney, W. G. (Ed.). (1991). *Culture and ideology in higher education: Advancing a critical agenda.* New York: Praeger.

Tierney, W. G. (2006). *Trust and the public good: Examining the cultural conditions of academic work.* New York: Peter Lang.

Tierney, W. G. (forthcoming). The challenge of college readiness. In W. G. Tierney (Ed.), *Rethinking education and* poverty. Baltimore: Johns Hopkins University Press.

Tierney, W. G., Bailey, T., Constantine, J., Finkelstein, N., & Hurd, N. (2009). *Helping students navigate the path to college: What high schools can do: A practice guide* (NCEE # 2009-4066). Washington, DC: National Center for Education Evaluation and Regional Assistance, Institute of Education Sciences, U.S. Department of Education.

Tierney, W. G., & Hagedorn, L. S. (Eds.). (2002). *Increasing access to college: Extending possibilities for all students.* Albany, NY: State University of New York Press.

Tierney, W. G., & Hentschke, G. C. (2007). *New players, different game: Understanding the rise of for-profit colleges and universities.* Baltimore: Johns Hopkins University Press.

Vedder, R. (2012, April 9). Why college isn't for everyone. *Bloomberg Businessweek.* Retrieved from http://www.businessweek.com/articles/2012-04-09/why-college-isnt-for-everyone

Vedder, R., Robe, C., & Denhart, J. (2013, January). *Why are recent college graduates underemployed? University enrollments and labor-market realities.* Washington, DC: Center for College Affordability and Productivity. Retrieved from http://centerforcollegeaffordability.org/uploads/Underemployed%20Report%202.pdf

White House. (n.d.). Higher education. Retrieved from http://www. whitehouse.gov/issues/education/higher-education

Wiggins, G. (2011, September 28). Common-core math standards don't add up. *Education Week, 31*(5), 22–23.

CONTRIBUTORS

DANIEL J. ALMEIDA is a Ph.D. student in Urban Education Policy at the University of Southern California and a Research Assistant in the Pullias Center for Higher Education. His research interests include issues related to first-generation college students, including college readiness, college completion, financial literacy, and grit. He earned a bachelor's degree from Dartmouth University and a master's degree in Higher Education Administration from Boston College.

BRYAN ADÁN RODRÍGUEZ is a Ph.D. candidate in Urban Education Policy at the University of Southern California. His research explores college access, K-16 policy, student farmworkers, and persistence among underrepresented students. His work has been published by the Journal of Hispanic Higher Education, Metropolitan Universities Journal, Pullias Center for Higher Education, and The Review of Higher Education. He holds a bachelor's degree from the University of California, Los Angeles and a master's degree from Harvard University.

LISA D. GARCIA is the Director of Outreach Programs in the Pullias Center for Higher Education at the University of Southern California (USC). She recently published a book, Undocumented and Unwanted: Attending College Against the Odds, which chronicles the experiences of undocumented immigrant students attending four-year institutions in California. As outreach director, she manages two college preparation programs that help facilitate undocumented and first-generation college students' successful transition to postsecondary studies. She continues to research issues of equity, access, and diversity pertaining to first-generation college students.

JULIA C. DUNCHEON is a Ph.D. candidate in Urban Education Policy at the University of Southern California and a researcher in the Pullias Center for Higher Education. Prior to pursuing her doctorate, she spent several years teaching history, government, and special education at a low-performing high school in Brooklyn, N.Y. Her research interests include college access and readiness, urban high schools, underserved student populations, educational inequality, and qualitative methods. She earned her B.A. from Wellesley College and an M.A. in Teaching from Long Island University, Brooklyn, N.Y.

WILLIAM G. TIERNEY is University Professor and Wilbur-Kieffer Professor of Higher Education and Co-director of the Pullias Center for Higher Education at the University of Southern California (USC), and a past President of the American Educational Research Association. Dr. Tierney is committed to informing policies and practices related to educational equity. He is involved in a project to develop interactive web-enhanced computer games for low-income youth that will equip students with knowledge about preparing for college. He is working on projects pertaining to the problems of remediation to ensure that high school students are college-ready, and a project investigating how to improve strategic decision-making in higher education. His recent publications include: The Impact of Culture on Organizational Decision-making, Trust and the Public Good: Examining the Cultural Conditions of Academic Work, and Understanding the Rise of For-profit Colleges and Universities.

INDEX

Note: Page numbers in *italics* indicate figures and tables.

215